The Manpower Connection

THE
MANPOWER
CONNECTION

EDUCATION AND WORK

Eli Ginzberg

Harvard University Press
Cambridge, Massachusetts
and London, England   1975

Library of Congress Cataloging in Publication Data

Ginzberg, Eli, 1911-
    The manpower connection.

    Includes index.
    1. Manpower policy—United States. 2. Labor and laboring classes—United
States. 3. Education—Economic aspects—United States. 4. Job satisfaction.
I. Title.
HD5724.G524   331.1'1'0973   75-11862
ISBN 0-674-54810-8

To the members, past and present,
of the
National Manpower Policy Task Force
in collegial fellowship

Preface

The chapters that comprise this book represent my efforts during the late 1960s and early 1970s to look beneath the surface in three critical arenas: education, work, and manpower policy. My approach has been informed by the continuing research of the Conservation of Human Resources Project at Columbia University, which I direct, and also reflects my close association with the policy arena stemming from my long-time chairmanship of the National Manpower Advisory Committee, my current chairmanship of the National Commission for Manpower Policy, and other governmental assignments.

In 1968 I published a collection of earlier manpower essays, entitled *Manpower Agenda for America* (McGraw-Hill). The present book gives more considered views based on additional research and a broader perspective. Details about the initial publication of these articles, all of which have been revised in varying degree, are given at the back of the book.

I am indebted to Alice M. Yohalem of the Conservation Project for her conscientious and skillful editing. She took responsibility for eliminating overlaps, bringing the material up-to-date, and clarifying ambiguities. Without her efforts this book would not have been published.

Ruth Szold Ginzberg made time in her busy schedule to improve the readability of the manuscript. To her also I am most grateful.

Contents

Part Three   MANPOWER

Tables

The Manpower Connection

Introduction

In the 1960s economists and other social scientists, returning to a long-neglected interest of their predecessors that had been initiated by Adam Smith, extended the established theory of investment to the acquisition of human skills and competences. Theodore Schultz, Gary Becker, and Jacob Mincer took the lead in elaborating a theory of human capital based on neoclassical economics. Starting with the assumption that people are constantly seeking to optimize their net position, they demonstrated that education and training, considered as investments, can explain differences in the lifetime earnings of different groups in the labor market.

The data had an overwhelming consistency—those with the least education earned the smallest incomes; those who had the most schooling tended to be in the highest earning category; those whose educational attainment was average were in the middle of the income scale. The new theory was one more demonstration of the power of economic analysis. Although political scientists, sociologists, and psychologists have had difficulty in developing cogent theories about such phenomena as the actions of modern states, the role of youth, or patterns of behavior, economists moved from strength to strength using their newly developed theories of human capital to explain not only determinants of lifetime earnings but also changes in the rates of birth, crime, divorce, and other critical dimensions of human and social behavior. While this introduction is not the appropriate forum in which to examine the validity of the various claims put forward by the human capital theorists, a few caveats may be appropriate in light of the focus of many of the chapters of the book.

Part One, *Education,* calls attention to recent developments that warn against a simplistic reliance on the human capital theory as an explicating mechanism. Not only is there no more than tenuous evidence of increased benefit to the individual and society from the rapid expansion of investments in public education, there is also no strong evidence which suggests that the new emphasis on career education will lead to lower unemployment, higher earnings, or a larger national product.

The first two chapters deal with basic weaknesses in educational planning that reflect confusion over goals; Chapters 3 and 4 focus on the difficulties of reforming urban schools; and Chapter 5 and 6 treat the lack of a realistic approach to occupational choice and career guidance.

The difficulties encountered throughout the United States in the attempt to improve the performance of urban schools demonstrate that significant gains in output do not always result from increased investments. Moreover, an examination of the economics of the proposed educational voucher system indicates serious shortcomings that threaten democratic values. It seems to be considerably easier to pinpoint the malfunctioning aspects of the educational establishment than to find ways to improve the schooling of low-income and minority youth.

Furthermore, neither the process of occupational choice nor the practices of career guidance add credibility to the rational assumptions of the human capital theorists. Career decision-making relies heavily on individual values and goals, while guidance often creates distortions in individual choice because of faulty information, pseudoprofessionalism among practitioners, and outright discrimination in the advice that many of them provide.

Let us quickly admit that the human capital theorists, agile as they are, would have little difficulty in taking account of these and many other imperfections. But the very flexibility of their theory, which permits them to encapsulate all types of behavior, eventually proves too much. For two hundred years economists have manufactured theories about society as if it were organized by independent men in the isolated pursuit of their individual interests, who calculate where their main chance lies and actively pursue it. A theory that predicates an underlying rationalism for much, if not all, social behavior cannot escape the constraints of its basic assumption. It does not prove itself by transmuting all actions into a cost or a benefit. Clearly, the real advantage of the human capital theory lies elsewhere. A more appropriate framework for the analysis of human resources remains to be fashioned.

A second important development of the 1960s and the early 1970s is the focus of Part Two, which relates to the arena of work—an old theme that has surfaced anew. The first international conference on "The Quality of Working Life" was held in 1972 at Arden House, Columbia University, and was attended by representatives of most of the developed nations. The conferees engaged in extended discussions about the state of knowledge about work, alternative routes of experimentation, and future lines of action that might be pursued to improve the quality of working life on the factory floor and in the office. Among the possible improvements suggested was an alteration of the existing patterns of interaction between workers and management and between workers and their machines, with the aim of providing workers with more scope for self-determination and more responsibility for the production of goods and services.

Concern that technology and specialization would rob workers of meaningful jobs dates back at least to Adam Smith and was a key point in the slashing attack of Karl Marx on the industrial capitalism of his day. Subsequently, Emile Durkheim predicted that increasing alienation would lead many to commit suicide. In the 1930s, Elton Mayo contributed to the fame of the Harvard Business School through his pioneering studies of factory work as a system of social interaction. In the early post-World War II years, the staff of the Tavistock Institute of London broke new ground by looking at a wide range of problems in the workplace through glasses tinted with Freudian psychodynamics. Later, at the end of the 1960s, a number of researchers and consultants, primarily in the rapidly industrializing countries of Western Europe, were able to persuade a group of enterprising companies to cooperate in new experiments aimed at determining how the "sociotechnical" approach could reduce workers' discontent and increase their morale and satisfactions, with corresponding gains in productivity.

The American Assembly, under a Ford Foundation grant, held a large national conference on this theme in 1973, again at Arden House. In the same year, the U. S. Department of Health, Education, and Welfare published a report, *Work in America,* which gave further visibility to the problems involved, as did the detailed reporting of the General Motors strike at Lordstown, interpreted by the media as a revolt of younger workers against the intolerable conditions of the assembly line.

The Conservation of Human Resources Project has been concerned with many dimensions of work, and a summary of its evolving understanding is presented in Chapter 7. The three subsequent chapters specifically address the recently rediscovered concerns noted above. These are discussed with deliberate caution and constraint, since I am convinced that the reform of the workplace will meet with only limited success. To improve conditions for the working man, it may be necessary to follow the more traditional methods of reducing hours of work, improving health and safety conditions, and increasing amenities.

The last five chapters in Part Two shift the focus from work to workers. They consider three major groups of workers, highly educated manpower, blue-collar workers, and women, as well as the manpower problems facing the armed services. Chapter 11 explores the disequilibrium between the enlarged supply of and the reduced demand for highly trained manpower. The serious tensions between the scientific leadership and the federal government are traced, and the early success of the scientist-statesman is linked to the troubles that ensued because of lack of public support for their goals and programs. The analysis also points to the built-in adjustment mechanisms in both the educational system and the economy, which are likely to prevent persistent long-term imbalances.

Chapter 12 considers the manpower challenges that face the Department of Defense with a 1974-75 total payroll of slightly under $60 billion. The central thrust of the chapter is to stress the extent to which effective manpower utilization depends in the first instance on effective organizational structures; secondarily on the incentive structures that contribute ·to or detract from the economical use of manpower; and finally on the commitment of the top leadership to a policy of effective manpower utilization.

During the Vietnam era, we saw the emergence of the "hard-hat"—the disenchanted, frustrated, blue-collar ethnic who was opposed to the emerging values of the youthful counterculture. The phenomenon was no sooner recognized than it was made to account for everything from the Wallace candidacy to the backlash against the blacks. Chapter 13 carries a warning on the danger of generalizing about half the American working population (blue-collar plus service workers), without taking account of the heterogeneity of their life experiences.

The forces responsible for the rapid increase of women in paid employment as well as some of the probable consequences for management, the economy, the family, and women themselves are considered in Chapters 14 and 15. While the human capital theorists have considered the larger participation of women in the labor market in terms of improved trade-offs between time spent in the home caring for children and housekeeping and time devoted to the world of work with its income-earning potential, our analysis is rooted in the transformation of the basic value structures of women (and therefore of men) and in the correspondingly radical changes in the institutional structures of the family, work, and the larger society.

The chapters in Part Three, *Manpower,* are devoted to the policy arena. The first chapter, 16, explores whether, a decade after its introduction, the federal effort to fashion a manpower policy via training and placing the disadvantaged can be judged a success. The answer is that it was truly more boon than boondoggle, although there are still wide margins for making future training more effective and for reducing the slippage between training and employment.

Chapter 17 traces the reasons why the federal government felt compelled to add a further dimension to its evolving manpower structure in the early 1970s through the establishment of a public employment program. The limitations of this route as a cure-all for excessive unemployment are reviewed and found to be substantial, if not determining. Without considering whether the widespread anxiety about the lowered productivity of the American economy is justified, Chapter 18 considers the potential of manpower programs, private and public, to contribute to removing the burden of technological change from the workingman. It shows that policies shifting the costs of change from the individual worker to society may prove to be a potent factor in facilitating more rapid technological and organizational advances.

The manpower approach is substantially enlarged in chapters 19 and 20. The former provides illustrations of diverse federal policies, from military procurement to social security, that impinge on the demand, supply, and utilization of the nation's human resources in both the short and long run. Chapter 20 describes a variety of approaches to the study of the manpower problems of the nation's large cities, many of which have been buffeted during the past two decades by many adverse developments. The ability of a municipality to take constructive action to solve many of its difficulties depends upon the use of a broad research strategy to support its decision-making apparatus.

The last two chapters address a broader range of issues, each of which is linked to the manpower theme. Chapter 21 criticizes the neglect of the strategic role of government in studies of the modern economy and society, a neglect that stems directly from the long-term bias of mainline economists who believe that Keynesian macrotheory grafted to Marshallian microtheory provides an adequate foundation for economic analysis. The error in this assumption becomes increasingly clear as inflation, balance of payments problems, and international monopolies play havoc with the stabilization efforts of the economic bureaucrats.

The concluding chapter recalls one of the most exciting periods of social intervention in the United States in this century. This was the short-lived but intense interlude of reform directed toward creation of the "Great Society," which was expected to broaden opportunities for many disadvantaged groups—the uneducated, the unskilled, the poor, minorities, women, the aged, and the ill. A retrospective analysis reveals that, although the promises were excessive, the resources limited, and the accomplishments modest, on balance the record is favorable. The efforts of a society that has the will to respond to the unmet needs of its citizens may fail, but the goodwill that accrues from addressing those needs assures that it will have a second, and even a third, opportunity.

The underlying theme of this book is that all efforts directed toward improvement of the nation's human resources require deepened knowledge and the political will to alter deeply rooted social structures. By calling attention to new frontiers, the emerging discipline of human resources can facilitate the building of the consensus required to remove inequities and to broaden opportunities.

Part One

EDUCATION

For a century or more the American people have had a love affair with public education, and the 1960s marked a renewal of the marriage vows. The word went forth that young people who remained in school long enough to obtain their high school or college diploma would have the inside track into preferred jobs and careers.

This advice does not appear to be in harmony with the facts. The following chapters point up some of the inconsistencies between the newly reaffirmed faith in more and more education and the harsh realities of the labor market. Specifically, they discuss reasons for the persisting difficulties experienced in educating low-income youth; the dangers of popular nostrums, such as career education and educational vouchers; the dynamics of occupational choice; and the urgent need for a redirection of career guidance.

1

Strategies for Educational Reform

The goals and performance of an educational system should be assessed by criteria related to the development of human resources. Among the criteria the first is freedom of inquiry, and the following personal reminiscence may emphasize its importance.

In 1928-29 I was a student at Heidelberg University, at a time when that institution was in the top rank of the world's great universities. Within the next few years, Adolf Hitler would destroy this center of learning, whose contributions to scholarship, science, and culture spanned more than five hundred years. To witness the Nazis' rise to power, to live through the tortured years of Hitler's regime (which occurred during the formative period of my life as an academic), made an indelible impression upon me. I learned that no educational institution, not even one firmly protected by a tradition of independence, stands immune from the dominant forces that shape the society of which it is a part. Those who devote themselves to the pursuit of knowledge and to the instruction of others must have the tolerance, if not the enthusiastic support, of the society that provides the resources to perform these missions.

The teaching profession must always attempt to instill pupils with a respect for truth and free inquiry. If teachers fail in this, they run the risk of becoming the henchmen of an orthodoxy whose leaders are more concerned with indoctrination than with the pursuit of truth. As we are learning today, free inquiry may be unsettling; hence those who know its worth must not abuse it. If they confuse the classroom with the political arena, they may not long enjoy the freedom society now grants them.

Freedom of inquiry is the first standard for evaluating the educational undertaking from the vantage of a human resources approach; the second is the degree to which educational institutions understand and are responsive to the variety of human potential.

Traditionally, our educational system has been concerned almost exclusively with the nurturing of cognitive abilities. Although cognitive abilities are critically important for individual and communal performance, they are not the totality of human capacities. Yet in American schools athletics is the only major exception to the rule of concentration on the development of cognitive skills. At the high school and college levels, a considerable amount of effort and resources is directed toward identifying young people with athletic potential as well as those with academic potential, toward nurturing and training them, and toward assuring that the successful among them are well rewarded. Our schools should have sought long ago to identify, train, and reward young people with potential for superior performance in fields other than the academic or athletic—politics, the arts, crafts, or interpersonal relations, for example.

A third criterion with which to assess the performance of an educational system is its contribution to the broadening of opportunities for self-development and career progression. Because income inequality remains a fact of contemporary life, we dare not conclude that educational opportunity makes little or no difference. The tens of thousands of young men and women from families of modest income who have graduated from public and private institutions and who have moved toward the top of the occupational ladder are proof that the role of education is a potent factor in social and economic mobility.

Parental education, occupation, and income continue to be powerful determinants of college attendance. Sons and daughters of upper-income parents have a clear and unequivocal advantage. Since more than four of every five young people graduate from high school today, and since there are sufficient places in the higher educational system for all who have the requisite academic preparation, one must exercise caution in downgrading the contribution of education to economic and social mobility. We have had considerably more success than any other nation, including Communist countries, in enabling young people to acquire educational credentials that provide access to better jobs and careers.

The fourth and last criterion is the amount of resources invested in education and the effectiveness with which these resources are utilized. The United States currently spends about $90 billion per year for education; this is about 8 percent of the gross national product (GNP). In 1929 educational expenditures represented only 3 percent of GNP. An increase of 160 percent in the share of national product directed to education over a period of forty years is noteworthy indeed. Aside from benefits to the individual citizen in terms of personal and career development, what does education contribute to the society at large?

The last three Presidents of the United States, taking their cue from economists and educators, stated in turn that any young person who wants a good life should stay in school and acquire a diploma or a degree. The figures never supported this claim and they still do not. All that they say is that, *on the average,* the more education a person has, the higher his lifetime earnings will be. Even if the figures supported the Presidents' claim, it would be objectionable if young people were to pursue education solely for its income-raising potential. When David Ben-Gurion was Prime Minister of Israel, he proposed that all who were interested in, and capable of profiting from, a university education should have the opportunity to pursue advanced studies even if they planned eventually to follow such mundane occupations as farmer, carpenter, soldier, chauffeur. He believed that education should be pursued for its own sake, not as an income-enhancing device.

From a human resources vantage we have briefly reviewed four criteria for judging the performance of an educational system. To what extent does it protect free inquiry, nurture a wide range of human potential, expand the opportunity matrix, and utilize scarce resources effectively?

Sources of Unease

There is widespread unease about the high proportion of students at every level of the system, from elementary to graduate school, who are bored with lectures and other material presented in the classroom and with assignments to be done at home. Boredom occurs when an individual is unable to see the purpose in an assigned task. At best, he will put out minimal effort; more typically, he will avoid performing what he regards as a pointless exercise. We cannot place the blame for boredom on the teaching staff. If a student sees no point to the learning process, even the most skilled teacher may fail to engage his interest and elicit his participation. Teachers aside, when an educational system contains a significant number of students who are bored and act accordingly, some facet of the system must be askew.

A second cause of unease derives from the fact that many high school, college, and graduate students flounder and fail to complete their studies. We cannot draw facile conclusions about dropouts, who often include some of a school's ablest students. They realize that they are not learning any skill or discipline and refuse to remain docile under this circumstance, even if it means leaving without a diploma or degree.

A third source of unease derives from the fact that major gaps continue to exist in the educational opportunities available to different groups in the population. It is the poor, the rural, and the minority-group youth who are most likely to be victimized. The schools they attend, the curricula to which they are exposed, and the teachers who instruct them often are inferior. The outcome can be read in the rejections for military service for reasons of educational inadequacy. Data for 1970 help to illuminate the wide national range in educational opportunity and acceptance for military service. In Minnesota, New Hampshire, and Washington, the rejection rate was between 0.7 and 0.9 per 100 men. In South Carolina and Mississippi, the rates were 25 and 22, respectively, or nearly thirty-five times as great. Such regional (and racial) differences are hard to justify in a country that prides itself on its democratic tradition and long-term support for public education.

Other data, however, indicate considerable progress in narrowing the differentials among groups. For instance, in 1940, whites in the age group 25 to 29 had completed an average of 10.7 years of schooling, in contrast to 7.1 years for nonwhites. In 1970, the figures were 12.6 and 12.2, respectively. The gap of 3.6 years had narrowed to 0.4 year. During the intervening thirty years, the educational achievement of nonwhites, measured in terms of years of schooling, had increased four times as fast as that of whites!

Another cause of public unease is the fact that, within a single decade (1960 to 1970), national expenditures per student in average daily attendance in elementary and secondary schools increased from approximately $500 to $1,000 in *stable* dollars. Both educators and lay leaders have expressed considerable concern about increasing voter rejection of higher local taxes to finance proposed school budgets. Since the late 1960s, taxpayer resistance has mounted to a point where some large school systems have had to close before the end of the semester because of lack of funds. However, this opposition must be placed in the context of the ten-year doubling in the *real* dollars expended per pupil. Many citizens are questioning the productivity of this additional money. They are asking for evidence that the average child is receiving a better education.

A fifth source of unease relates to the appropriate role for the school in the transformation of American society. The busing issue will not disappear. It is worth pointing out, however, that whereas 7 percent of all school children were bused in 1929, 43 percent were bused in 1970; and most of this increase reflected increased school consolidation, not desegregation.

Additional sources of unease, relating primarily to the effectiveness of increased public expenditures on behalf of education, warrant some brief comments. We have been pursuing the path of compensatory education. The federal government has been appropriating about $1.5 billion a year to this end. An advisory committee to the President and the Congress has reported that only about one-third of this amount initially reached the youngsters for whom it was intended. Moreover, the committee concluded that educators are only beginning to learn what is involved in designating an effective compensatory program.

Many legislators have become disenchanted with educational leaders because, acting on their advice, the law-makers expanded government support for graduate programs only to find that the country now faces a surplus of educated manpower. In seeking funds for expansion, the educators neglected to consider what part of the new output of doctorates would be fed back into the educational system to cope with increased enrollments. They did not realize that the expansion of enrollments would soon level off for a variety of demographic, economic, and intellectual reasons and that, when this happened, new doctorates would be a glut on the market.

There has also been growing restiveness with the economists' theory of human investment, which correlates educational attainment and lifetime earnings and which was adopted by many educators to strengthen their arguments for increased funding. Long before Christopher Jencks, it was noted that about one-third of all high school graduates without college experience earn over $10,000 a year, while the same proportion of college graduates earn less. Even more striking is the finding that about two out of every five males with five or more years of education beyond high school earn $15,000 or more per year, while this is the case for only one out of twenty women. Clearly, for many people, the payoff from education remains to be proved.

Directions for New Strategies

Having set forth some operative criteria for assessing an educational system and having identified some of the sources of unease with the present structure, I shall now propose some directions for new strategies.

First, schools must be adjudged failures unless they accomplish three tasks: they must nurture curiosity, teach basic skills, and provide guidance in choosing among options.

If learning depends on evoking and directing the curiosity with which all humans are endowed, then the school's task is cut out for it. It must develop curricula and teaching methods that will pique children's native curiosity and must avoid, at all costs, assignments that suppress or eliminate this inborn trait. It is difficult to identify the means by which we can take advantage of youthful curiosity, but surely it is a characteristic that warrants more attention than it has yet received. A study of how students spend their free time out of school may be a useful clue to whether their assignments in school are stimulating their curiosity. An ominous note: the average American who now has more than twelve years of schooling reads about one book a year! More effective development and use of curiosity should be high on the agenda of educational research and practice.

A second area calling for new approaches relates to the critical transition from home to school. In general, the school does a reasonably good job of receiving a youngster from a middle-class home whose parents have prepared him for school. But it is no secret that the school does a poor job with respect to the large numbers of poor and minority children who have fewer family supports. We need a restructuring of kindergarten and grades one through three; we need new curricula and new teaching methods. If the first four years of schooling were to be treated as a block in which youngsters can move at their own pace to acquire basic skills, where care is taken to avoid stigmatizing a child with premature failure, and where those who encounter difficulties have access to extra supports, the entire experience would be less intimidating and the outcome more productive. Evidence to the contrary notwithstanding, I refuse to accept the thesis that children from disadvantaged homes cannot profit from well-designed and well-executed educational programs.

Thirdly, as the Fleischmann Report (1973) on educational financing in New York State recommended, it is essential that the states assume more responsibility over schools within their jurisdiction to assure that all pupils acquire a minimum level of competence in basic skills. This recommendation parallels one advanced almost two centuries ago by Adam Smith, who argued that it is the responsibility of the state to provide basic education for all its citizens. Smith suggested that a man's entrance into productive employment be dependent on his prior acquisition of basic knowledge and skills. In Switzerland the army returns recruits to their cantons for additional instruction if they fail the educational screening test.

We also need to do much more to provide effective links between the school and the world of work, particularly for the nonbookish minority who have little or no intention of going on to college. The recent emphasis on career education is a move in the right direction. This does not necessarily mean that occupations should be a unit of study in elementary, junior, or senior high schools. Nor does it mean that every student should acquire a manual or white-collar skill in school or in a school-sponsored program. Neither does it mean introduction of the

Swedish system whereby all students spend some months at work during their high school years. Rather, it means that a concern for the relation between education and work should permeate the curriculum at all levels; that good educational and occupational guidance services should be available; and that after the ninth grade, students with little interest in or aptitude for academic work should be afforded alternative opportunities for development.

Educators made an error when they promised the country to take care of all young people in the schoolroom until they are 18 years old. A significant minority of boys and girls cannot profit from so prolonged an exposure. They need opportunities to work, to earn money, to be associated with adults in purposeful activities for at least part of the time. Such alternative developmental experiences cannot be provided by educators alone within the confines of the school. A much enlarged program of work/study requires the cooperation of employers, trade unions, and the community. This is the single most important challenge facing American education, and it is one that requires action on a broad front.

Finally, we need to make a series of adjustments to ensure that the educational system becomes more accessible to young and mature adults when they see the possibility of profiting from additional education and training. This implies a great many changes: in the policies adopted and the funding provided by legislative bodies; in the manner in which schools operate to facilitate reentry of pupils who have dropped out or have temporarily terminated their education at lower levels; in the willingness of employers to provide time for workers to continue or return to their studies.

Concluding Observations

It will require hard work on the part of researchers, administrators, and teachers to determine whether and to what extent these strategies hold the promise of improving the productivity of the American educational system. To nurture curiosity, to improve linkages between school and work, and to provide easier access of adults to continuing education and training are essential steps in enhancing the role that education plays in the development of human potential. And it is this task above all others that educators must continue to address.

The educational system cannot be a substitute for the family; it cannot cure poverty and racism, assure individuals good jobs and good incomes, control delinquency and crime, or usher in a brave new world. But teachers can make their students more intelligent, more considerate, and more sensitive to their own problems and to the problems of others.

Years ago, John Maynard Keynes expressed the hope that the day would come when economists would be as useful as dentists. I have the same hope for educators.

Career Education:
Many Questions, Few Answers

Under the leadership of Commissioner Sidney Marland, the U. S. Office of Education arrived at a concept of "career education" early in the 1970s. At a meeting with the National Manpower Advisory Committee (NMAC) in 1971, Dr. Marland discussed the rationale for this new educational program, its major features, and the gains envisioned.

According to Commissioner Marland, a national program of career education is desirable because of the need to find a new focus for our large educational effort. He cited the relatively low productivity of the $85 billion education industry, which is reflected in the high proportion of young people who complete their schooling without a marketable skill. The aim of career education is to provide both new focus and new direction to all levels of the educational system by relating a pupil's education and training to his life and career objectives.

The Office of Education envisioned four major models for career education:

(a) Transforming elementary and secondary schools to place career planning at the center of their efforts.

(b) Developing industry-related education and training so that work/study programs will become possible for many young people as early as age 13 or 14.

(c) A home model, making use of modern technology such as television, to facilitate the education and training of housebound women.

(*d*)   An institutional effort directed at people who are in training centers, hospitals, or prisons.

The putative gains from this large-scale reform would include prevention of failure in school, development of a sound self-identity, deflection of unqualified youngsters from the mirage of college, improvement in the status of jobs that do not require a college degree, and facilitation of movement between school and work in accordance with changing expectations and needs.

The Response of the National Manpower Advisory Committee

In response to Dr. Marland's proposal, the NMAC emphasized the necessity of eliciting support from the academically oriented educational community, because vocational educators alone cannot restructure the school establishment. In any event, the committee stated, the acquisition of basic knowledge and skills must underlie any reform of the educational system.

Proponents of career education were warned that this reform must be mounted with the realization that little new money, if any, will be made available by a resentful electorate which feels that it has already been oversold on education. Paper planning in Washington must not be confused with broad support in the hinterland. National interest in and support for career education is modest, which suggests the need for dialogue and citizen involvement in order to engender enthusiasm. Moreover, the capability of the federal government to bring about specific reforms at state and local levels is limited. Multiple field models to serve as demonstrations would be a desirable way to bring the concept to the people. There is always a danger that (as frequently occurs) the federal government will perform enthusiastic prelaunch efforts and finance a few interesting experimental and demonstration projects, but will fail to fund the long-term efforts required for carrying out a major reform. It would be desirable to study European experience in depth, since West Germany, Sweden, the United Kingdom, and other countries have experimented selectively with career education.

Educational planners were urged not to oversell the new approach as a system that will improve employment and career opportunities for all people. Since employment opportunities are limited and unemployment rates are at an unacceptable level, many people will be unable to find suitable work regardless of the nature of their education and training. Furthermore, since it is presently impossible to develop sound manpower forecasts, career education must include possibilities for retraining and subsequent adaptation to a changing economy. The members of the National Manpower Advisory Committee cautioned that education must be viewed as a consumption as well as an investment good. Many members of the work force are already conspicuously overtrained for available jobs, and they are correspondingly discontent.

Specifically, the committee warned that care must be taken to avoid the use of work/study programs as a back-door entrance to the use of child labor. It questioned the assumption that business will cooperate in providing expanded opportunities for these programs. Furthermore, it predicted that, without guidance and counseling, which are critical to this type of effort but which are conspicuously weak in the career arena, the program is unlikely to succeed. Nor is it likely to succeed unless employers begin to attach less importance to certificates and credentials.

Finally, the NMAC expressed concern that career education may be used to discourage disadvantaged students from seeking admission to college. If it were used in this manner, it would close out opportunities for some students to improve their socioeconomic position through higher education.

A Critique

A careful review of Dr. Marland's proposal and of the reactions of the committee leads me to present the following observations.

Although our present educational effort may not stand up well to a cost/benefit analysis, I believe that it is worthwhile to appraise the productivity of public investment in education in relation to other large-scale programs such as defense, welfare, and health. There is no reason to believe that education is doing less well than these programs, although it may not be doing any better.

The only important one of the four models with which the Office of Education is experimenting appears to be industry-related education and training efforts that would enable even young people in their early teens to engage in work/study programs. The other models do not appear to have a central core on which significant improvements can be based.

With regard to projected gains, only that which looks forward to permitting people to move back and forth between school and work in accordance with their changing expectations and needs holds significant promise. "Failure," "identity," "mirage," "status"—these are loaded concepts, but they are not solid enough to support sound reforms.

Observers of the Washington scene know that the formulation of new programs with new objectives is much easier than their effective implementation. This is especially true in areas where the federal government has relatively little influence over decisions, or money to buy support or acquiescence. The dangers of oversell are always present; the difficulties of succeeding are always underestimated.

The American economy is antiyouth in that employers, if they have an option, prefer to hire people in their twenties rather than those in their teens. Trade unions, pressed by their members for job security, also look askance at facilitating the inflow of young people into a job market that is already short on jobs and long on people. We must conclude, therefore, that the key to successful career education—the expansion of work/study programs—runs counter to deep-seated trends and tendencies. It will take much time and the accumulation of considerable evidence to prove, at least to me, that business will cooperate with the educational world to provide the work opportunities that career education requires if it is to succeed.

Granted that the educational system has many defects, including the important finding that a great many students who pass through the schools fail to acquire marketable skills, we must not assume that even well-functioning schools can assure successful career outcomes. They cannot. The past error of pleading with young people to remain in school on the assumption that a diploma assures happiness and prosperity should not be repeated in a new form. The best career education cannot assure a good job, a decent income, or a satisfying career. The educational system can do better or worse in preparing people for work and careers, but the performance of the economy and of the labor market is not responsive. surely in the short run, to alterations in the quality of the labor supply. Our economy has seldom operated at a less than 5- to 6-percent unemployment level in recent decades, and recently it has been at much higher levels. Improving education is not the best answer to a shortfall in jobs!

There is also a danger that the educational reformers will make their task too easy by assuming that, if the emphasis on academic education is reduced in favor of career education, all will be well. The simple fact is that schools that do not teach their students how to read, write, talk, calculate, think, are failures. They are malfunctioning, and their students are victimized. No matter how enthusiastic one may be about career education, one cannot—dare not—ignore the perennial challenge to the schools, which is to meet society's implicit and explicit demand to teach students basic cognitive skills. People who lack these skills not only will be impoverished in their personal lives, but also will be handicapped in pursuing their careers.

The 1960s saw the breakthrough of a new methodology, studies in human capital. Economists transferred their theories of investment and rates of return from technology to people. In the process they provided a powerful rationale to special-interest groups, which were pressuring for expanded financing of education and other types of social services. Some simple-minded converts believed that every increase in educational spending would be reflected in an increase in economic wealth. Many politicians in the developing and developed nations, disappointed by the performance of their economic systems, have begun to take a hard look at this doctrine, and some are now convinced that it is misleading. Millions and billions of dollars spent on schools may return little by way of increased national wealth in a short or even intermediate period. At best, the relations between education and the economy are significant only in the long run.

Educators, having been through this unfortunate experience in the recent past, would be well-advised to proceed cautiously in the future. All education that is worthwhile has some bearing on how a person can earn his livelihood. But a meaningful educational experience cannot rest solely or even primarily on a calculation of differential future earnings based on educational achievement. To attempt such a calculation is to confuse education with job training, personal development with market earnings, a good society with career achievement. If educators do not know better than to appraise education in terms of the earnings of their graduates, all critiques of education and educators have been too gentle!

One final comment. I strongly approve of career education. The thrust of these caveats is to help prevent career education from promising more than it can deliver. I have pointed to the barriers that must be removed to make it operational, to the excessive claims about its potential effectiveness, to the challenges the educational system must still meet, and to the danger of confusing the goals of education. Whether career education will be just another governmental program strong in slogans and weak in effectiveness will depend on the extent to which the educational leadership takes these warnings to heart.

3

The Reform of Urban Schools: Illusion or Reality?

Increasingly, our large city schools are mired in a swamp of insoluble problems. First, a disturbingly large number of students in urban school systems acquire little knowledge or information and rarely learn a skill. Second, increasingly heavy financial investments are made for teachers and teaching materials, on the assumption that more money will result in improved schools. Again I contend that, while money is not unimportant, more funds will not necessarily bring about the desired results.

As with any large and complex system, a great amount of the working time of the officialdom (administrators and teachers) must be devoted to keeping the system operating at a tolerable level. Administrators must see that fires are not set, that one student does not knife another, that children are not pushed down a flight of stairs. One might begrudge the amount of time that must be devoted to these "law and order" issues, but there does not seem to be any alternative.

Given the present distribution of income and the residential patterns of various population groups, there is no prospect that the inner-city schools will be substantially desegregated unless the whole schooling process is transferred to buses. James Conant made this point more than ten years ago, but few liberals wanted to hear it and still fewer wanted to acknowledge it. Since black and Puerto Rican youngsters account for 60 percent or more of all pupils in the public schools in Manhattan, for example, there simply is no way to establish a racial balance in the lower grades.

Wherever trade unions are established, or where employees have similar controls over the conditions of their work, seniority tends to prevail. This means that the more experienced teachers do not have to teach in ghetto schools unless they want to. While many younger teachers are enthusiastic, their enthusiasm soon gives way to despair when they are assigned to ghetto schools, especially those where the supervision is inadequate.

In addition, physical plant and facilities tend to be below average in the low-income areas of the city. One need not argue that the quality of physical facilities is critical to education, but bad facilities surely do not make instruction or learning easier. Moreover, the high mobility characteristic of many minority-group families places an almost insurmountable burden on the school system, which must attempt to care for and teach so many children who enter and leave several schools during the course of the year.

Next, as Ellen Winston remarked at the White House Conference on Education in 1965, it is difficult if not impossible to teach a hungry child. It is even more difficult to teach a child who comes to school after insufficient rest. Yet many children in ghetto areas are both hungry and tired.

The fact that many parents are unable to participate in the education of their youngsters presents a further deterrent to a child's learning. In many homes there is no father, and the mother may be hard pressed to cope with the realities she faces. She simply does not have time and energy to oversee homework or to visit school. There is little reinforcement at home of the school's attempt to teach the importance of reading and writing.

Finally, young children are aware of tensions and hostilities. At present, when the race issue is to the fore, many pupils see the teacher as the enemy and stubbornly and adamantly refuse to follow instructions.

The Dilemmas

With these facts before us, and I believe they *are* facts and not impressions or prejudices, let us attempt to understand the dilemmas they represent.

The first point is that we have romanticized the past effectiveness of public education. It is not true that the public schools were effective in their attempts to educate the children of European immigrants in the nineteenth and twentieth centuries. Conflicting value systems had an adverse effect on the ability of these children to learn. The memoirs of Abraham Cahan provide unequivocal evidence that a considerable number of Jewish youngsters on New York's lower East Side found school to be an unhappy experience and profited little from it.

Although conflicts resulting from racial differences are more intense and intractable than ethnic or class conflicts, it would be a mistake to blame racial conflict for the poor performance of ghetto schools. After all, for a great many years, only black teachers were teaching black students in the South, with mediocre results.

We are told that the "conforming" child is the one with whom the school is best able to cope. With thirty or forty youngsters in a class, it is not surprising that teachers place heavy stress on obedience and find active youngsters difficult to handle. But life in the ghetto is rough, and even young children may already be disturbed. In many schools they are forced to sit still and may not leave their seats without permission. I suspect that one important nonfit between child and school is the ghetto pupil's need for activity and the school's insistence on immobility.

Another parameter derives from the fact that many students face a communications problem right from the start. While educators realize and try to adjust to the fact that some youngsters come from foreign-speaking homes, they seldom realize that the English spoken in the black ghetto is distinctive.

Young people appear to learn under only one of two conditions. Either they fear the authority of the teacher and learn because they are cowed into it, or they identify, respect, and even love their teacher and learn because they want to win his or, more likely, her praise. Since we no longer beat children in school to make them learn and since there is little love between most ghetto children and their teachers, these children have little incentive to learn.

If children do not master the basic skills early in their schooling, it is more or less inevitable that they will fail later on and, as they fail, will lose interest and motivation. Most educational systems refuse to confront this issue straightforwardly. Although they know that many children are unable to perform at an advanced level because they have not mastered the prerequisites, teachers continue to move them along to higher grades. After a while, the system has made so many adaptations that it forgets that its primary mission is to ensure that certain basic skills are acquired by all children.

Because so many children fail so early, many teachers assume that these children, or more probably, all the children in the school, have fundamental deficits; as a consequence, many teachers give up even trying to teach, thereby proving their own assumptions.

Our insistence that children remain in school until they are 17 or 18, together with the fact that many of them do not master the skills upon which further learning is based, is a clear invitation to mounting trouble; the increasing rise in truancy is telling evidence of this.

Learning requires discipline. More importantly, it requires self-discipline. If children come to school sleepy and hungry, they will find it hard to stay awake and attend to their teachers. And if they are poor and hungry, what is their motivation for learning? As Bert Lahr asked, "What's the use of learning to count if you have nothing to count?"

The Program of the Utopians

Having inspected these dilemmas, let us take a look at the program of the utopian reformers.

First, they recommend that all poor youngsters have an opportunity to attend a Head Start program. Since only about 10 percent presently do, this would mean a tenfold expansion of the program.

Next, they advocate that we put much more money into school plant and equipment and that we raise teachers' salaries in order to attract and retain better teachers. I do not know how much they want to spend, but it is important to remember that the American public at the present time is investing about $90 billion in all forms of education.

Their third contention is that classes ought to be small. Perhaps they should, but so far nobody has demonstrated that class size makes a real difference in outcome. There probably is a maximum class size above which the effectiveness of the teacher is reduced. One does not have to be in favor of very large classes to be skeptical about very small ones.

Another platform in the reform program is to provide free breakfast and lunch for all children, or at least for the poor. Still another recommendation is to abandon the six-hour school day and to continue certain educational activities until the early evening, as well as on Saturdays and holidays. It would be hard to argue against a broadening and deepening of school programs; certainly this should be tested to learn if there is a strong demand for such activities.

The proponents of reform place heavy stress on increased parental involvement and more community control to overcome the lack of reinforcement to which we alluded earlier. In some cities, community control has been the prelude to community conflict; in other instances, efforts to involve parents have not been successful because some parents are afraid of the authority the school represents and others have little time to devote to school concerns.

There is a strong plea for improved services, that is, for more school psychologists, guidance personnel, and speech therapists. Since many children in urban schools come from disadvantaged homes, it would be hard to downgrade their needs in this area.

Another building block in the reformers' edifice is the need for a curriculum sensitive to the problems of minority groups, so that a ghetto child can develop a positive self-image. In turn, teachers are asked to learn more about the culture of the young people whom they instruct.

The reformers also point to the need for strengthening of vocational education programs. Since many youngsters find it difficult to profit from academic instruction, it is easy to be attracted to this proposal.

The final recommendation that the reformers repeatedly advance is for more individualized programming. After all, they say, schools deal with human beings, not statistical abstractions.

A Critique

A few brief comments on the reforms outlined above.

First, there is not enough money available nor will enough money become available to implement even half of these specific proposals. No matter how large a reduction is made in the budget of the Department of Defense—and in 1974 its budget request rose—there still would not be enough money to introduce all of these reforms.

Even if money were less of an issue and class size were reduced, we would face a manpower constraint. It is reasonable for the schools to seek to attract and to hold larger numbers of fine teachers, but we cannot expect them to hire a sufficient number of talented instructors to cover an increasing number of small classes.

Time plays a role. Even if we could begin now to reform the instruction of teachers to produce greater sensitivity to the cultural backgrounds of minority children, it would take a long time (Paul Mort used to say forty years) for the innovation to work its way through the system.

Fourth, it is not possible to establish strong vocational education programs in all high schools. We will be lucky if we can establish one or more skill-training centers in each city. Good vocational education is expensive in terms of money, personnel, and equipment.

Community control and related matters may offer some leverage against the bureaucratic rigidities that currently characterize schools in many urban centers, but the simple fact is that the unsatisfactory state of American education is in no small measure an outgrowth of community control.

There are, as we have seen, serious questions about many of the measures that are supposed to turn an unsatisfactory system into a satisfactory one. It is likely that similar questions can be asked about the "realistic" approach that follows, but at least it looks for answers to complex problems.

A Realistic Approach

My first recommendation is to place a performance requirement on the school system. Under the constitution of the State of New York, for example, every child is entitled to certain basic educational services. I would like to see every state enforce such a provision, that is, I would like state commissioners of education to measure the extent to which local boards of education meet their responsibilities. Although it is argued that current achievement tests are tests of performance, they are not used in this manner. I would like the state commissioners to require each school to explain the subnormal performance, if any, of its students and to explore how the amount of slippage can be reduced.

My second recommendation relates to the gains that might accrue from ungrading the first three school years which, together with kindergarten, would provide children from differing backgrounds with more flexibility during the initial adjustment period. I suspect that ungrading, with some differential allocation of resources, would enable more children to acquire basic skills. Moreover, it seems to me that a considerably larger research input is required to improve the curriculum for the first years. For example, we know much less than we ought to know about the teaching of reading.

Conventional wisdom holds that the best way to improve educational output is to increase pedagogical input. I see little prospect that the American people will vastly increase their expenditures for public education. The schools will have to continue with the same proportion of talent they have been able to attract in the recent past. We may, however, be able to supplement this. There would be many advantages, for example, if interested college students could be pursuaded to spend a semester or a year as teachers' assistants in ghetto schools. It would be relatively easy to combine such teaching experience with reading and writing assignments that would justify giving students college credit in a wide range of fields, from English to social sciences. The infusion of this new stream of manpower would have several benefits. The student teachers would be volunteers, they would be enthusiastic, and they would not be a threat to the permanent bureaucracy.

I would also like to see free breakfasts—as well as free lunches—for poor children. Since we cannot do very much in the short run about providing improved housing for the poor, we can at least take action on the food front.

Despite my reservations about the consequences of more community participation, I think it would be advantageous if more parents were encouraged to come to school and talk to the administration and the staff about the progress of their children and about how they might be helpful. Most city school systems suffer from excessive introversion.

I want to emphasize the desirability of more work/study programs, although they will not be easy to introduce or expand, given the lack of interest of most employers in young workers. However, it is more practical to introduce work/study programs than to increase vocational programs, which are very costly both in money and in staff.

The teaching profession has done itself a disservice by asking the community for more money with the promise that this will permit it to serve the needs of all young people. I do not think that the profession can deliver on that promise. Schools can serve many youngsters well, but they are simply unsuitable environments for certain adolescents who need instead opportunities in the real world.

One of the weaknesses in our society at large, and in our schools in particular, is the poor linkage between one subsystem and another. Recent efforts to improve this linkage for poor children have been impressive. Increasingly, we are telling them that, if they make an effort in high school, and if they perform adequately, we will assure them a place in college.

Even if all of the foregoing suggestions for improvement were to be implemented, the schools would probably continue to fail many children; consequently, we need second-chance institutions. I agree in theory with those who say it is better to have the basic institution, the school, perform effectively than to have inadequate schools and new training programs for young adults. But the simple fact is that we do not know how to prevent all failures, any more than we know how to prevent all diseases, and therefore we must invest considerable funds in therapeutic and rehabilitative efforts. Among the specific adjustments I would like to see are community colleges that would provide special programs for high school dropouts if they can demonstrate, in one fashion or another, that they have matured and would welcome a second chance.

As more tracks are built into an educational and training system, it becomes important to have a good guidance system to help people find their way through the labyrinth. It is easier to define than to structure such a system, since it would need better information than is currently available and more empathetic counselors—persons who are willing to use community resources and who are skilled in group and interpersonal interchanges.

As long as racism continues to confound our society, we will confront difficulties on the educational front, as on every other front. And as long as poverty afflicts large numbers of Americans, the schools will be handicapped in their efforts to perform effectively.

4

The Economics of the Voucher System

A voucher system involves a governmental authorization up to a stipulated amount for the individual to purchase a service in the market. One of the first proponents of a voucher system for education in the United States was Milton Friedman, who in 1955 (in *Economics and the Public Interest,* ed. Robert Solo, Rutgers University Press) argued that its adoption would lead to a series of improvements: greater individual (parental) freedom through broadened consumer choice; increased efficiency and economy through introducing competition where monopoly had earlier held sway; and greater diversity through an increase in entrepreneurship. Friedman knew that conditions of scale might inhibit the introduction of multiple schools in sparsely settled areas, and he recognized that a voucher system would be welcomed by groups committed to the maintenance of segregation. But he argued for "freedom," even if it would force blacks to wait for a changed attitude among whites before they could attend desegregated schools.

The Center for the Study of Public Policy, otherwise known as the Cambridge group, headed by Christopher Jencks, developed a planning document for the Office of Economic Opportunity that explored whether the voucher system might be used to speed certain specific educational objectives: increased diversity in curricula and teaching methods; desegregation; increased opportunities for minority children to attend better schools; greater parental choice; more disclosure of information from schools competing for public support; and public funds for the financially vulnerable parochial school system. Since the Cambridge group has been principally concerned with better education for children from low-income families and minority groups, it seems fair to say that if this "redistributive" effort cannot be accomplished, these proponents of the voucher system will not be interested in experiments testing its other potentialities.

Lessons from a Pluralistic Economy

Our society has been attempting for several decades to establish better conditions for the poor and otherwise disadvantaged on a series of fronts: housing, welfare, income, and health, as well as education. The results of these experiences deserve attention, even if we ignore certain refinements. The following generalizations can be ventured about these governmentally engendered efforts to bring about substantial improvements in the quantity and quality of services available to the poor and disadvantaged:

(*a*) The programs involve expenditures of many billions of dollars annually.

(*b*) The expectations on which they are based are seldom, if ever, fulfilled.

(*c*) Congress is hesitant to assume large financial commitments previously carried by state and local governments.

(*d*) The expenditure of increased sums does not ensure the delivery of more and better services to a targeted population, such as the poor.

(*e*) Many white families, in the North as well as the South, will forego the advantages provided by governmental subsidies if these can be enjoyed only in close association with blacks.

It is irresponsible to move ahead with even an experimental program of educational vouchers without facing up to the results of current efforts at distributive justice. In recent years, the American people have expended many tens of billions of dollars with only modest success to achieve objectives closely related to those of this latest version of educational reform.

Recent Educational Reforms Reappraised

Let us now take a look at the efforts that have been launched and implemented in recent years to achieve the goal which is the essence of the proposal for educational vouchers, that of improving the schooling available to youngsters from low-income and minority families.

In quick review, we note first the introduction of governmental financing for preschool programs. Head Start made it possible for the children of many poor families to attend nursery schools, a type of schooling formerly available only to children of parents who were able and willing to pay. But with minor exceptions, this departure has provided a service that involves little commingling of children from different backgrounds, since Head Start has been overwhelmingly engaged in establishing new institutions to serve only the disadvantaged. There would have been no significant expansion of Head Start for children of low-income families had the government stipulated that the poor and the black be admitted in large numbers to existing, predominantly white, middle-class nursery schools.

A second major thrust has been the effort, led by the federal government and reinforced by state and local governments, to make supplemental resources available to schools whose pupils are primarily from disadvantaged homes. Two findings are important. Despite legislative dicta, much of the additional money ended up in programs available to children from middle- and even upper-income homes. Similarly, advisers to the Department of Health, Education, and Welfare have determined that many of these grants resulted initially in no appreciable gain in the educational achievement of the children who were the target of the effort.

Through a combination of legislative, judicial, and administrative pressures, reinforced in certain areas by political leverage and public opinion, some progress has been made to broaden the opportunities for black youngsters to attend predominantly white schools, where the level of student achievement has been considerably higher than in all-black schools. For a variety of reasons, including cost and length of transportation, student and teacher hostility, fear, and preference for remaining with one's own group, many black families who were given the opportunity to enroll their children in predominantly white schools did not avail themselves of this option.

In many communities black leaders have recently become more interested in securing control over ghetto schools in the belief that they have more to gain thereby than by pursuing the goal of desegregation, which is often logistically impossible and which in any case would fail many black children by stressing white, middle-class values. These leaders are saying to their local boards of education: give us the tools and we will do the job of educating our youngsters.

Finally, in harmony with the temper of the times, many parochial and private schools, which formerly were closed to blacks or admitted only a select few, have changed their admission policies to admit many more, both paying and scholarship students.

Let us distill these findings from two decades of educational reform:

(*a*) It proved easier for the federal government to start a separate preschool program for disadvantaged children than to insist that they be admitted into existing institutions which were not able to cope with large numbers of such youngsters.

(*b*) It proved easier for government to provide several billion dollars of additional educational funding annually than to assure that the money accrued to the advantage of the targeted disadvantaged population.

(*c*) The black community has become increasingly uneasy about the practicality or desirability of school desegregation and, accordingly, in many localities has opted for control over ghetto schools.

(*d*) The proportion of black students in parochial and private schools, on a paying or scholarship basis, has increased substantially in recent years.

A Closer Look at Educational Vouchers

We are now in a better position to look more closely at the proposal for instituting a system of educational vouchers and at the prospects for the achievement of the planners' priority objectives.

The Cambridge group's proposal has the following components:

(*a*) The voucher system would cover the full operating costs of education, thereby encouraging the development of a diversity of non-public schools.

(*b*) The vouchers for disadvantaged children would be worth more than those for middle- and upper-income families, thereby facilitating admission of the disadvantaged to preferred private schools.

(*c*) Discrimination would be controlled by administrative surveillance; the participating private schools would be compelled to admit at least half of their student body by lottery.

(*d*) Vouchers would be given directly to parents who, having received information from the educational authorities about competing schools, could make an effective choice.

Let us look at what is implied by these desiderata. With regard to a full-cost voucher system, the proposal carries an increase in governmental operating expenditures for public education of approximately 10 to 15 percent, or about $5 billion annually, for elementary and secondary education alone. This means, of course, an increased burden on the taxpayer. Moreover, a full-cost voucher system would lead to the maintenance of the present parochial schools and to their proliferation. Since most blacks are Protestants and most parochial schools are Catholic or Jewish, it is difficult to see how this system would benefit blacks.

The objective of assuring more blacks and other disadvantaged children access to good private schools hinges on the establishment of new schools and their ability to provide better education at the average cost per pupil in the public school. Under a voucher system, the subsequent withdrawal of sizable numbers of white and black pupils from existing public schools would raise the existing per capita cost. Advocates of the voucher system might respond that, even if the average cost were increased, it would be accompanied by an improvement in quality. In any case, the voucher system in itself would not contribute to narrowing the substantial differentials in per capita expenditures that currently exist among states and among localities within the same state.

The contention that vouchers for disadvantaged children would facilitate their acceptance at private schools because they would be worth more than vouchers for advantaged children has the following implications. The Cambridge group indicates that the special financing would come only from the federal government. Whether it would in fact be forthcoming is, to put it conservatively, moot. Moreover, the assumption that it is easy to determine which families would be entitled to a more valuable voucher does not hold, given the variability in both income and expenditures over short periods. Moreover, as the Cambridge group realizes, the fact that a student is black or poor does not necessarily imply that he will be more difficult to educate. If that is so, why should the community provide the school with an override in tuition?

If the proposal were acceptable to taxpayers, it might go a small distance toward facilitating the admission of disadvantaged children to desirable private schools. The limits on these admissions would be the numbers and proportions of underprivileged children that these schools would be willing to admit, and these of course derive from the pressures that might be exercised on the schools.

The Cambridge group expects discrimination to be controlled by administrative surveillance and by a lottery for admission but, as noted earlier, the majority of private schools are presently under religious auspices. It is highly improbable that any level of government would seek to force these institutions to accept large numbers of children of other faiths, or that minority groups would press for their children to be admitted to such institutions.

The better nondenominational private schools currently spend 50 to 150 percent more per pupil than the public schools. Yet, under the proposal, no school within the voucher system would be permitted to charge additional tuition. The impact of such a regulation should be clear. If affluent parents are willing to invest several thousand dollars annually in the education of their children, these high-tuition schools would not participate in the voucher plan. One possible consequence would be a *reduction* in the number of minority children whom these schools would accept if an alternative were to become available.

This brings us face to face with the challenge of discrimination. In communities where a small number of minority children seek admission to a private school, predominantly white schools might be willing to accept 50 percent of all admissions on a lottery basis, on the assumption that the proportion of minority pupils would fall between 10 to 20 percent. But it is doubtful that most schools would participate if the eventual distribution of white and black students would be close to 50-50.

It is assumed by the proponents of this system that, once parents are provided with information about schools by the educational authorities, they will be able to make an effective choice. The Cambridge group acknowledges that right now it is impossible to provide definitive information about the performance of a school for several reasons: disagreement about the goals of education; the need to balance short- and long-run outcomes; the inability to distinguish what the child brings into class and what the school does for him; the absence of reliable measuring instruments.

One must consider the possibility that community leadership might attempt to persuade ghetto parents to opt for one or another alternative. Moreover, it is venturesome to postulate that many ghetto parents will have the time, energy, interest, and background necessary to make informed judgments, even if the available information were much better than now appears likely. The question of relevant information would be more complicated if many new private schools spring up as a result of the introduction of a voucher system. How can we learn about the performance of these schools until several years have passed, even if the criteria are limited to what the children report?

Some Economic Speculations

The voucher plan, at least as prepared by the Cambridge group, aims to improve the school opportunities available to the black and the poor by increasing their prospects for entering existing private schools and by simultaneously encouraging the creation of new ones. With regard to the first objective, we have seen that it is predicated on the provision of more tax money for education in general as well as on the willingness of taxpayers to expend extra sums for the education of the disadvantaged. Even if these two assumptions are realistic, we have noted that more is required. The existing private schools would have to adjust their admission policies and procedures to accept a large number of disadvantaged children. While some would enter the system, the question remains, how many? We have argued that the number would be small because of the following facts. Most private schools are under denominational auspices, and the better nondenominational schools are unlikely to join the system if they expect that the proportion of black and poor children would exceed 20 percent or so. Therefore, the voucher plan must be assessed specifically from the viewpoint of its contribution to the establishment of new schools that would be superior to those currently in existence.

Economists have long proceeded on the assumption that entrepreneurship is a scarce resource. To expect to find many people capable of bringing new schools into existence, staffing them, and structuring curricula attuned to the needs and interests of the student body is contrary to experience. Thus, if existing private schools are unlikely to accept many disadvantaged youngsters under the voucher plan, and if well-run schools are difficult to establish, there is little basis for following the voucher route.

There are additional dimensions to the establishment of new schools. The Cambridge group is as silent on the matter of funds for new construction as it is on the purchase of units that are currently part of the governmental system. It is unlikely that hard-pressed taxpayers will view with favor the appropriation of additional funds for new construction on the ground that "competition" will have beneficial effects on performance. Moreover, if educational costs are not to be increased unnecessarily, a regional planning mechanism would have to assess the need for additional capacity and to choose among competing institutions, public or private. The decision would almost certainly favor the public sector.

A possible alternative would be the sale of existing public schools to private sponsors. Milton Friedman contemplated this in his original proposal. But such sales are unlikely, among other reasons because most sponsors do not have the requisite capital. Moreover, we must allow for strong resistance from the educational leadership, as well as from taxpayers, to dismemberment of the public system.

A matter related to a potential shift in ownership involves the long-range contractual commitments held by teaching and administrative staffs in public schools which cover tenure, increments based on years of service, pension rights, and related employment benefits. The chaos of 1968 in the Ocean Hill-Brownsville section of Brooklyn should serve as a warning that, even if school buildings could be sold or transferred to a new management, the legal commitments to staff represent a barrier that makes such transfers exceedingly difficult.

The basic premise underlying the voucher system is belief in the benefits of increased competition. Still, economists recognize that effective competition presupposes some approximation of equality of bargaining power. And that is missing in the case of the poor and the disadvantaged. Because they have more income, are more powerful politically, and practice housing discrimination, middle-class whites have succeeded in removing themselves from close contact with disadvantaged blacks. It is fatuous to believe that the white community will permit a voucher system to remove the barriers they have laboriously erected to protect themselves and their children from what they consider to be undesirable contact with the disadvantaged.

The other nub of the voucher proposal is to make more funds available to improve the quality of education available to disadvantaged children in the ghetto, preferably outside the present rigid educational system. As we noted previously, the presumption against such an effort's succeeding is powerful in light of the shortages of entrepreneurial talent, lack of command over facilities, and long-term employment arrangements with the present staff.

Gimmick versus Institutional Reform

The voucher system is a gimmick. It pretends to offer a solution to problems presented by segregated schools and ineffective education for the poor and disadvantaged. Let us remember that it has taken about two decades of pressure on the part of the federal government to make some headway in desegregating public schools in the South. While much remains to be accomplished, the last several years have seen progress. In the North, the situation has worsened as a result of demographic changes and housing patterns. More and more black children attend schools where most of the student body is black. The incontestable fact is that significant desegregation of Northern public schools hinges on redistribution of the urban minority population. Without housing desegregation, not much progress can be expected on the educational front—particularly in the elementary grades.

During the past decade, various levels of government have sought to increase their educational expenditures for disadvantaged pupils in the hope of improving their experiences and adding to their skills. The results to date have been unimpressive. The voucher plan does not address this problem of improving the performance of ghetto children through larger expenditures per capita, other than to facilitate the establishment or expansion of schools outside the public system. For reasons that have been adduced above, the outlook for new sponsorship is not propitious. Moreover, the question remains whether new sponsorship would lead to improved educational fare and results for the disadvantaged child.

Desegregation and improved education for black and other poor chil-

.dren are not social objectives that can be easily accomplished in a society that remains heavily racist, is unbalanced in its population distribution, and has found little relationship between additional educational inputs and educational achievement. That a gadget such as a system of educational vouchers will succeed in resolving a problem with which the courts, Congress, and state and local legislatures have had but modest success, despite resort to police power and the expenditure of many billions of dollars, is a presumption based on faith, not facts.

A Trial Balance Sheet

Recourse to a voucher system, even under the safeguards recommended by the Cambridge group (which will not necessarily be adopted or enforced by many jurisdictions), promises the following:

(a) To shore up parochial schools.

(b) To encourage black nationalists in the ghetto to organize and operate their own schools.

(c) To ease the costs of upper-middle-class parents who now send their children to private schools.

(d) To increase the number of mediocre private schools.

(e) To weaken an already weak public educational system in cities with a high proportion of minority residents.

(f) To broaden the access of some black and poor students to parochial and private schools.

(g) To counter the forces operating to enforce desegregation in public schools.

There are good reasons for citizens to be concerned about our halting progress in speeding school desegregation and about improving the quality of education for the ghetto child. Effective reform of the large city school systems will not be easy. Some years ago, an unpublished report of a White House Task Force unanimously recommended establishment of a competitive system of education in each major metropolis to be subsidized by federal funds for a period of a decade or more. Here was a remedy cut to size. The voucher system is not. Moreover, vouchers threaten many values that need reinforcement, not impairment. The country needs more institutional reforms, not more gimmicks.

Restatement of the Theory of Occupational Choice

In 1951 my colleagues and I formulated a theory of occupational choice that was published the following year in a book entitled *Occupational Choice: An Approach to a General Theory*. Now, more than two decades later, I have arrived at a reformulation of the theory in light of research undertaken since then by the Conservation of Human Resources Project at Columbia University. In contrast to my earlier view, which saw a permanent closure of the process of occupational choice at the time of entrance into the work force, at some time between the ages of 20 and 25, I now believe that the choice process is coexistent with a person's working life—that the issue may be reopened at any time. This is not a minor gloss, but points instead to a fundamental restatement of the previous position.

Review and Revision of 1951 Theory

To set the stage for this restatement, let me summarize the three key elements of the original theory. Occupational choice, we said, is a decision-making *process* that extends from prepuberty until the late teens or early twenties, at which time the individual makes a definitive occupational commitment. Many educational and related decisions made along the way have the quality of *irreversibility:* a student who is pursuing a prelaw curriculum cannot suddenly shift tack and seek admission to medical school, for example. Third, the resolution of the choice process always ends in a *compromise,* as the individual seeks to find an optimal fit between his interests, capacities, and values, and the world of work.

"Process" reappraised.   The restructuring starts by acknowledging that the process of occupational decision-making is not limited to a decade, but may extend through a person's working life. This revised conclusion about the choice process was reached as a result of continuing research. The original study had focused primarily on youths from upper-income homes who had sufficient time, money, and options to work out their choice problems—with the result that many ended up in professional careers. We did not appreciate, until a subsequent study of the career patterns of highly educated middle-aged men, that even those who enter a profession may move on to different types of work, either related or unrelated to their original choice.

Another factor that suggested a reappraisal of the matter of timing was an investigation into the occupational choices and career development of women. The male model of preparation for and choice of work, usually followed by a clear transition to full-time work or a career, does not fit the female prototype. Many women interrupt their educational preparation to marry, and their career development is frequently marked by shifts between work and home. Moreover, because the careers of their husbands traditionally have taken precedence over their own, women have been forced to modify or alter their career objectives.

A study of changes in midcareer also contributed to a better understanding of timing. As a result of this research, my colleagues and I learned that many people who had selected their careers early in life and had pursued them for a number of years—even decades—with marked success, sought new fields of endeavor as a result of changes within themselves or within their work environments.

We were able to identify three principal factors involved in the dynamic lifelong choice process. First and most important is the feedback mechanism between an original career choice and work experience. If the satisfactions that were sought originally are not forthcoming, or if work experience suggests other career possibilities that promise greater satisfactions, it is likely that a new choice will be attempted. The probability of venturing a change and of succeeding in realizing it is affected by two related factors: the degree of freedom available through family circumstances, and the pressures or options arising out of the job situation.

"Irreversibility" reversed.   Later research indicated that the second critical element of the original theory, irreversibility, also needed modification. While the multiple educational and occupational decisions a

young person makes between childhood and young adulthood do have a cumulative effect on his or her occupational prospects, we now believe that these decisions are not determining.

There are several reasons pressing for revision of this facet of the theory. The first is the elongation of the preparatory process. Since 80 percent of the age group graduates from high school, and since half of all graduates enter postsecondary education or training, decisions made prior to age 20 do not appear to be as determining as we had predicted, at least for the two out of five whose options remain open.

To a lesser degree, this is also true of those who do not have the qualifications for or the interest in entering formal education or training after high school. Many of these young adults spend two to four years in military service as a result of which their horizons may be broadened, they usually acquire some skill, and they are entitled to valuable benefits that may encourage them to pursue specialized training. Others among dropouts and terminal high school graduates have an opportunity to enter one or another type of publicly supported training, which may influence them to reassess their occupational objectives.

Most important, I have come to recognize that the career development of noncollege entrants will be materially affected by the type of employment they obtain. If it is in a large company with an internal labor market where training and promotional opportunities are geared to seniority, the key career decisions will be made at a later time; earlier occupational decisions will be of relatively little significance.

Little is left of our original emphasis on irreversibility. The principal challenge that young people face during their teens is to develop a strategy that will keep their options open, at least to the extent of assuring admission to college, or to a preferred job.

"Compromise" reconsidered.   This brings us to a reconsideration of the third element of the original theory, which held that crystallization of occupational choice involves a compromise between personal preferences and the constraints of the world of work. While I still believe that few individuals make occupational choices that satisfy all of their principal needs and desires, I now think that a more correct formulation is that of *optimization.* Men and women seek to find the best occupational fit between their changing desires and their changing circumstances. This search is a continuing one. As long as they entertain the possibility of shifting their goals, they are constantly considering a new balance in which the potential gains are weighed against the probable costs. Our studies have persuaded me to move from the static to the dynamic, from compromise to optimization.

Reformulation of the Occupational Choice Theory

Herewith, in brief, is the reformulated theory of occupational choice:

———— Occupational choice is a process that remains open as long as one is able to make or expects to make work- and career-related decisions. This process may continue throughout a person's working life.

———— While the successive decisions that are made during the preparatory period will have a shaping influence on a subsequent career, later experiences on and off the job may also materially affect one's work and life and thus can result in new career decisions.

———— People make decisions about jobs and careers with the aim of finding the best possible fit between their principal needs and desires and the opportunities and constraints in the world of work.

My reformulated theory, then, states that *occupational choice is a lifelong process of decision-making in which the individual constantly seeks to find the optimal fit between career goals and the realities of the world of work.*

The fact that an individual remains in the same occupation does not imply an unchanged occupational choice. Consider the professor who, after being granted tenure, radically reduces the time he devotes to scholarly endeavors and seeks his major satisfactions from consulting, or on the golf course. Or the colonel who, passed over for promotion to brigadier general, spends his last four years in the military service passively avoiding trouble until he qualifies for retirement.

Moreover, many who make one or more radical changes in their organizational employment—the physician who leaves private practice to become a public health administrator and who, after a few years, shifts to a senior staff position in a hospital—may still be pursuing the same occupational goal. If, as I now believe, the process of occupational choice is as long as one's work life, it is necessary to distinguish between the individual's latent and overt occupational behavior, so that the critical elements of continuity and change in career development can be isolated and evaluated.

Also important in this connection is the fact that for every individual, the passage of time is a critical factor. On the one hand, major changes occur over the years: he accumulates skill and work experience; his interests and values may shift; his personal and family circumstances may change. Moreover, prospective employers look differently at a young adult just out of school, at a worker in his prime, and at a person who is entering the last third of his working life.

In the original version of our theory we paid little attention to these facts, as we focused primarily on young white men from middle- and upper-middle-income homes who were college bound or college educated. We had deliberately selected this group because it had a wide range of options as a result of family income, sex, intelligence, race, and educational opportunity. In the two intervening decades our research increasingly concerned disadvantaged populations—the undereducated, the ineffective soldier, blacks, women, the poor—with the consequence that we became increasingly sensitive to the manner in which inequalities in income, malfunctioning institutions, and prejudice and discrimination, reduce the options and increase the constraints that many people face in choosing their occupations.

Constraints on Occupational Choice

We paid particular attention to the inhibiting and often crippling role of dysfunctional institutions in the occupational choices of large segments of the population. Children born into low-income families have relatively little prospect of developing and realizing an occupational goal that requires a college or professional education. The exceptional person can make it, but the vast majority will be unable to surmount the multiple hurdles in their way.

Low family income is not the only factor that narrows options; parental education and values are often constraining. We were impressed with the fact that many parents in relatively comfortable blue-collar families do not encourage their offspring to acquire advanced educational credentials, thus cutting them off from many high-level occupations and careers.

Educational inadequacies.   All too frequently young people from low-income homes do not develop interests, acquire skills, or formulate realistic aspirations. Instead of liberating these youngsters from the adverse environment into which they were born and brought up, schools too often operate to ensure that at the end of their educational experience these disadvantaged youngsters are firmly entrapped in a constricted lifestyle.

While considerable progress has been made in lowering discriminatory employment barriers against women and minority groups, this progress is frequently not reflected in the educational system, either in curriculum or in guidance. Consequently, a great many able young women and members of minority groups are encouraged to pursue programs that will restrict their later career options. Because school administrators and teachers do not keep up with the changes in the marketplace, they contribute to faulty decision-making on the part of many young people.

Lack of linkages.   While I believe that a significant improvement in the occupational decision-making process, particularly for the less affluent members of the community, requires major reforms in the educational system, I do not wish to focus exclusive attention on the reform of the school because of the important role played by experiences in the world of work in an open-ended occupational decision-making process. Particularly important are linkages among institutions, for instance, among different levels of the educational system; between high school and later training; between high school and the armed forces; between military and civilian careers; between home and work; between mental hospitals or prisons and the labor market. Movements between and among these different sectors are the essence of adult work experience. Consequently, if the transition from one sector to another is facilitated, there is less likelihood of slippage and concomitant waste of talent and personal frustration. Since full-time commitment to the labor market typically occurs after a young person has moved back and forth among school, the military, the civilian labor market, and homemaking, the importance of smoothing the pathways among these sectors is vital to satisfactory career resolutions.

While education is the open sesame to many prestigious occupations and careers, extended education does not assure worker competence. There is a real difference between evaluating educational background to determine whether a person has the basic knowledge required for a present or prospective assignment and using educational attainment as a screening device. Yet many employers who confuse certification with ability not only inflict hardship upon job seekers but ultimately hurt themselves.

Conclusion

The reformulation of the theory of occupational choice grows out of two decades of empirical research in manpower economics, much of which has been focused on the occupational problems of disadvantaged populations. These efforts have helped me to understand that the model used in the original investigation, a group with maximum options, could not support the subtitle *An Approach to a General Theory*. Consequently, we have sought to broaden our knowledge of the ways in which critical reality factors such as income, sex, and race operate to limit occupational choices.

The original formulation was based on a developmental approach; my reformulated theory stands on sociopsychological formulations. I have sought to make room not only for the individual as the principal actor in the decision-making process, but also for external forces, past and present, that set the parameters within which the individual must make his choice.

My greater sensitivity to reality factors in the present formulation does not contravene my conviction that the individual remains the prime mover in the decision-making process. Although young people who grow up in adverse circumstances have fewer real choices in shaping their lives and careers, everyone has some options and most of us have several.

The critical issue is whether individuals explore the better options that are available to them, especially since few choices can be exploited without cost. Unless a person is able and willing to put forth effort, he may not realize his potential. Although inequalities based on sex, race, income, and learning are pervasive and can have a crippling impact on the career and life choices of many people, many other Americans are not seriously handicapped. They have a variety of alternatives, and a high proportion among them are able and willing to make the investment required to realize their choices.

6

A Critical Look at Career Guidance

Guidance is a young profession, a little more than sixty-five years old. During its brief existence it has undergone several major changes in orientation. It began by helping low-income youngsters—most of whom were no more than 14 years old—to find jobs after stopping school. That was in 1908. In the thirties, emphasis was on "matching men and jobs" by attempting to assess the aptitudes of the unemployed and fit them with skill requirements for specific positions.

After World War II, the profession adopted a developmental approach heavily dependent on psychology. The whole person—his attitudes, feelings, and aspirations—became the center of concern. The guidance counselor became, in effect, a therapist. No longer was he chiefly concerned with specifically vocational problems. The net result of this change is that present-day guidance has an exaggerated and unrealizable ambition: to add significantly to human happiness. Today, *career* guidance represents a minor commitment of the counseling profession.

A study of career guidance is complex, since it is provided at thousands of sites and in many different kinds of settings. Its practitioners have widely varying educational backgrounds, and the potential clientele represents diversity in age, race and ethnicity, income level, place of residence, and stage of career development.

For three years in the late 1960s, our Conservation of Human Resources Project studied how guidance performs its functions and how well it meets society's needs. The study group investigated practitioners, the institutional frameworks in which they work, and the effectiveness of guidance as a tool in career decision-making. The researchers made recommendations—to the profession and to the public—for strengthening guidance and for expanding its use.

Logistics of Guidance

An estimated sixty thousand persons work as guidance counselors in the United States. Perhaps as many as two-thirds of them are employed in secondary schools. The next largest group works in vocational rehabilitation agencies and the Federal-State Employment Service. A small number of counselors work in elementary schools, colleges and universities, community service or profit-making organizations, or are self-employed.

This distribution reflects an inadequate allocation of guidance resources for the large number of persons with serious career problems, including members of minority groups, college students, young out-of-school adults, returning veterans, mature women reentering the labor force, experienced workers seeking to change jobs or careers, and older persons approaching retirement. Guidance today is preoccupied with youth to the neglect of adults; it is overly concerned with educational goals and underinvolved with the problems of the workplace.

Counselor Training

Most school counselors are former teachers, because almost every state requires that a school counselor have a teaching license. This pattern has no counterpart in any other professional field, with the possible exception of public health where the leadership—but only the leadership—is recruited from medical school graduates. Inasmuch as teaching licenses are required for school counselors, those who wish to enter counseling must first undertake teacher training and then enter counselor education programs. The requirement that school counselors have teaching licenses is expensive, redundant, and largely unnecessary. In addition, most school counselors acquire either a certificate or a master's degree by attending part-time graduate programs that contain a heavy dose of didactic instruction in psychology and very little instruction about occupations and the labor market.

Guidance counselors in vocational rehabilitation agencies and the Employment Service come from a wider array of occupational backgrounds than do school counselors. Some begin their careers in industry, social work, or teaching, while others enter counseling immediately after college. A significant number have worked in some other capacity for their present employers before becoming guidance counselors. The educational credentials of rehabilitation agency and Employment Service counselors range downward from doctorates in clinical psychology followed by a year's internship to less than a college degree.

Of course, not all counselor training takes place in graduate schools. In every occupation skills are acquired on the job. Counselors can grow in expertise and understanding as they work with their clients. An important consideration here is the quality of professional supervision a counselor receives; he may or may not be able to learn from highly trained and experienced colleagues. Supportive learning environment is probably more characteristic of guidance and professional counseling in the Veterans Administration and in well-run community agencies than in the typical school or Employment Service setting where counselors often are supervised by administrators who know little about guidance.

The training of guidance counselors usually takes place in schools of education or in allied departments. Faculty and courses frequently are borrowed from cognate departments of psychology or sociology and are adjusted, often poorly, to the needs of students of guidance. Many students attend classes part-time while they earn a living, which makes it difficult for them to become fully engaged in their studies. There is overemphasis on the classroom to the neglect of field work. These are only a few of the problems at the education and training level.

Problems of School Guidance

As we have seen, most guidance counseling takes place in junior and senior high schools. At these sites the focus of counseling is upon helping students to achieve emotional maturity. High school counselors also spend time helping upperclassmen decide on suitable colleges and fill out applications.

Recently guidance has been making strong inroads into elementary schools. While there is no question that elementary schools need strengthening, there is a serious question whether provision of more guidance personnel is a realistic response. Curriculum change, ungraded classes, remediation, and similar innovations in the elementary school system appear worthwhile but, except for some instruction about the world of work by the classroom teacher, there is no rationale for an elementary school service devoted to individual career decision-making. If there are missing pupil personnel services at lower grade levels, they may have to be supplied; but the unique skills of the career guidance profession are not relevant for very young children who are a long way from making an occupational choice. If money were of no concern, it might be worth experimenting with elementary school guidance; but since funds are limited, other unmet needs should take priority.

Moreover, elementary schools are not handling their principal function well. They are not providing many children with the fundamental skills essential to later performance. It is certainly more important for pupils in the lower grades to learn to read, write, and compute than to receive a service that is only peripheral to the learning function.

The great preoccupation of counselors with emotional development is based on the assumption that young people need help in clearing away the psychological underbrush that litters their pathways into the world. If this is done, the profession believes, young people will be better able to make sound choices.

Actually, a high proportion of high school counselors are not engaged in any type of guidance. Instead, they are heavily involved in helping their principals keep the schools orderly. They deal with disturbed students, those in trouble with the police, or youths with drug problems. In other words, they are "cooling it" for the administration. Admittedly these are necessary tasks, but when performed by guidance personnel, the counselors' effectiveness is reduced. Many students come to consider counselors as administration stooges, rather than as student advocates.

It is always difficult for a staff member to alert a superior about institutional malfunctioning. Nevertheless, it is part of a professional's responsibility to point out shortfalls to both insiders and concerned outsiders. Just as the medical profession has no right to refrain from publicizing the existence of preventable lead poisoning in many children, counselors have no right to observe maltreatment or mishandling of pupils without calling it to the attention of those in authority, in or out of the school. They must be able to judge what they can and cannot remedy themselves. Counselors cannot change the incomes of ghetto residents or eliminate prejudice, but they can press for nondiscriminatory assistance and instruction and they can make an effort to protect disadvantaged youngsters from adverse influences.

I have been charged with emphasizing career guidance and neglecting guidance directed to human potential and personal development; my response is that I do not believe that any one group is able to deal with a person's total situation. Moreover, in light of the country's investment in education and the critical importance of work, a focus upon individual career decisions covers a great deal of important territory. There are other groups with special expertise in handling psychological, social, and learning problems. The major focus of the counselor at the school level should be on educational and career planning.

Another problem concerns the receptivity to counseling, especially among captive clients like students. It might be advantageous if students were presented with a view of guidance in terms of the potential help it offers and given the option of accepting or rejecting these services. The reluctant client has little motivation to make effective use of the proffered help. Like all services, guidance can benefit only those who understand its potential value.

Since the paths of many youngsters have been narrowed or closed because of family poverty, minority status, poor schooling, and the like, their prime need is for substantive advice about jobs, skill training, community colleges, and services that can help them find a way to make a living. Guidance counselors might be able to broaden the options of these young people if counseling were better oriented to their needs.

Those who can best afford self-exploration—young people from the middle and upper classes—have the largest number of options, but the assumption that guidance significantly enhances their prospects for a satisfying life is open to challenge. Suburban high school students, who generally have the greatest access to guidance services, see counselors on the average of two to four times a year during six years of junior and senior high school for less than twenty minutes per session. At the beginning of the 1970s, the national ratio of counselors to students was in the neighborhood of 1 to 550. With the current amount of counseling available to each student, it would be astonishing indeed if guidance could significantly change his life.

The fact is that young people from high-income homes have more leeway than the poor both to make mistakes in their career planning and to recover from their errors. Young people from high-income families, for example, can stay in school longer and can eventually achieve a satisfactory resolution of their career problems by revising their plans (several times, if necessary) if they are dissatisfied with their initial choices. They learn about their strengths, interests, values, potentialities, and limitations through a dynamic process that starts at birth and stretches over a long period; and they have continued inputs from family, friends, and peers. The process of exploration is much shorter for disadvantaged youngsters who must make early decisions about how to support themselves.

Inadequacies of Career Information

Even if counselors were able to offer extensive vocational assistance, there would still be little they could do for the large numbers of young people who pass through an educational system that fails to teach them essential skills and prepare them for work. Correcting this situation requires basic institutional realignments of priorities and resources. Counseling alone—either in or out of the school system—cannot make up for the deficiencies of the educational system.

Nevertheless, the profession could help young people to make the important and often difficult transition from school to work. Today printed information about various careers all too often is perfunctorily distributed. Most of these materials have not been prepared specifically for students, nor are they frequently read by them. They seldom tell a student what he wants or needs to know about jobs in his neighborhood, such as how to get them, how much they pay, or what kind of future they hold.

Other occupational information that counselors use also is seriously deficient. Materials such as the *Occupational Outlook Handbook*, for example, are unsuited to the needs of high school dropouts or to high school graduates who are ready to enter the labor force. Of limited use also to students who plan to continue their education or training, they tend to be too general in describing the nature of specific jobs, the alternative paths into work, the probable limits of advancement in each field, and linkages among occupations. Moreover, employment and wage data are given in national aggregates, rather than in detail for regional and local labor markets.

The guidance profession places disproportionate stress on tests and other instruments, such as checklists and inventories, to learn about the individual's aptitudes, interests, and values. As a result, guidance personnel focus on personal characteristics to the neglect of occupational realities.

Recently there have been experimental efforts to computerize information for career decision-making. At best, these efforts are premature. The cost of computer installations can be justified only if they are in steady use and are fed data that are updated constantly, as in the job banks of the Employment Service. At worst, the computerization of information for career decision-making focuses attention on gadgetry and deflects the attention of the guidance profession from the critical tasks of deepening understanding of the process of making choices and improving the quality of information on which career judgments are based.

Counseling as a Profession

Guidance generally is deficient in the kind of standards that mark other professions. Usually the hallmarks of a profession are strong educational and training institutions that both instruct and indoctrinate future practitioners; professional responsibility for determining the shape and direction of one's work, subject to peer judgments and control; and career opportunities that attract and hold able people in the profession. In the guidance profession these characteristics are the exception, not the rule.

On the job, most guidance personnel have their work cut out for them, not by themselves, but by others. They are subject far more to the administrative exigencies of the school or agency for which they work than to professional goals and guidelines. Guidance personnel must make it clear to administrators that their responsibilities are to their clients and not to the institutions within which they perform their services. Since they have no strong professional identity and since there are many competing groups with similar goals, guidance personnel often experience identity crises. There has been little understanding of the large institutional framework within which guidance operates and little interchange with key groups who affect outcomes. For example, counselors and teachers tend to have minimal opportunity or desire to interact. And even relations between counselors and colleagues who are psychologists or social workers are often neglected. Worse still, there are practically no interchanges between counselors and economists, sociologists, and labor market specialists. When it comes to career opportunities, there are few rungs on the guidance ladder; for most persons, there is no place to advance unless they leave the guidance field.

Recommendations to the Profession

Despite many weaknesses, guidance has the potential for providing important services that are sorely needed by many persons. The Conservation of Human Resources Project has made a number of proposals, based upon its study, that are directed toward helping the guidance profession realize its full potential. These recommendations fall into two categories—those addressed to the profession itself, and those directed to the public which, by its attitudes and actions, determines the demands made on and the support available to the guidance field.

The profession should take the following steps:

——Abandon its psychotherapeutic focus and return to its initial concentration on educational and career guidance. In the Employment Service and at other sites where career guidance is emphasized, it is clear that the profession can perform a vital function for the unemployed, minorities, veterans, and others whose employment has been erratic or nonexistent.

——Firmly link counseling services to other kinds of client support. For example, unless the counselor can deliver concrete help to students with inferior educational preparation, he is wasting his and their time. Students who need remedial education, help in entering a training program, and aid in getting a job are likely to look upon nonspecific advice as worthless. Among the many lessons learned in administering the Manpower Development and Training Act is that some clients, particularly the disadvantaged, need intensive, wide-ranging supportive services. These may include orientation to work, day care for their children, transportation, skill training, job counseling, job referral, and even some assistance with medical and other problems prior to and during the initial stages of employment. The counselor can be the link between his client and the services available in the community.

—— Initiate major reforms in the education and training of guidance counselors. A full-time one-year graduate program would be preferable to the present pattern of part-time study. The curriculum should include emphasis on the world of work and pathways into it; on mobilizing and using community resources; and on supervised field work. Less psychology should be offered in favor of more economics and sociology so that students can develop a more knowledgeable view of the world with which their clients must cope. All students should be required to participate in practicums under supervision. Finally, counselor educators themselves should be recruited from a variety of disciplines, instead of primarily from subspecialties of psychology as is now the case.

—— Seek to change the almost universal regulation that only teachers can become certified school counselors. In this way the flow of recruits into counseling can be widened to include individuals from a variety of backgrounds.

—— Expand guidance resources for both young and mature adults, and retard the slow but steady trend toward bringing guidance services into the elementary school. Properly trained guidance counselors primarily concerned with career development have little to contribute to young children. Moreover, school psychologists and other pupil personnel specialists are increasingly available, and they are better able than guidance counselors to deal with the problems that beset elementary pupils.

Recommendations to the Public and the Government

There is much that government now does in the field of guidance that it should continue to do, only better. For instance, the federal government recognizes that guidance should be an integral part of an Employment Service that aims to provide broad services to its clients, including large numbers of disadvantaged persons. Nonetheless, the federal government has not assumed leadership to see that the guidance function is performed effectively rather than perfunctorily.

Similarly, government plays a critical role in collecting the labor market and occupational data that provide key inputs for career guidance. But the federal government, in association with state and local governments, has not taken the essential next steps to make such information useful at the local and regional level where people study, work, and live. Until this is done, the informational base available for career guidance remains seriously deficient.

As far as the public is concerned, there is much that it can and should do to strengthen the effectiveness of guidance services. It must encourage schools to draw more heavily on local resources (employers, trade unions, professions); it must exercise oversight to see that discriminatory attitudes and advice are not tolerated; it should press for evaluations that will reveal the effectiveness of the services young people and adults receive. And it should do what it can to encourage linkages among the key institutions involved in assisting people with respect to the world of work and encourage innovative efforts to improve these institutions and the linkages among them.

Concluding Comments

In light of the diverse population groups who could benefit from guidance services, it has been suggested that the guidance function be performed as part of a broad community service, rather than confined to its present settings. I oppose such a move, primarily because of my familiarity with the realities of public finance. Since schools, the Employment Service, and the Veterans Administration have managed to establish a claim for guidance services as part of their operating budgets, the removal of guidance from these settings would risk loss of much of the financing that is presently available. While theoretically it would be desirable to separate guidance from its present institutional bases, realistically the risk is too great.

However, there is no reason why community-based guidance services should not be organized to serve paying clients. I doubt there are quality services in any field that do not require a direct consumer contribution to cover at least part of the costs. One of the troubles with guidance is that it is so heavily dependent on the public purse. If it really has so much to offer the American public, some part of the public should be willing to defray some part of the cost.

The problem is that the people who have the most need for guidance services are those with the least ability to pay. Obviously services for the poor and near-poor should be subsidized. Nevertheless it is interesting to speculate why guidance has made so little headway in the private and nonprofit sectors. Presumably the consumer is reluctant to pay for what guidance can offer.

More than ever before, our society needs strong career guidance services. We are concerned that there be open pathways to employment and equal opportunity in employment, and we are no longer willing to leave such matters to the vagaries of birth and chance. At the same time, there are rapidly changing requirements for industrial jobs, altered market conditions for professional manpower, new paraprofessional occupations, and many other labor market trends that make occupational choice and adjustment more difficult. Clearly we need quality career guidance.

What is here recommended harks back to the early days of the guidance movement when occupational considerations were to the fore. This is why guidance in elementary schools appears counter to what we view as the central purpose of guidance and why we question its expansion. We believe that it expanded primarily in obedience to Sutton's Law—that is where the money is!

The guidance profession can also be criticized for being too ingrown, for neglecting the needs of adults, and for failing to make effective use of community resources.

We are now at a crossroads with much experience behind us and a clearer view of the alternatives ahead. With the cooperative efforts of the profession, a concerned public, and more alert governments, we can use what we have learned to strengthen career guidance so that it can provide more and better services to a public that needs them.

WORK

The nine chapters that comprise Part Two address two distinct but related themes. The first four chapters deal with an old subject that has recently acquired increased visibility—work and its discontents—and the ways in which the conditions of the workplace can be improved to contribute to the quality of the workingman's life. This theme can be traced back to Adam Smith and it has come to the fore most recently in the form of the sociotechnical approach in Great Britain, Norway, and the United States.

In the remaining five essays, the focus is shifted from work per se to workers and the major problems resulting from such diverse trends as the shifting requirements for educated manpower, the changing roles of women, the position of the blue-collar worker in the perspective of changes in twentieth century America, and the special manpower challenges facing the armed forces. In each instance, manpower analyses are used to uncover the deeper dimensions of the problems; at the same time, consideration is given to the institutional forces that precipitated the issues and that must be altered before effective solutions can be designed.

7

Work: The Eye of the Hurricane

Webster's defines work as the "exertion of strength or faculties for the accomplishment of something." According to this definition, playing tennis or even sexual activity is work! Perhaps so for the tennis professional or the prostitute, but not for others. Moreover, eating fits this definition of work and creates an additional problem: unless one eats, one cannot work. How, then, can we distinguish between the essential preconditions for work and the performance of work? Even if we can make an operational differentiation between eating and working (see Leo Bartemeier's essay, "Eating and Working," in the July 1950 *American Journal of Ortho-Psychiatry*), where can we draw the line between learning and working? For example, is the surgical resident being educated or is he working, or is he, in fact, doing both? Certainly overlap exists between work and recreation: an obvious example is the businessman who negotiates a deal in a restaurant or on the golf course.

Once we became aware of the analytical complexities of defining work, my colleagues and I eschewed the phenomenological challenge and proceeded with the following pragmatic approach.

We see work as a socially necessary activity for almost all men and for a growing proportion of women who must "sell their labor power," to use the Marxian phrase, to earn income that enables them to support themselves and their dependents. The overriding dimension of work is social compulsion. This is not to deny that people derive gratification from work per se: people on the upper end of the income ladder ascribe less importance to extrinsic rewards, such as income and job security, and more importance to intrinsic or concomitant goals, such as personal fulfillment and interpersonal relationships.

We recognize that this pragmatic approach does not resolve many important questions, such as why housewives are not included in the work force by the census takers even though they may spend as many as eighty hours a week running their households and rearing children. In addition, many other people do not fall into clearly defined labor force categories: the college athlete who receives a full scholarship; the writer who is supported by an allowance from home: the professor who gets a consultant's fee for traveling overseas during his summer vacation.

Although no simple or even complex definition can capture the multiple facets of work, our research has developed new understanding about certain of its aspects, primarily in its conventional sense as an income-producing activity.

Gleanings

My colleagues and I have focused on one or another dimension of work in our research investigations during the past three decades. However, neither as a group nor individually have we so far presented a broad treatment of the theme. It is a weakness of academics to narrow their focus, but they do so because a wider area is more difficult to master, particularly inductively. Moreover, reasonable men weigh the successes and failures of their predecessors: since the formulations of even Marx, Freud, and Veblen with respect to work are limited in insight, substance, and validity, it behooves others to proceed circumspectly. That is why we have taken one step at a time.

We received our first research grant at Columbia University in 1939 to study unemployment in South Wales and in New York City. The propositions set forth below represent gleanings from a continuing research program since that time, interrupted only by World War II, although studies initiated earlier were published during the war.

The first study, noted above, probed the individual family, community, and national consequences of a continuing high level of unemployment. Thus lack of work was our initial route into the study of work. We documented in considerable depth the disorganization in the lives of adults and children when the conventional breadwinner, the father, lost his job and despite repeated efforts was unable to find another. Work was no longer the fulcrum around which his life and the lives of the other members of his family were organized. We did not speculate whether, in a postindustrial society, there could be an equivalent for work. In the 1930s such a prospect was not considered. We were overwhelmingly impressed by the need of men to be able to spend their energies in purposeful activity and to discharge their roles as family providers. When they were robbed of this opportunity, especially when entire communities suffered an erosion of their economies, as in South Wales, life slowly ground to a standstill and one day could no longer be distinguished from the next, nor one year from another.

The study of the long-term unemployed in New York City added important increments to our understanding. It alerted us to the important satisfactions that men derive from contacts with co-workers, not only on the job, but while traveling to and from work, and through social relations off the job. It indicated that work provides not only satisfactions for the worker, but also for his wife—who knows that she can count on many hours when the house is hers, alone. The pleasure a worker derives from buying presents for his wife and children also helped us to recognize the importance of the extrinsic satisfactions derived from work.

Despite conventional belief that men who do not work spend much of their free time in intensified sexual activity, our studies demonstrate the opposite. When a man's ego is undermined by his inability to perform his accustomed role as breadwinner, his libido is diminished, not heightened. Moreover, we learned that some wives who had engaged in sexual relations with their husbands when they were employed, balked when the men no longer brought home a paycheck. As one woman put it, "FDR wears the pants in this family—he gives us our money!"

In the unemployed families we studied in both locations, husbands and wives were living together. While this was of considerable support to their children, early developmental disturbances did exist among children who were growing up with unemployed fathers—and in parts of South Wales, no men worked.

Let us call attention briefly to the use we made of some suggestive data presented by Kinsey about the important linkage between work and sex. In "Class and Sex Behavior," we developed a hypothesis that explains a finding Kinsey had not explored, namely, that the premarital sexual behavior of upwardly mobile persons resembles the group they eventually join, not their group of origin. We found the explanation in the value system that informs the lives of the upwardly mobile: their long-term perspectives; their ability to forego immediate gratification; and their capacity for sublimation. The linkage between a value structure and sexual behavior is suggested by the many estranged members of the present younger generation who challenge the existing middle-class orientation with its emphasis on material goals, long periods of preparation, and the authority of teachers. They express their disdain by turning their backs on study and work in favor of immediate gratification via sex and drugs.

After the end of World War II, a restructured research team started to study occupational choice and adjustment to work, since our earlier investigations into unemployment had alerted us to the critical role that work plays in ordering the lives of individuals and societies. We soon discovered that occupational choice was a sufficiently complex phenomenon to warrant our full attention. The principal finding from our systematic investigation of this subject was that occupational choice is not a single decision, but the outgrowth of a decade or more of sequential decisions. In time these decisions become less readily reversible, and final choice represents a compromise between what the individual wants to do and his access to educational and employment opportunities. In carrying out this investigation, we identified some of the linkages between the process of occupational decision-making and the complex arena of work satisfaction.

During the early 1950s our research at Columbia broadened and deepened its focus from concern with the psychological factors to an institutional approach.

A few illustrations will indicate our new interest in the historical, sociological, and political aspects of work. It has been accepted doctrine since the days of Karl Marx, although Adam Smith had earlier discussed the same theme, that excessive specialization has the effect of alienating the worker from his work. The new romantics on the left, from Fromm to Marcuse, have given renewed life to this doctrine. However, we were unable to find support for it in our extensive investigation of the lives of American workers in the early part of the twentieth century. The life stories of laborers, operatives, skilled workers, and white-collar workers identify many aspects of their work to which they objected, often vigorously, and which they fought to change. But they were not alienated: they accepted what they were doing, even if their work entailed disemboweling cattle or attaching fenders day after day, week after week, year after year. They never questioned that it was useful work and that it had to be done. Most importantly, they accepted the fact that, without more education or some special skill, it was practically inevitable that they would be engaged in routine tasks. The error made by theorists who postulate that most assembly-line workers are alienated is that of projecting their own values and aspirations upon the mass of blue-collar workers, just as affluent Americans err in assuming that most Asians and Africans are miserable because they have an annual income equal to only one-fortieth of their own.

However, the fact that we were unable to find objective evidence of widespread alienation among American workers during the first half of this century does not mean that the young people who are joining the labor force today will tolerate the oppressive pace and the other disagreeable concomitants of the assembly line. The odds are that they will not!

The interest that prompted General Dwight Eisenhower to establish the Conservation of Human Resources Project when he became president of Columbia University grew out of his concern about the large-scale manpower problems revealed during World War II when 18 million young Americans were screened for military service and only about 16 million were accepted. Ineffective performance in terms of the interplay between individual shortcomings and institutional malfunctioning was the focus of a series of studies published during the 1950s.

In brief, these several investigations made the following contributions to an understanding of work:

Ineffective performance cannot be traced to the individual alone without taking account of organizational and societal determinants.

It is presumptuous for psychiatrists and psychologists to contend that they can prognosticate on the basis of their screening instruments whether or not a man can perform effectively.

While most men can encapsulate severe stress, even breakdown, and eventually return to their previous level of performance, some are permanently incapacitated by unanticipated stress.

Most people are able to meet minimum work requirements and to discharge their basic responsibilities if they have adequate leadership and, in the event of difficulties, some interim support.

Remorseless racial discrimination can so disturb the value system, expectations, and behavior patterns of members of a minority group that it will ensure their ineffectiveness.

In our view the surprising finding about blacks was not the large number who failed but the larger number who, despite severe deprivations, maltreatment, and isolation, were able to surmount these barriers.

Prior to World War II, the staff had explored the misfit between college-educated women and their later work experience. A renewed interest in women and work grew out of our investigation of occupational choice, which demonstrated striking differences in the manner in which males and females approach the problem of careers. In the middle 1950s, the National Manpower Council directed its attention to the broad subject of womanpower, and its findings and recommendations helped to place the subject high on the nation's agenda. Its report demonstrated that the exigencies of World War II had initiated a revolution by encouraging the employment of middle-class married women, a revolution that was likely to continue (as in fact it has). It noted serious hindrances to the effective utilization of women's potentials and skills, and recommended action to remove arbitrary barriers.

In the mid-1960s, as an outgrowth of our general interest in the relation between talent and performance, we returned once again to the subject of women and produced two studies that made further contributions to our understanding. Talented women have a greater number of options than their male counterparts in assigning a role to work in their lives. Since many women desire and plan for both motherhood and a career, there is a much greater degree of ambiguity in their work decisions as a result of their realizing that their eventual careers will be greatly influenced by the attitudes and support of the men they marry. Although many talented women deliberately settle for less success in the occupational arena in favor of greater gains elsewhere, others refuse to make this accommodation.

A counterpart study of talented men led us to look more intensively at the problems of work satisfaction, a subject that has long attracted the interest of psychologists and sociologists but that had not, in our view, been adequately researched. We developed criteria that distinguish the work orientation of men in terms of whether their primary goal is autonomy, power, social relationships, or ideological involvement. This was followed by a schema of work satisfaction that is related to five major individual concerns: the nature of the work, the scope for self-expression, freedom of action, social contribution, and rewards and extrinsic concomitants.

Since the United States had taken the lead in developing arbitration (a new institution to deal with conflicts in the work arena), the Conservation Project staff decided in the early 1960s to review systematically the awards of leading arbitrators in an attempt to understand more about the interplay between social values and the rights of employers and employees. We found in the decisions of leading arbitrators a determination to expand the reach of democratic values by treating workers first and foremost as men; next, as citizens; and only thirdly as employees who had entered into a contractual relationship to provide labor power in exchange for wages and other perquisites.

The concept of laissez-faire had been in retreat for more than a century, but the American worker's insistence on recognition as an individual, apart from his status as an employee, was underscored by this critical review of leading arbitration awards. Here were warning signs of changing worker expectations and behavior that have only recently become manifest in industrial centers and that may eventually transform the American industrial scene.

The macrodeterminants of the revolution in work also attracted our attention and were dealt with selectively in a series of studies in the 1950s and 1960s. We touched upon a great many themes, from the impact of affluence on the expectations of new entrants into the work force to the corrosive influence of large organizations upon employees. We noted, in particular, the subtle shift from a society in which men from different backgrounds used to compete in the work arena to one in which life chances were largely determined at birth and in school. To compound the difficulties—and the inequities—organizations have come to rely increasingly on educational certification, which tells us more about a person's father than about his own abilities.

Although it is not possible here to do more than trace the outlines of our research investigations into work over the last thirty years (they have been presented in more than thirty books), the above summary serves its purpose if it helps the reader to identify the major themes that have been pursued.

Propositions

Our investigations of work showed it to be so complex that we avoided a premature commitment to a general theory. Now we are approaching the point where we will be able to pull together much of what we have learned and place it within a framework of the world that may come to be. The propositions set out below are based on the conviction that fundamental shifts are occurring in the role of work in the lives of individuals and of societies, not only in the developed industrial nations but also in countries that are beginning to experience a quickening of their economies. Our concentration here, at least initially, will be on what is happening in the United States, and to a lesser degree, in the advanced economies of Western Europe.

——It is erroneous to postulate a marked decline in the work ethic in America and especially to attribute it to youth alone. We believe that changes have been under way for some time in the ways in which large numbers of Americans of all ages relate to work.

——Similarly, we believe it is an error to single out any particular occupational group, such as blue-collar or service workers, and argue that they have lost pride in workmanship and are no longer willing to give a day's work for a day's pay. Our counterpoint is that, if such trends can be validated, they can be found in all occupational groups, although not necessarily to the same degree. The work attitudes and behavior of professionals and other white-collar workers have much in common with those of workers in other categories.

——The American work ethic may be altered as small-scale independent enterprise gives way still further to large organizational structures characterized by hired management, salaried professionals, and bureaucratized staffs. It is difficult to discern whether a new work ethic will develop as a result of these organizational changes, particularly when taken in conjunction with transformations occurring in the wider economic, political, and social spheres.

Nevertheless, we can expect that, as a society moves away from a subsistence standard of living, and if we are more successful in establishing and maintaining a high level of employment, people's attitudes toward their work and careers will be significantly altered. The majority of the present work force has had no experience prior to the mid-1970s with a prolonged high level of unemployment, and average family income has risen to above $10,000. While many Americans still are under- or unemployed and live in poverty, the majority is largely free of these twin scourges. As American workers become increasingly affluent, their relation to the work arena is bound to be appreciably different from that of their fathers, and particularly their grandfathers, who lived under oppressive threats.

——Allowance must also be made for the successful efforts of ever-larger groups of workers—professional and managerial, other white-collar, blue-collar, and (recently) service workers—to develop structures through which they are able to influence the conditions under which they work, output norms, rewards, promotion ladders, and job security. Clearly, as workers are able to exert more leverage on these several fronts, they will certainly use their power to bring about changes they consider desirable. The structures they develop may also affect the quantity and quality of work and the manner in which rewards are distributed.

——In the past, most men began working regularly in their early teens and continued until they dropped in their tracks. Today, more and more young people do not get regular jobs until they are in their early or mid-twenties. There is little doubt that this markedly elongated preparatory process affects their expectations and responses as members of the labor force.

——The outstanding characteristic of large organizations is their ability to survive the loss of any worker, including the man at the top. They have been able to accomplish this by attracting and retaining a large group of potential executives who are assessed and promoted over time, and by organizing work so that it can be performed no matter what happens to any man or group of men. But these adaptive approaches are expensive. Too little attention has been paid to the way in which employee initiative, energy, and motivation are drained by the way in which large organizations function.

——An interesting clue to what may well be a deep malaise is seen in the small but growing number of people who have had successful careers but who decide in midstream to make a break and seek a new occupation. While the reasons for these attempts at breakaway are many and diverse, they seem to be rooted in varying degrees of dissatisfaction with the work these individuals have been doing.

——It is often difficult to assess the specific contribution of the individual in our society, because work is increasingly performed in groups and because the key to group cohesion and performance lies in "political arrangements" among the members and the leadership. Thus personal acceptability is often confused with technical competence. Recognizing this fact, as they must, many men decide early in their careers that rewards will come from conformity and agreeableness, not from innovative ideas or the expenditure of extra energy.

——Another important concomitant of how large organizations operate, and one that has an impact on how people work, is the restricted room at the top—a limitation that quickly becomes clear to most employees. Once they recognize it, many recalculate the probabilities of attaining one of the key prizes and the costs that attach to the effort. Until there is evidence to the contrary, it is reasonable to postulate that most men early seek a niche where they can enjoy peace, security, and modest rewards. Once they make such a decision, it must infuse all aspects of their work.

——About 40 percent of all working persons are women. We know little about what different groups of women want from work, except that many of them have begun to fight against the discrimination to which they have been subjected. Moreover, most working women are married, and changes in their career aspirations and behavior will inevitably lead to changes in the lives of their husbands and children.

——Finally, we must recognize that the close links that formerly existed between work and income have been loosened with consequences that are just beginning to surface. The welfare mess is one tip of the iceberg. There are many others: middle-class youth who shun employment while living on family allowances; ghetto youth who refuse low-paying jobs in favor of more glamorous and better-paying illegal activity; potential workers who are unwilling to accept certain types of jobs; assembly-line workers who prefer a lower pay check and more leisure. There is no need to add to this list to make the point that, once a substantial proportion of society is able to shift its preference away from work, the consequences are likely to be momentous.

Eye of the Hurricane

The foregoing propositions add up to one unequivocal conclusion. The traditional American work ethic can no longer be relied upon to give direction and momentum to the work goals of many people. This concluding section will demonstrate that so radical a transformation in

values is linked to other changes in critical aspects of modern life. Specifically, new attitudes and behavior toward religion, sex, materialism, and
the family are being propelled by the same forces that are altering views
about work.

These, apparently, are the common elements:

————The broad challenge to the legitimacy of established institutions;
————The unwillingness of many individuals to accept authoritative
prescriptions for their goals and behavior;
————The loosening of the bonds of institutional identification;
————The presumption that the individual is the sole judge of what is
right and proper for himself.

Here are some brief illustrations of these elements that suggest the rapid
rate at which the moorings of Western society are being cut. Catholic
priests ask to be released from their vows of celibacy; nuns march in public protest against their bishop; graduates of West Point apply for separation from the Army on grounds of conscience; soldiers refuse to go out
on patrol; students ransack the files of their college president and release
to the press his personal correspondence; professors negotiate like hard-
ened trade unionists; a spouse precipitously walks out of a marriage of
twenty years' duration.

One should not be surprised, therefore, that many people no longer
assume that they must work as hard as they can; certainly, many do not
feel it necessary to work regularly. If the work that is available interests
them, if it holds promise of utilizing their skills, if it pays a decent wage
and offers an opportunity for advancement, then they may feel it is
worthwhile.

Moreover, workers are accelerating their challenges to management's
authority. In their view, since nothing can be produced and no profits
earned without their participation, they should have a role in all decision-
making that impinges on their interests, from determining shift schedules
to setting output norms and establishing criteria for promotion and separation. Management's prerogatives are questioned daily and, each time
a new labor contract is negotiated, the employer's scope for decision-
making is narrowed.

The bonds of identification between the worker and the institution that
employs him are constantly being loosened. This holds for the professor
at an Ivy League college and the physician at a major teaching hospital as
much as for the factory operative and the service worker. Many employees deliberately avoid investing much energy or effort in the organization
for which they work because they believe that it will always put its own
interests above those of the individual. These pervasive new attitudes and
behavior toward work indicate that more and more individuals look to

themselves rather than to the organization to protect their goals and interests.

The crisis that the Western world may be approaching is not limited to the work arena but encompasses all major institutions from the family to the state. Industrialization, urbanization, and democracy require that men seek to realize their goals through institutions. But a malaise now characterizes ever-larger numbers of persons who question the ability of the established institutions to be responsive to their goals. They find themselves in latent or overt conflict with these institutions. Men are not refusing to work, but they are seeking to use their energies in new ways to provide greater satisfactions. A hurricane is building up with work as its eye. It is impossible to see which institutions will collapse and which will withstand the strong winds. And it is impossible to know how the landscape will look after the debris is removed and new structures are put into place. But of one thing we can be sure: the landscape will be different.

Pertinent Studies*

Listed below are publications that have resulted from the several research studies carried out by the Conservation Project over the past three decades. They provide the foundation for most of the generalizations developed in Chapter 7.

Grass on the Slag Heaps: The Story of the Welsh Miners (New York, Harper, 1942).

The Unemployed (New York, Harper, 1943).

Occupational Choice: An Approach to a General Theory (New York, Columbia University Press, 1951).

The Uneducated (New York, Columbia University Press, 1953).

Psychiatry and Military Manpower Policy (New York, Kings Crown Press, Columbia, 1953).

The Negro Potential (New York, Columbia University Press, 1956).

The National Manpower Council, *Womanpower* (New York, Columbia University Press, 1957).

Work in the Lives of Married Women (New York, Columbia University Press, 1958).

Human Resources: The Wealth of a Nation (New York, Simon and Schuster, 1958).

The Optimistic Tradition and American Youth (New York, Columbia University Press, 1962).

Democratic Values and the Rights of Management (New York, Columbia University Press, 1963).

*Except where otherwise indicated, Eli Ginzberg is the senior or sole author.

Talent and Performance (New York, Columbia University Press, 1964).

The Troublesome Presence: American Democracy and the Negro (New York, Free Press-Macmillan, 1964).

The American Worker in the Twentieth Century: A History through Autobiographies (New York, Free Press-Macmillan, 1964).

Educated American Women: Self-Portraits (New York, Columbia University Press, 1966).

Life Styles of Educated Women (New York, Columbia University Press, 1966).

The Middle Class Negro in the White Man's World (New York, Columbia University Press, 1967).

Ivar E. Berg, *Education and Jobs* (New York, Praeger, 1970).

Robert W. Smuts, *Women and Work in America* (New York, Schocken, reprinted 1971).

Career Guidance (New York, McGraw-Hill, 1971).

Dale L. Hiestand, *Career Changes after 35* (New York, Columbia University Press, 1971).

8

The Changing American Economy and Labor Force

Various theories have been advanced about the present role of work in American life. An assessment of their validity requires basic data about the employment-related dimensions of the American economy over the past few generations. The data alone will not prove or disprove any theory, but will provide a framework within which alternative formulations can be tested.

Before we look at the facts of economic life, some words of caution are in order with respect to the current hypothesis that the American worker has become increasingly discontented with his work. The broad changes in employment conditions since the onset of World War II are well known: hours of work have been reduced; real earnings have advanced significantly; the work environment has improved; job security is stronger; discrimination against women and minorities has decreased; there is less pressure on workers to conform to arbitrary demands of supervisors; and a significantly higher proportion of workers are in white-collar occupations.

Although these trends do not prove that the working population in the United States is less unhappy about work than its fathers or grandfathers, they do suggest that any thesis that assumes increasing disenchantment must be supported by a careful examination of changes not only within the workplace but also outside—in the background, education, expectations, and values of the present generation of workers. This we intend to provide.

The Changing Contours of the American Economy

In the half-century after the end of World War I the American economy witnessed a doubling in the size of its work force—and also showed striking changes in the work environment. Table 1 presents the changes in the industrial distribution of workers during this period.

Table 1.   Employment[a] by industry division, 1920 and 1970

	1920		1970	
Industry	Number employed (in 000s)	Percent employed	Number employed (in 000s)	Percent employed
Agriculture[b]	11,120	29.1	3,462	4.7
Mining	1,230	3.2	622	0.8
Manufacturing	10,534	27.6	19,369	26.1
Construction	848	2.2	3,345	4.5
Services	14,476	37.9	47,281	63.9
Total	38,208	100.0	74,079	100.0

SOURCE: U. S. Bureau of the Census, *Historical Statistics of the United States, Colonial Times to 1957,* Washington, D. C., 1960, p. 7364; and *Manpower Report of the President,* March 1973, U. S. Government Printing Office, p. 225.

a Wage and salary employment.

b Includes self-employed and unpaid family workers in addition to wage and salary workers.

In 1920, more than one of every four workers were in agriculture; by 1970, this was true of approximately one of twenty-five. The declining importance of agriculture as a source of employment is the outstanding change in the American economy over the last half-century. Mining also experienced a significant absolute and relative decline. Manufacturing had almost the same relative share of employment at the end of the period as at the beginning, but construction employees more than quadrupled in number and doubled in relative importance. The sizable reductions in agricultural employment and in mining were absorbed primarily by the service sector, particularly by trade, personal, professional, business, and government services.

To summarize the shift that took place: in 1920, the goods-producing sector—agriculture, mining, manufacturing, and construction—accounted for more than three out of every five workers; in 1970, this sector accounted for about one in three, a decline of almost 50 percent.

Closely related to the shift from agriculture to the service sector was the migration of a large part of the black population and of many poor white families from the rural South to urban centers, primarily in the North and West.

A second significant change in the American economy during the first half of the century occurred with respect to the organizational structures within which work is carried on. Of the three principal entrepreneurial sectors—private, nonprofit, and government—the unequivocal finding is the marked shrinkage in the role of the private sector.

During the four decades between 1920 and 1960, private sector employment declined from slightly over 90 percent of the total to less than 80 percent. Correspondingly, government increased its share from about 7 percent to over 15 percent of total employment, and nonprofit institutions increased their share from under 3 percent to approximately 5 percent. Calculations for 1963 showed further declines in the private sector and increases in the "not-for-profit" sector (government and nonprofit combined). These calculations were replicated for the late 1960s and showed a continued upward drift in the employment role of the not-for-profit sector.

The foregoing data relate to direct employment. If the analysis is broadened to include the role of government in generating employment among private contractors from whom it buys, the shift to the not-for-profit sector is even greater. In 1960, direct and indirect employment in the not-for-profit sector involved not less than one in every three workers, and may have been closer to two in five—up from one in seven, thirty years earlier.

Hidden beneath this steady expansion of employment in the not-for-profit sector are a host of trends that are only slowly being recognized. These concern wage distribution; unionization of government employees; job instability on governmental programs, which are subject to sudden termination; establishment of work norms aimed at productivity increases and quality control; social and political tensions arising from tax resistance, on the one hand, and pressures for more and better public services, on the other.

Another dimension of the changes that have been occurring is revealed by trends in ownership structure. In 1945, there were slightly more than 6.7 million proprietorships and partnerships with receipts of about $80 billion and profits of $12 billion. A quarter-century later, there were almost 4 million more proprietorships and partnerships, with over $400 billion in receipts and profits of $44 billion. In the earlier year, there were 420,000 corporations with $225 billion in receipts and $21 billion in profits. Twenty-five years later, there were some 1.7 million corporations—with receipts of about $1.7 trillion and profits totaling $81 billion! Slightly more than 1 percent of all active corporations accounted for over

56 percent of corporate receipts in 1969. During the two decades following World War II, the largest 200 corporations in manufacturing increased their share of total value added by two-fifths, from 30 to 42 percent.

In 1971, employees (14.3 million) of the 500 largest manufacturing concerns represented three-quarters of total manufacturing employment, and workers in the 50 largest retail firms (2.4 million) comprised slightly more than one out of every five retail employees.

Despite the substantial decrease in the number of persons who make their livelihood in agriculture, individual proprietorships and partnerships have increased substantially in other sectors since the onset of World War II. Over the same period, the large corporation has come to dominate in manufacturing and it has made a significant impact in retailing, which traditionally has been a small-enterprise arena. Corporations also loom large in service sectors that are capital intensive, such as transportation and utilities. Nevertheless, the data do not confirm the widespread impression that all or most Americans work for large corporate enterprises. Many do, but many others do not.

Table 2 describes changes in the occupational distribution that are linked to these sectorial, entrepreneurial, and organizational changes. The table shows that, while there was an 86-percent increase in total employment between 1920 and 1970, the rate of growth of white-collar and nonhousehold service workers was much greater, the blue-collar increase was less, and farm employment dropped precipitously. Not only did the white-collar category experience the highest rate of growth, but each of its subgroups rose at a higher rate than employment as a whole. Professional and technical workers increased the most, followed closely by clerical employees. Sales workers show the least proportionate gain in the white-collar group, although they more than doubled in number.

The proportionate decrease in blue-collar workers over this period despite increases in craftsmen and operatives resulted in part from a 25-percent decrease in nonfarm laborers. The growth in the service sector was overwhelmingly caused by the substantial increase in nonhousehold employees. The 73-percent decline in farm workers equally affected farmers and farm laborers.

In terms of employment distribution, white-collar employment increased from one worker in four to almost one in two, while agricultural workers, who represented more than one worker in four in 1920, had dropped to one in twenty-five by 1970. The specific occupational groups showing the largest proportionate increases in their share of total employment in this period were professional and technical workers, service employees except private household workers, and clerical workers in that order.

Table 2.   Employed persons, by major occupational groups, 1920 and 1970

Occupational group	1920[a]		1970[b]	
	Number employed (in 000s)	Percent employed	Number employed (in 000s)	Percent employed
White-collar workers	10,529	24.9	37,997	48.4
Professional and techni- cal workers	2,283	5.4	11,140	14.3
Managers and administra- tors	2,803	6.6	8,289	10.5
Sales workers	2,058	4.9	4,854	6.2
Clerical workers	3,385	8.0	13,714	17.4
Blue-collar workers	16,974	40.2	27,791	35.3
Craftsmen and kindred workers	5,482	13.0	10,158	12.9
Operatives	6,587	15.6	13,909	17.7
Nonfarm laborers	4,905	11.6	3,724	4.7
Service workers	3,313	7.9	9,712	12.3
Private house- hold	1,411	3.4	1,558	2.2
Other	1,902	4.5	8,154	10.1
Farm workers	11,390	27.0	3,126	4.0
Farmers and farm man- agers	6,442	15.3	1,753	2.2
Farm laborers and foremen	4,948	11.7	1,373	1.8
Total	42,206	100.0	78,626	100.0

SOURCE: U. S. Bureau of the Census, *Historical Statistics of the United States, Colonial Times to 1957,* Washington, D. C., 1960, p. 74; and, *Manpower Report of the President,* March 1973, U. S. Government Printing Office, p. 141.

[a] "Economically active population" 10 years of age and over.
[b] Employed persons 16 years of age and over.

There were three broad occupational developments in this half-century. First, advances in technology generated new occupations such as computer programmer, office machine operator, TV and airplane mechanic, and welder. Second, the economy was able to absorb an increased number of educated persons in such fields as college teaching, engineering, accounting, and social work. Third, large increases in secretaries and typists, workers in commercial services, and hospital workers reflect such factors as a rising flow of paper work, the transfer of services from the home to the market, and the growth of the health industry.

During the last fifty years, then, the industrial structure, organizational forms, and occupational distribution of the American economy have undergone large-scale alterations. Because so many different changes took place, it is difficult to summarize them all and even more difficult to assess their significance from the vantage of workers' satisfaction with their jobs.

As we have seen, the most significant alterations in the occupational distribution of the labor force were a striking reduction in the proportion employed in agriculture, a sharp decline in the proportion engaged in nonfarm laboring jobs, and large relative and absolute increases in the numbers of professional, clerical, and service workers.

Associated changes occurred in employment sectors and organizations. There was a major shift of the economy from goods to service production. Manufacturing declined in importance as a source of employment, and the role of government as a direct and indirect employer expanded rapidly. Although the large corporation grew in importance, particularly in manufacturing, transportation and utilities, and retail trade, proprietorship remained a significant form of business enterprise in agriculture, construction, trade, and services.

These changes per se can be used to support a large number of inferences. For instance, is the shift of agriculture to be read as a significant diminution of opportunities for a person to be his own boss in the face of the continuing high level of proprietorships in other sectors? Is the rapid growth of professional and technical employment to be interpreted as providing expanded opportunities for many to shape and direct their own work when we know that many professionals are in tightly controlled employment settings? Does it make sense to talk about a decline in the proportion of blue-collar workers when a closer look reveals that the decline is primarily among nonfarm laborers and that it is more than offset by the increase in service workers, who often do much the same type of work? Should blue-collar and service workers be treated as a single group whose relative size has not changed over the period?

Clearly, caution is in order in drawing broad inferences from these gross data. And there is further reason to avoid generalizations. How workers view their work depends not only upon the nature of their jobs but also upon what they bring to their jobs—background, education, expectations, values—in short, what they are seeking in work and what they find. We must look more closely at changes within the working population.

The Changing Characteristics of the Labor Force

Just as the American economy has undergone a great many changes since the end of World War I, so has the American worker. Here are some of the gross differences between the typical wage earner in 1920 and one in 1970. To begin with, the American worker in 1920 was more likely to have been born abroad or, if born in the United States, to have at least one foreign-born parent, than the average worker in 1970. If he or his parents had immigrated, it is likely that he was impressed by the good fortune of being in this country where, even under adverse conditions, the prospects for a poor man were better than in the less developed and more stratified society of the Old World. Even men who had the least desirable jobs, who earned barely enough to feed their families, who lived in slums, who had no knowledge of English, realized that they were better off than if they remained in their native lands where life was often intolerable.

Many workers born in this country had been brought up on farms or were but one generation removed from the farm, and they knew at first or second hand what it was to struggle with the vagaries of nature and the fluctuations of the market. Even if industrial employment and city living left much to be desired, it was generally preferred to life on the farm.

The typical worker of the 1920s had completed elementary school and had attended high school for a year or so before starting work. Aside from a limited number of professional and managerial occupations that required an extended period of formal education, most jobs made physical rather than intellectual demands. Even a craftsman could develop a high level of skill on a minimal educational foundation.

In 1920, many middle-aged workers had personal recollections of the deep depression of the 1890s that had caused a great deal of distress. Younger workers had had personal experiences with the adverse conditions that led to widespread unemployment in 1907, and again in the years immediately preceding the outbreak of World War I. The threat or reality of unemployment was embedded in the experiences and expectations of the American worker. In fact, 1920 saw the end of the wartime and postwar boom. The collapse of the economy led to widespread and persistent unemployment.

The early decades of this century found most blacks locked into

Southern agriculture, where they operated small farms as tenants or sharecroppers. Many black women worked as domestics to supplement their families' marginal income. If white women worked, it was only for the period between leaving school and marriage or the birth of their first children. In urban communities, white single women provided much of the labor force that met the rapidly expanding demands for office, retail, domestic, and commercial service workers. At the professional level, unmarried women were a key source of elementary school teachers.

Let us examine the characteristics of the contemporary labor force against this background. While some of today's workers were born abroad and others have foreign-born parents, a much higher proportion of the total were born here. In fact, with the exception of those in a relatively few urban centers such as New York, Chicago, and Los Angeles, the typical worker today is not only native-born, but is likely to be at least third-generation American.

Among the white urban population, rural ties are more distant than in 1920. Even though there are some recent immigrants from rural areas in all large cities, the proportion is much smaller than at the end of World War I.

The educational preparation of the American worker has undergone a major transformation over the past half-century, as evidenced by the fact that in 1970 almost four out of five of the relevant age group had graduated from high school, compared to about one out of six in 1920. In the earlier year, only one in six high school graduates went on to get a college or first professional degree. A half-century later, the proportion approached one in three.

If the focus is narrowed to the thirty years between 1940 and 1970, the median years of schooling completed by the entire population aged 25 and over was 8.6 in the earlier year, at that time just one semester beyond graduation from elementary school. By 1970, the median had increased by about 50 percent to 12.2 years, or a little beyond high school graduation.

At the outbreak of World War II, 38 percent of persons aged 25 to 29 years had graduated from high school and under 6 percent had a college degree. The comparable figures for 1971 were 77 percent and 17 percent, a doubling in the proportion of high school graduates and about a three-fold increase in the proportion of college graduates.

Obviously, the past half-century has witnessed a radical change in the educational attainment of American workers. Instead of discontinuing formal education after elementary school, as had been the custom earlier, the predominant group of young people now joining the labor force have acquired high school diplomas, about half of all high school graduates enter postsecondary education, and more than one in five obtain college degrees.

To these differences in family background and education must be added another difference between the American worker of then and now. This can be subsumed under the heading of expectations about the economy and particularly about employment. We earlier noted that periodic depressions with attendant large-scale unemployment were part of the experience and expectations of American workers prior to World War II. But in the thirty-three years from 1940 to 1973 the American economy avoided a serious depression—although it experienced recessions that constricted the job market but did not usually result in sharp reductions in disposable income because of multiple transfer payments.

At the present time, two of every three workers are under 44 years of age and the majority of workers were born after the onset of World War II. Rough calculations suggest that not more than one of ten workers currently in the labor force actually held a job or looked for one during the 1930-1933 debacle. Thus, first-hand experience with the job market during a severe depression had all but faded from the consciousness of American workers.

Until the severe recession of 1974-1975, workers—if not personally or socially handicapped—assumed that they could find a job. They assumed that, at worst, they might be out of work for a relatively short period. Until the recession, the unemployment rate for white male household heads had not exceeded 3 percent—and reached that figure only once, in 1971. In the late 1960s, it ranged between 1.4 and 1.7 percent.

Special Groups in the Labor Force

In the early decades of this century an analysis of the labor force would usually proceed in terms of white males. Only if the employment problems of Southern agriculture or the expanding needs for office, sales, and service workers were the focus, were blacks or women taken into consideration. In the post-World War II era, it was (and still is) not possible to concentrate on white male workers in an assessment of the labor market. Women have come to account for about 40 percent of the civilian labor force, and blacks are no longer concentrated in Southern agriculture. In addition, in recent decades increasing attention has been paid to youth, especially those with educational or other handicaps, who are encountering difficulty in making the transition from school to work. Even an abbreviated comment on the changing role of work in American life must address the circumstances of these three groups, not only because of their increased importance in the labor force, but also because of changes in the political and social climate that have led the American public belatedly to recognize and attempt to avoid pervasive discrimination in the work preparatory structure and in the labor market.

Blacks.   With regard to blacks, the post-World War II period has been a marked absolute and relative improvement in their employment, income, and education. At the same time, the most recent data reveal gaps between the average economic position of whites and blacks.

The most striking improvement has occurred in the educational arena. In 1940, whites aged 25 to 29 had approximately half again as many years of schooling as did their black counterparts—10.3 years versus 7 years. By 1970, only four-tenths of one year separated the two: the white average was 12.6 years; the black mean had risen to 12.2 years. In other words, during this thirty-year period, the white gain was 2.3 years while that of the blacks was 5.2 years. But wide gaps remained. The proportion of white college graduates aged 25 to 29 was 17.9 percent in 1971 in contrast to 6.4 percent of blacks of similar age. And the discrepancies are much greater beyond the baccalaureate. To the extent that many of the best jobs in the economy are reserved for those who have completed a long course of general and professional education, the blacks still lag the whites, and by a considerable distance, despite substantial gains in recent years.

The education a person receives is one of the determinants of his future income; another is the type of employment he is able to obtain. Blacks have long encountered overt and extensive discrimination in the labor market throughout the United States. While such discrimination is still present and oppressive, the 1960s witnessed intensified efforts in both the public and private domains to reduce and remove employment barriers. The extent to which these efforts have been successful can be read in the improvements blacks have made in gaining access to higher-level occupations, just as the difficulties they continue to face can be deduced from their continued overrepresentation at the lower end of the occupational structure.

In both 1960 and 1970, blacks accounted for 11 percent of all employed persons. During this decade they increased their representation in professional and technical jobs from 4 to 7 percent; among managers and officials, from 3 to 4 percent; in clerical jobs, from 5 to 8 percent; as craftsmen and foremen, from 5 to 7 percent. However, blacks continue to be significantly underrepresented in each of these groups and remain concentrated at the lower end of the occupational scale. Currently, blacks account for 23 percent of all nonfarm laborers, 42 percent of all private household workers, and 19 percent of all other service workers. Only among the farm workers are they equal to the white workers, accounting for only 11 percent of the much-diminished farm labor force.

There are other distressing aspects to the black employment experience. For instance, white males in the prime working ages have a labor force participation rate of between 94 and 97 percent; the black male rate is between 86 and 93 percent. As far as unemployment is concerned, the black rate has been roughly double that of whites throughout the past decade—and this holds true for both men and women.

The single most dramatic index of racial discrimination has been the median income of black families as a percentage of that of white families. In 1950 the median family income of Negroes was 54 percent of that of white families. In 1964, when the comprehensive Civil Rights Act was passed, the ratio stood at 56 percent. By 1970, it had risen to 63 percent. However, the national median hides two important facts. First, it obscures the more pronounced gap in the South, where the black median in 1970 was 57 percent of the white, compared with other parts of the country where the percentage varied from 71 in the Northeast to 77 in the West. Second, it is not sensitive to the experience of the younger age groups who have benefited most from improved educational advantages and lessened discrimination. In the North and West, in 1970, the median for black families with a head-of-household under the age of 35 was 96 percent of the white median; where both husband and wife worked, it was 104 percent.

The significant improvement in the condition of black workers in the 1960s reflects diverse forces, including the largest sustained boom in the history of the American economy; widespread public efforts to remove long-established discriminatory practices; more favorable geographic distribution of the black population; and the absence of any competing labor source. Still, the gains that have been made should not be permitted to obscure the disadvantages that continue to afflict most blacks: lower family income, fewer college entrants, and persistent discrimination.

Women.   The kinds of discrimination that affect women in their preparation for work and in their labor market experiences both parallel and differ from those which afflict blacks. As far as education is concerned, until recently a higher proportion of females than males received a high school diploma, but by 1970 7 percent of males 24 years and over had completed four years of college compared with 5.6 percent of females, a difference of 20 percent. At the master's and doctorate levels, 5.4 percent of males have degrees compared with 2.2 percent of females. These educational differences do little to explain the gross differences between the occupational distribution of men and that of women as shown in Table 3.

The table demonstrates that males are broadly distributed among the several occupational groups and that females are concentrated within a few fields of work. More than one in three women are employed in clerical occupations and more than one in five are service workers. The

Table 3. Employed persons 14 years old or over, by major occupational group and sex, 1970

Occupational group	Male		Female	
	Number employed (in 000s)	Percent employed	Number employed (in 000s)	Percent employed
White-collar workers	20,054	41.0	17,943	60.5
Professional and technical	6,842	14.1	4,298	14.5
Managers and administrators	6,968	14.2	1,321	4.5
Salesworkers	2,763	5.6	2,091	7.0
Clerical workers	3,481	7.1	10,233	34.5
Blue-collar workers	23,020	47.0	4,771	16.0
Craftsmen and kindred workers	9,826	20.1	332	1.1
Operators	9,605	19.6	4,303	14.5
Nonfarm laborers	3,589	7.3	136	.4
Service workers	3,285	6.7	6,427	21.7
Farm workers	2,601	5.3	525	1.8
Total	48,960	100.0	29,666	100.0

SOURCE: U. S. Bureau of the Census, *Statistical Abstract of the United States: 1972* (93rd ed.), Washington, D. C., 1972, p. 230.

proportion of male managers and administrators is over three times that of females, and the proportion of male craftsmen is almost twenty times that of females. On the other hand, women are about five times more likely than men to be clerical workers and over three times as apt to be in service jobs.

Only in the professional, sales, and operative occupations is the pattern of male and female employment more or less parallel. It should be emphasized, however, that these data refer to gross classifications. For instance, the largest number of women professionals are school-teachers and nurses, while engineers are the largest male professional group, and males predominate in medicine and law, the highest-earning professions. In sales, males have close to a monopoly in the lucrative industrial equipment and high-ticket items, while women hold lower-paying positions. There are twice as many female as male operatives in nondurable manufacturing, where pay scales are considerably lower than in durable manufacturing, where males predominate.

Traditionally, women have been concentrated within certain specific occupations. About one of every four employed women is a secretary, retail sales clerk, bookkeeper, elementary-school teacher, or household worker. Half of all women workers are employed in twenty-one types of jobs, while employed men are distributed over sixty-five specific occupations. The American job market has been bifurcated by sex, as well as by race.

Combined public and private efforts to reduce and eliminate discrimination against women in the world of education and work have begun to take hold. One result is indicated by a comparison of entrants to medical and law schools. In the mid-sixties, women accounted for about 10 percent of the entering classes of medical schools and 3 percent of law school classes; in 1972, women comprised 20 percent of the entrants to medical school, and 12 percent of the first-year law students.

The earnings of women workers averaged about $3,500 in 1971, compared to male mean earnings of approximately $8,000. However, almost two-thirds of the males, but only two-fifths of the females, worked full-time, full-year. Moreover, as we have seen, women are concentrated in low-paying occupations. If the comparison is confined to those who worked full-time, full-year, the findings are still striking: men's mean earnings were about $10,400 and women's were $5,900, less than three-fifths of the men's. Equally striking is the fact that, of all persons with money earnings in 1971, 31 percent of the men, but less than 4 percent of the women, earned $10,000 or more. A still more revealing comparison is between the average income, by educational level, of men and women who worked full-time year-round in 1971. In the case of high school graduates the mean was $10,700 for men and $6,000 for women; for college graduates, $15,600 for men and $8,600 for women; for those with five or more years of college, $18,000 for men and $10,800 for women.

While females clearly suffer discrimination in the labor market, it should be noted that the married woman's social and economic status is often derived from the occupation and earning of her husband. Moreover, middle-class white women learn about the levers of power and how they can be manipulated from their fathers, brothers, and husbands, a source of knowledge usually unavailable to members of minority groups who are on the periphery of the society and economy. One must be careful, therefore, not to equate racial and sex discrimination. While they have much in common, they differ in many essentials.

Youth.   The third special employment problem that warrants attention is the predicament of young people, particularly young people whose racial or ethnic background, education, or criminal record presents handicaps as they seek to establish themselves in the world of work.

The initial source of the difficulty of these disadvantaged young people is embedded in the demographic turnabout that occurred after World War II. During most of the 1930s the birth rate was about 18 to 19 per 1,000, and in 1945 it was 20.5 per 1,000. By the end of the 1940s and until late in the 1950s, it hovered between 24 and 25 per 1,000 and reached a peak of 25.2 in 1957. Thus, throughout the early post-World War II period, the birth rate was over a third higher than it had been in the prewar decade. This rise in the birth rate resulted in a substantial increase in the proportion of families with three or four children and a corresponding decline of childless or one-child families.

The high birth rates of the late 1940s and the 1950s produced marked increases in the teenage population of the 1960s. The 16- to 19-year-old group expanded by 46 percent within a single decade. Although this demographic change had multiple effects upon such areas as secondary and higher education, military manpower policy, the crime rate, and drug addiction, our concern is primarily with its employment-related dimensions. The critical finding is that, in the face of a 20-percent increase in the female work force between 1952 and 1972, the number of teenagers at work increased by over 100 percent!

The postwar baby crop also contributed to a rapid increase in the numbers of workers in the 20- to 24-year age group. The number of male workers in this category rose from about 5.1 million in 1947 to 7.8 million in 1972; the corresponding numbers of females were 2.7 and 5.3 million. Even though the American economy enjoyed a long period of expansion in the 1960s, reinforced by additional manpower needs of the armed forces, the demographic explosion among teenagers and young adults required a high level of job creation if all who sought work were to find it.

Although many young people succeeded in finding the full- or part-time employment they wanted and needed, a significant number were unable to make a successful transition from school to work. The story can be read in rising unemployment rates and in the widening gap between unemployment rates of 16- to 24-year-olds and those of older members of the labor force. A rough rule of thumb for determining unemployment rates for any year in the late 1960s to early 1970s is to take the national unemployment rate and double it for youth, and double it again for minority youth. In other words, when the national unemployment rate was 5.5 percent, the youth rate was 11 percent, and the rate for minority youth was 20 percent. During the past decade male teenagers from minority groups have had unemployment rates in the 25- to 35-percent range, while female rates were close to 40 percent. It should be noted that these rates are understated, since many young people who have dropped out of school have not started or have abandoned the search for work and therefore are not counted as members of the labor force.

In all industrial countries, the youth unemployment rate tends to be somewhat higher than the average rate because of the job changes young people make as they try to find congenial, or at least acceptable, work. However, the data suggest that the demographic explosion, together with labor market constraints, have resulted in an unusually high youth unemployment rate in the United States. The rise in demand for white-collar workers had an adverse effect upon many poorly educated youngsters who were untrained for clerical or other types of office jobs. As long as employers were able to find adult women to fill their expanding needs, they were loath to hire young people.

Protective legislation, long on the books, made it difficult for employers to hire youth for certain types of jobs. Because of rising racial consciousness, some better educated minority youth were reluctant to accept dead-end jobs in such occupations as domestic service or unskilled manual work. Lack of a high school diploma or the existence of a police record had a particularly harmful effect on the employability of many minority youth from low-income homes. Many economists believe that the high minimum wage was a further obstacle to the employment of young people, although the evidence is not conclusive.

The years ahead promise some relief as the demographic bulge diminishes. The rate of increase of the white teenage population will decline from 46 percent to 9 percent. Unfortunately, the increase in the number of nonwhite teenagers will be about as large in the 1970s as the 44-percent increase in the 1960s. Even with an easing of the pressure of total numbers, the transition of young people from school to work will remain difficult, particularly for those who enter the job market with one or more handicaps.

We have seen that discrimination continues to place limitations upon the employment of blacks and women. This is reflected in their concentration in less desirable and lower-paying jobs. Although the decade of the 1960s saw substantial gains by blacks and, later, by women, wide gaps between these groups and white males remain and are not likely to be substantially reduced in the near future. Many young people are having difficulty in getting a firm toehold in the world of work, among other reasons because of the recent rapid increase in their numbers. The demographic outlook is becoming more favorable, but many minority youth, especially those who do not acquire a high school diploma or who lack the skills demanded for white-collar work, will continue to have difficulty in finding satisfactory jobs that hold promise of advancement.

In Search of Perspective

The reason for the earlier caveat about drawing inferences about work satisfaction from data about transformations in the American economy and its occupational structure should now be evident. Yet inferences that may lead to greater understanding are the touchstone of social research. Let us look backward to see whether a limited number of propositions can be precipitated, and then let us look ahead to see whether any tentative forecasts can be made.

The period since World War II has seen an increasing number of married female full- or part-time workers. This suggests that, given the opportunity to earn money income, more and more adult women will choose work for pay over homemaking and voluntary activities. Of course, many women who work have no option because they are heads of households and are responsible for supporting themselves and their dependents. Many others who work have an urgent need for additional family income. Nevertheless, many women work primarily because they prefer to have a job or pursue a career.

A second major trend characteristic of the post-World War II era is a substantial increase in the years of school attained by new entrants into the labor force and a corresponding shift in their industrial and occupational attachment. Compared with earlier periods, a greatly increased proportion is employed in the service sector and as white-collar workers. Despite the much larger number who entered the labor force as high school or college graduates than in the past, their wages and salaries have not suffered. The returns from education achieved remained high throughout the period, although some of the better-educated entrants were unsuccessful in getting or holding jobs commensurate with their education. While many white-collar jobs are prestigious in name rather than in fact, the expansion of professional and managerial employment has provided attractive work and work environments for many new job-holders. The world of the office is less physically demanding and less enervating for most people than the world of the factory, the mine, and the farm, and in the last quarter-century there has been a major shift of the economy away from machine-controlled occupations.

Work always represents an admixture of pluses and minuses in the sense that those who enter an employment relationship give up their time, accept direction and supervision in the use of their energies, and submit themselves to rules and discipline, in return for wages, benefits, opportunities for advancement, and concomitant social satisfactions. During the postwar period, there was a conspicuous lack of pressure by workers to reduce their conventional daily or weekly hours. In fact, overtime became the pattern; overtime hours worked averaged more than 10 percent of standard hours. The reduction in working time that did occur came about through paid holidays and longer vacations, as a result of the worker's demand for blocks of leisure in which to enjoy his higher real earnings. The absence of broad pressure to reduce the workday and workweek may be interpreted as evidence that most employees did not find their work life particularly oppressive. Otherwise they would have traded additional income for additional free time.

Workers organize themselves into trade unions to improve their bargaining position vis-à-vis employers, not solely with the aim of raising wages and improving fringe benefits but also in order to broaden their control over their immediate working environment. The postwar period saw a slow growth of organized labor, so slow in fact that, even after allowance is made for other factors such as sophisticated employer-opposition, less encouraging governmental attitudes, and weakness at the top of the trade union movement, we must conclude that the great mass of unorganized workers were not ready to pay the costs of organizing. Apparently they did not feel that their present conditions were so hard or that the union could obtain sufficient benefits to justify the turmoil of organizing.

However, we cannot read the evidence as proving that all was right in the world of work, or even that conditions were improving so rapidly that an era of contentment was about to dawn. That was not the case; the sources of discontent were legion. Workers and employers in every sector of the economy were in conflict—often latent, periodically overt—about wages, conditions of work, productivity, and other critical dimensions of the employment relation. Just as soon as old sources of difficulty were ironed out, new ones emerged as a result of changes in the economy, the society, and the workers themselves. In a modern democratic society, a dynamic of discontent is embedded in work relations.

Against this background of recent changes in the world of work it is possible to identify several areas where discontent is likely to become manifest in the years ahead. It is not clear that the employment advantages of extended education will continue. A recent report by the Carnegie Commission on Higher Eudcation suggests that over one-quarter of the college graduates and prospective college graduates in the 1970s will have to settle for jobs that were formerly held by nongraduates. If this results in wage compression, there probably will be rising orders of dissatisfaction among the better-educated workers.

Expanding experiments with flexible working hours, rising union objections to compulsory overtime, and the expansion of forced and optional early retirement, suggest that we may be entering a new era of trade-offs between work and income and between opportunities for older and for younger workers. It would be strange indeed if increasing family income did not lead, sooner or later, to a reconsideration of the hours question. The preferences of workers are likely to run afoul of both technological and cost considerations and to result in compromise solutions—but not unless employers and employees learn to appreciate each other's priority needs and preferences.

The pervasive troubles all modern economies face in reconciling high-level employment with reasonable price stability underscore the necessity for modifications in collective bargaining and in market mechanisms as they influence price and dividend determinations. Workers will not forego their search for equity, but the domain of the struggle has begun to widen to include a role for government. No one can see clearly the new structures that must be put into place or what will be required to ensure that they become functional, but we can prognosticate that this will be an increasingly important arena of conflict.

During the 1960s there was a major thrust to reduce and remove educational and employment discrimination against minorities and women. The several levels of government have pursued various actions to expand opportunities for groups previously barred outright or severely handicapped in their efforts to gain access to desirable jobs and careers. In the last few years, the initial emphasis on assisting black men to improve their employability has been broadened to include women, the Spanish-speaking, and many smaller minority groups such as American Indians. While governmental efforts have unquestionably helped reduce discrimination in the labor market, the rate of progress has been uneven, slowed in many cases by the small number of qualified minority members in the hiring pool, by the recalcitrance of trade unions in accepting outsiders, by the relatively few job openings in such areas as the academic world, and, above all, by a growing concern that the rights of the majority be protected while corrective actions aimed at helping minorities proceed.

Despite these and other difficulties, it is reasonable to expect that the issue of discrimination will be at the forefront of negotiations in the years ahead, and conflicts are likely to continue as individuals and groups struggle over the division of employment opportunities.

Finally, the combination of more education, more jobs (up to 1974-1975), and higher family income is loosening the monolithic relationship that existed for so long between people and work. In an earlier day men had to work to survive. This is less true today. At the upper end of the income scale, families support their children well into their twenties. At the lower end, many young people manage to exist without regular jobs largely by engaging in illegal activities. Since more and more married couples are working one or the other spouse may drop out of the labor market for a time to return to school, to raise a child, or to pursue an avocational interest. To the extent that people want more degrees of freedom to structure their lives and their time, we must anticipate additional discord in the work arena between employees who seek greater options and employers who are locked into production schedules and the market.

Modern societies can absorb a considerable amount of conflict. As workers attempt to find a new balance between work and other activities, they will modify the existing reality and develop new expectations, thereby setting the stage for still further changes.

9

Work Restructuring and Manpower Realities

This chapter explores from different vantage points the interface between the restructuring of jobs and the nature of the labor force. First, it provides a theoretical assessment of the extent to which manpower and economic parameters affect changes in the conditions of work. Next, it presents an explicit analysis of major manpower and labor market transformations in industrialized societies and of their influence upon the quality of working life. Finally, it discusses the impact of the labor market on restructuring the workplace and the impact of selective societal trends on alterations within it.

Some Basic Theorems

Actions initiated by individual employers, by the labor movement, and by national governments to improve the conditions of working life have both potentialities and limitations.

The individual employer is disinclined to enter into any large-scale investment in the absence of a clear estimate of the amount and duration of payoff. Significant improvements in plant conditions frequently call for sizable investments with no guarantee—or even likelihood—of a proportionate increase in productivity. Nevertheless, since employers compete for labor, management may invest in improving the conditions of working life to the extent that it feels workers will seek jobs in a better designed and better managed plant. The higher the proportion of wages to total costs, however, the more cautiously will the employer experiment with programs that may further increase his wage bill. The possibility that a new program may lead to a reduction in his labor costs will be treated with skepticism. Pari passu, an employer whose wage costs account for less than a quarter of his total costs (as in large process industries) may be more inclined to take a chance. He has less to lose, and if the new program works he may have bought himself a period of relative industrial peace.

Although an employer's role is critical to any improvement in the quality of working life, one must not overlook the fact that in most industrial societies the cues to the distribution to the work force of an incremental surplus come, directly or indirectly, from trade unions. In the United States, union leadership has the first and final word on whether the surplus is to be paid out in higher wages, better fringe benefits, lower hours, more vacations, or in improving the health, safety, and work conditions in the plant. To date, most unions have opted for shorter hours and higher wages and benefits, and for restrictions on managerial rights to unilateral determinations affecting working conditions. Most labor leaders are convinced that they have had a major influence upon improvements in the conditions of working life, although they have been only peripherally concerned with the structure of production and styles of management. They have been influential in certain areas: moderation of the speed of assembly lines; limitation of weight-lifting requirements for men and women; rest periods; restriction in the powers of foremen; procedures for layoffs and callbacks. There is no question that, if trade union members decide that problems affecting life in the work place are to be moved to the top of their agenda, this is where the future action will be.

Until the unions move, the speed with which individual employers will initiate new programs to improve working life is limited because of major constraints from the competitive market; the protection of managerial prerogatives; and other demands of trade unions. Nonetheless, under governmental initiative the same forces that constrain experimentation can encourage it.

Modern governments have played a key role in strategic areas of work such as health, safety, amenities, hours, minimum wages, compensation systems, unemployment insurance—all of which have been broadly directed to improving the lot of workers. Yet governments have not always had a free hand, because strict enforcement of both existing legislation and administrative policies can put the marginal employer out of business, and his workers out of jobs. It requires not only courage but judgment on the part of bureaucrats to know how rigidly to enforce the law. Governments also must balance the potential costs citizens must bear for the support of major alterations in the existing patterns of work against the benefits they are likely to receive. Reluctance to introduce legislation reducing the workweek from 40 to 35 hours, for example, results from the putative loss of output that such a step would entail. Politicians believe, probably correctly, that given a choice, most of their constituents prefer higher income to fewer working hours. Another constraint on government action is international competition. Although the extent of dependence on international trade varies among countries, no major nation can be indifferent to the implications of domestic legislation that threatens to raise the costs of its products.

Thus government efforts are circumscribed by the need to protect weak enterprises that provide large numbers of workers with a livelihood; by the desire to avoid changes that may prove costly in terms of reduced output; and by a disinclination to jeopardize the international competitive position of export goods.

These several theorems derived from the experience of modern industrialized societies indicate that, although there are margins for innovation to improve the conditions of work, the margins are limited because of the fear of increased costs and the uncertainty of gains in productivity. Companies and countries alike tend to be cautious and to opt for the unsatisfactory present in which they have learned to survive, rather than for the problematical future that may spell failure.

Manpower Trends

A number of major trends in the labor market have a direct bearing on the quality of working life. It often has been observed that most social change does not result from policies and programs designed to check a particular danger or respond to specific opportunity, but is the consequence of underlying forces which, individually and in combination, alter the shape of things to come. The thrust of this section is that changes in the manpower arena in the principal industrial nations of the world have already materially affected the quality of working life and give every promise of continuing to do so.

The first of these changes has been the shift from a goods-producing to a service-producing economy, a shift that warns against the use of the manufacturing prototype for analytical purposes, and especially warns against the assembly-line prototype, which currently describes the working environment of less than 2 percent of all employed Americans. Although certain services, such as banking, communications, and insurance tend to be provided in large-scale enterprises with many of the characteristics found in manufacturing, a high proportion of all workers in the service sector are employed in small organizations.

With each passing year, a smaller number of workers remains in a working environment in which output is strictly controlled and work patterns are determined by machines. If it is indeed dysfunctional for a human being to be an appendage of a machine, and if the exigencies of the production-profit system have led employers to set exhausting work norms, it must be acknowledged that fewer and fewer workers labor in such environments. An increasing proportion of all workers earn their livelihoods under conditions where the employer has difficulty setting norms, establishing the pace, and exercising close supervision.

A second major trend is the demand of modern economies for larger numbers of highly educated and well-trained personnel. In the United States the growth of professional, technical, and kindred workers has outpaced that of every other occupational group. Many of these workers are self-employed, and some work without direct supervision. Others are employed in large organizations where they may be members of teams whose work goals are set by team leaders, or they may even punch time clocks, as do many physicians who work in clinics that depend upon third-party reimbursement. Their assignments are often narrow and routine. Nevertheless, the conditions under which most of these service employees work differ markedly from those of the production-line worker. Professionals, in particular, possess considerable orders of freedom to determine how they work, when they work, and the quality of their output, and while all manpower projections are problematic, the odds favor a continuing absolute and relative growth in professional manpower.

A third critical change relates to women, whose participation in the labor forces of advanced industrial societies is increasing steadily. While the majority of female workers has tended to be employed less than full-time full-year, the career orientation of many of those who are fully employed, particularly married women, seems to differ from that of the male prototype. The trade-off between income and time is critical for the married woman with homemaking responsibilities, as is the trade-off between commitment to her job and commitment to her family. The important point is that females are accounting for an increasing proportion of the total labor force, and this fact lends a new dimension to the model of the traditional worker.

The later entrance of people into the labor force and their earlier exit from full-time employment is a fourth trend whose influence and impact has not been given proper attention. Little is known about the consequences of starting full-time work at age 24, instead of at age 14, but one may speculate that the longer the period of occupational exploration, the higher one's expectations. Similarly, with retirement benefits increasingly available after twenty to thirty years of work, many workers in their early and middle fifties can change their life styles by shifting to a new type of work. To the extent that this trend continues and accelerates—and acceleration appears likely—it is necessary to deal with the quality of working life from a longitudinal perspective.

A variation of occupational shifts because of early retirement is the recent trend toward the pursuit of second careers prior to retirement age. While still relatively few in terms of the total labor force, increasing numbers of workers are finding it possible and desirable to change their occupations in midstream. No longer satisfied with their first choice, they look around for new and more stimulating fields of activity. Sometimes they return to school or make other serious efforts to prepare themselves for a career change. Earlier vesting of pensions, larger governmental expenditures for adult education and training, and higher personal incomes and savings will unquestionably accelerate this tendency.

A sixth trend relates to the steady decrease in hours worked per year. Although there has been no recent large-scale decline in the average workweek in the United States, both in Europe and in this country, total hours are decreasing because of more holidays, longer vacations, and paid absences to attend to personal affairs. In the long run there will probably be further reductions in the hours worked per year.

Finally, post-World War II developments on both sides of the Atlantic point to the accelerated growth of large organizations, in business as well as in the nonprofit and government sectors. Universities with 50,000 students and hospitals with 2,000 beds are no longer exceptional. The recent movement toward mergers in the United States has seen the disappearance of a large number of small, successful, well-managed firms that could not withstand the lure of attractive purchase offers. Although small new firms are being formed constantly, the trend is toward the continuing growth of large companies where the decision-making process tends to be concentrated at the top, among other reasons because that is the only place where critical determinations about the long-term interests of the organization can be made. Unlike smaller firms, such large organizations tend to be more bureaucratic, to subscribe to rationalization of work, and to be more rigid and less personal.

This list of major trends affecting the work environment could easily be extended beyond the seven that have been briefly discussed. For example, the growth of white-collar unionism undoubtedly will provide additional leverage for many workers to influence their working environment; the steadily rising level of educational attainment will unquestionably produce more young workers with high expectations and with new and different orientations to work; and rising levels of family income, together with improved social welfare benefits, will provide people with new degrees of freedom in making decisions about work, jobs, and careers.

Impact on Work

The critical thrust of work restructuring is to bring about a better fit between the individual and the organization, with the joint aim of optimizing the goals of the worker and of his employer. To this end, restructuring experiments have been directed toward enlarging the scope of the worker with respect to planning, self-control, and self-regulation—that is, toward autonomy and a broadening of options. The premise is that, in exchange for more satisfying employment conditions, the worker will become more committed to the organization.

What can be said, then, about the impact of the aforementioned trends on the quality of working life? The shift from goods to services suggests that in advanced industrial societies rigid, highly subdivided, tightly controlled production lines will provide the work setting for an ever-smaller proportion of the total work force, but it tells little about the potentials for autonomy among brokerage clerks, salesgirls, telephone operators, and sanitation workers.

The absolute as well as relative increase in professional and technical workers suggests the need for more sophisticated measurements of output, and for less reliance on tight controls, if the potential contributions of these workers are to be optimized. There is little evidence that large organizations are willing to run the risks of providing brainworkers with the autonomy they desire, although a sophisticated company will adopt personnel policies for its professional staff that resemble an academic setting more than a factory environment.

Women's agitation against employment discrimination is indicative of the long way that employers have to go to improve the opportunity structures for females. Whether they work because of choice or necessity, there is rising discontent among the female labor force at all occupational levels because generic problems in the work setting are exacerbated by sex bias.

Delayed entrance into the labor force and potentially earlier departure represent a marked increase in the freedom to make life plans, but it is a freedom that cuts two ways: the more time, effort, and money that young people invest in preparing for work and careers, the higher their expectations and the greater their potential source of dissatisfaction if their goals are not fulfilled. Similarly, if men have the option to retire early, employers often have the option to force early retirement.

Another broadening of options is the trend toward second careers, which is enabling increasing numbers of workers to move out of fields that no longer command their interest or engage their talents. Here again, it does not follow that the choice of a second career will live up to expectations.

The reduction in working time also can be seen as a broadening of options. If workers find their work oppressive or uninteresting, the possibility of spending fewer hours on the job permits them to seek satisfactions elsewhere. Despite its merits, however, this alternative does not enhance the quality of life in the workplace itself.

Even the trend toward larger organizations is equivocal with respect to the subject at hand. Those who reach the top in the large and more complex organization (or get close to the top) probably find their work of increasing interest. On the other hand, for many in middle management, the environment is not so attractive because they have less opportunity to advance and less scope for participating in policy decisions than in smaller organizations. Thus the trend toward bigness may have a negative impact upon the quality of working life. Of course, the dysfunctional aspects of size are not restricted to those on the managerial level. All workers in large organizations are locked into personnel systems and must adhere to company policies that leave them and their supervisors little room to maneuver in a manner that will alter their working environment.

Conclusions

Managerial initiatives to provide greater autonomy and broader options for workers to obtain improved performance must be considered within the context of labor market forces that are themselves continuously transforming the work environment. Our review suggests that manpower trends have important implications for the success of work restructuring efforts. At a minimum, they point to the need for a broadened framework for any consideration of improvements in the quality of working life.

It is essential to recognize that workers' adjustment to the world of work changes as the workers themselves change; hence there is need for longitudinal perspective that permits the evaluation of such changes. Also, it is wrong both to neglect differences in the work orientation of men and women, and to ignore the strong career drives of many women. The effects of the vastly extended period of education and training prior to labor market entry upon the skills workers have to offer, upon their expectations about work, and upon their values, must also be part of a comprehensive study of the quality of working life. Finally, a broadened framework must allow for an interpretation of the interplay between work and nonwork, specifically with respect to alterations in such basic areas as authority, legitimacy, equity, and status. Unless the work arena is studied within the societal context, we shall continue to fly blind, not knowing whether or not conditions in the workplace are responsive to the aspirations and expectations of the worker.

10

The Humanizing of Europe's Assembly Line

Those of us who study the problems of jobs, work, and manpower lately have been required to turn our attention from the issue of employment itself to that of work satisfaction—or, more properly, work dissatisfaction. Note, for example, the enormous amount of attention paid to the wildcat strike at the Chevrolet Vega assembly line at Lordstown, Ohio, and to the rising rejection of collective bargaining agreements by union locals whose members believe that their national leadership is disregarding unsatisfactory working conditions. There is also the growing interest among leading corporations—AT&T, General Foods, Polaroid, Procter & Gamble, Chrysler—in experimenting with job redesign, enrichment, rotation, enlargement, and with decentralized decision-making, all of which are aimed at removing some of the major sources of employee discontent with work conditions. Even the enthusiastic public response to the revival of Charlie Chaplin's movie, *Modern Times,* suggests popular empathy with the plight of the industrial worker.

In Europe, as I learned in the early 1970s during a trip through the Netherlands, Sweden, Norway, France, and Italy, and in Israel, the subject of work satisfaction is attracting even more attention than in the United States. I talked with managers, labor leaders, government officials, and research personnel about some of their new experiments in work structuring. In addition, I spent many hours in plants observing a number of these experiments, which ranged from autonomous work groups in a television assembly unit to efforts at job enlargement and enrichment in automotive assembly plants.

One of the things that strikes an American studying industrial and economic conditions in other countries is the way in which each society is caught up in its own historical time schedule. Thus, over and over again, European managers waxed enthusiastic over their discovery of the "new" doctrines of decentralization and consultative management, doctrines that have flourished in the United States at least since the end of World War II. On the other hand, almost without exception, European managers are far more sensitive than their American counterparts to the play of ideological and political forces that place severe limits on their ability to remedy workers' broad discontent through restructuring the work they perform.

The role of social science in this regard has been significant. In the early 1950s, the Tavistock Institute in London described a new synthesis, composed of the technology of Frederick W. Taylor and Elton Mayo's perception of the factory as a network of social relations, which has come to be called the sociotechnical approach. In the early 1960s, the institute became associated with Einar Thorsrud of Norway, who was about to launch a cooperative effort among management, labor, government, and social scientists to modify the work environment in order to make a tangible improvement in the quality of life. Ten years of active experimentation followed; Thorsrud is now the acknowledged leader among European practitioners of sociotechnical methods.

Motivations for Restructuring Work

The workers and representatives of management who take part in such experiments are, of course, pursuing—or believe they are pursuing—their own interests. The interests of management, while diverse, are easy to discern. On the one hand, they stem from the fact that many companies have come to face great difficulty in recruiting industrial workers, particularly from their native labor force. For most of the last decade, the majority of the countries of Western Europe (and Israel) have been confronted with a labor market that has ranged from tight to very tight. All of the European countries I visited, Italy excepted, have had to import foreign workers; and in Italy the automobile plants in Turin were staffed increasingly with labor recruited from the southern part of the country. Industrial employers had also sought to expand the number and proportion of female employees, but this group turned out to be a rather shallow labor pool. Relatively few women can be enticed into blue-collar jobs, especially if heavy, noisy, and dirty work is involved.

Recently, each of the labor-importing countries has become aware of the social and political disabilities involved in having a large foreign labor force in its midst. There are very real drawbacks if the foreign workers remain for only a year or two; and if they seek to settle more or less permanently, all sorts of difficulties arise with respect to such elements as the provision of housing and schooling, and the social and political relations between the immigrants and the host society. When tight labor markets begin to loosen and unemployment increases, great pressure develops to restrict the importation of foreign labor. Employers who have come to depend on such labor see themselves caught in a bind: they are unable to recruit local labor and they run the risk of having their foreign supplies cut off. If, through changes in work structuring, industrial employment could be made more attractive to the native population, employers might be able to surmount their recruitment problems.

Another inducement for management to restructure work has been provided by such factors as increases in absenteeism and turnover, and other evidence, imagined or real, of low motivation and low morale. There are as yet few hard data to back what are general impressions. Actually, other factors having little or nothing to do with actual job dissatisfaction seem to offer just as reasonable an explanation for counterproductive worker behavior. In Italy, for example, a recent change in the social security system no longer requires that a worker who takes a day off because of illness be examined by a physician, and many workers now view the liberalized sick benefits as paid time off.

In addition, management has looked for ways to increase productivity in order to compensate for higher wage costs. Trade unions in France and Italy have been successful in achieving major reforms, such as transferring blue-collar workers to the monthly payroll and upgrading a significant proportion of unskilled and semiskilled workers. Work structuring offers a prospect of offsetting the cost of these innovations.

As European companies have grown in size and complexity, their managements have become more professional. One consequence of this trend is increased attention to established organizational relationships and supervision. Many companies have found themselves burdened with excessive layers of supervision, which slow decision-making, retard productivity, and prove burdensome to those at the bottom of the hierarchy. Experimentation with work structuring by enlarging the responsibility of the worker on the line often provides an excuse for making fairly radical organizational changes, including collapsing several layers of supervisors. Moreover, in Sweden, where hourly wages are the exception in industrial establishments, earlier each change in the production system usually provided the occasion for intensive negotiations between management and labor about norms, piece rates, and bonuses. One tangential benefit of work structuring has been to reduce, if not eliminate, such complex negotiations.

In Western Europe and Israel, then, there is a minority of managements who, faced with a range of problems centered around recruitment and utilization of manpower, have decided that they have little to lose, and perhaps much to gain, from experimenting with changes in work structuring. If successful, they believe their companies will benefit in terms of increased productivity and profits, as well as in improved worker satisfaction.

As for the workers, why have they been willing to participate in experiments that could not be launched and surely could not be successfully implemented without their cooperation? What have they seen as their own possible gain? To begin with, most factory work in Europe—as in the United States—leaves much to be desired. It is characterized by excessive noise, poor ventilation, machinery that breaks down often, poor supervision, infrequent rest periods, and a host of other conditions workers find irksome. As a result, any effort on the part of management to address itself to these problems will be seen as a boon, provided the workers are convinced that the new approach is not aimed at getting them to produce more without commensurate adjustment in wages. Since most experiments require the cooperation of only small numbers of worker volunteers, it is usually easy to counter their fears.

The volunteers frequently respond to improved communications and expanded decision-making power, which are integral parts of many work structuring experiments. They like the idea of having more say about the specifics of the production process, and they enjoy the regularly scheduled conferences at which they learn about how their work fits into the larger picture. They also like the fact that the experiments relieve them of one or more layers of supervision and that they are given more opportunity to use their initiative. In the case of autonomous work groups—a leading form of experiment—the members frequently relish the camaraderie that develops, and most of them find themselves under less pressure than when the pace of work was set by the machine.

There are additional reasons why workers support the experiments. Most important is their conviction—in many cases justified—that if the experiment proves itself, they will be able to earn more through upgrading, higher wage rates, larger bonuses, or all three. Sometimes they see in these experiments the promise of reaching other long-deferred goals, such as getting rid of piecework or being placed on the monthly payroll, thereby enjoying the same perquisites as white-collar workers.

The experiments also expand the scope and responsibility of the local labor representative. In most European countries and in Israel, either the national unions or the national trade union organization (L. O. in Sweden and Histadrut in Israel) have long dominated the collective bargaining process. The worker in the plant and his local trade union representative are both pawns in a strategy of national negotiations. But no significant changes in the restructuring of work can be made without local trade union participation. While the national trade union leaders have seldom been enthusiastic about these experiments, they generally cooperate because they recognize the mounting evidence of local restiveness and see the experiments as a relatively safe outlet for the drive for greater local autonomy. And it is, after all, risky for the leadership to drag its feet, for the union must play a key role in any serious program aimed at improving the work environment.

A word about the research community and governmental officials. Thorsrud explained his initial interest in work structuring in terms of his disenchantment with radical political solutions—that is, with the Soviet and Yugoslav versions of Communism—and his equal distaste for the banality and materialism of industrial capitalism in its American version. He was impressed with the desirability of infusing fresh life into the social democracy of the Scandinavian countries, which were finding it increasingly difficult in the post-World War II years to advance into new terrains. The more pragmatic members of the Western European research community, while less concerned with the larger problems of values and politics, shared Thorsrud's desire to find an alternative to the confrontation and conflict that have for so long characterized labor-management relations.

It was only one small step, therefore, for some political leaders such as Jacques Chaban-Delmas, the former French premier, to join the ranks of the new converts. In outlining his platform for election in 1974, Chaban-Delmas made reform of the working environment one of his key planks, specifically stressing a superior profit-sharing plan, worker participation at board level, and improvements in the workplace.

In Sweden, the establishment coalition consisting of representatives of management, labor, government, and the research community prepared a working paper, "The Quality of Working Life," for the Stockholm conference on the environment, the only presentation directed specifically to this subject. These are exceptional examples. The subject is still too esoteric to have caught the imagination of most politicians or governments.

A Tentative Balance Sheet

With about a decade of experimentation in Norway and the Netherlands, and with briefer but more intensive efforts in the other countries, it is now possible to begin to draw up some kind of balance sheet on the changes in the work environment.

The first thing one notices is how slowly the experiments have proceeded in both Norway and the Netherlands. The senior staff of Philips in the Netherlands is aware of this and finds its experience with small-scale experiments at job enlargement and autonomous work groups in radio and television production to have been exaggerated out of all proportion. A visitor to Eindhoven-Philips headquarters concludes that the firm has pursued some interesting experimentations for their own sake—since the management hesitates to make any real jump from experimentation to policy. There have been no radical changes in the basic production system and it is questionable whether there will be. A manager pointed out that the successful autonomous group that was assembling twenty-six television sets a day could produce thirty, but refused to do so. When asked whether he had discussed a reduction in hours or a higher bonus with the members of the group, he looked aghast!

In Norway, on the other hand, the slow pace reflects Thorsrud's determination to advance only in unison with the principals: management, labor, government. He is committed to the idea that the planning, the success, and the errors of work structuring must be left to those who have to live with the changes. The Norwegian experimenters believe that other entrepreneurs regard them as deviants, enamored of a method that makes no sense to sound businessmen. Nor have the national trade union leaders shown much enthusiasm for the new approach, although one or another has been willing to participate. The modesty of the Norwegian record, therefore, reflects a conjunction of Thorsrud's determination to seek progress only with the active participation of all the principals and the difficulty of eliciting the cooperation of any large number of these principals.

The efforts in the other countries are too recent to justify any clear-cut conclusion. Still, certain notes come through loud and clear. First is the critically important fact that, with the possible exception of a large office machine and electronics concern in Italy, nowhere has management been sufficiently convinced by the experimental results to have made any fundamental alteration in its production processes. Until managements move to alter their basic operations, the entire approach remains in the realm of the abstruse.

This is not to say that there have been no significant spin-off effects. Many firms have come to appreciate the considerable gains to be made in moving toward decentralization, flattening their organizations, and removing one or more layers of supervision. More importantly, they have come to recognize that there are also gains to be realized from improved communications with their work force and from involving employees in decisions that bear on their own working conditions.

There are further spin-offs as far as workers and their trade union organizations are concerned. Many workers have actually secured important improvements in their working conditions. At Volvo in Göteborg, Sweden, the men who operate the big body presses that have an excessively high noise level, now can take a break in a special noise-proof retreat in their immediate area. And Olivetti, south of Turin, Italy, has linked work structuring to upgrading a thousand or more workers, with corresponding increases in their wages.

Moreover, one finds in these several countries links between work structuring experiments and reductions in hours, shifts from piecework to hourly or monthly pay, improved bonuses, and other priority objectives of trade unions. Such objectives might well have been achieved by the trade unions without these experiments, but the gains would have come more slowly.

While no *national* trade union leader talked glowingly about the experiments per se (Ben Aharon, the former leader of Histadrut, was convinced of the need for fundamental changes in the work world but in terms of protecting the dignity and intelligence of men), much favorable comment came from *local* labor leaders who were directly involved in introducing changes at the workplace. It seems likely then that the experiments are doing little to reduce the basic tensions between national unions and their locals that exist in the United States, Western Europe, and Israel. However, by providing new scope for local leaders, they may be easing relations somewhat.

Thus, the results have not been total gain or total loss. Indeed, before choosing to be either an optimist or a skeptic, one must attempt to place work structuring in the larger context of those political, social, and economic forces that will be the major factors in determining the transformation of industrial societies in the decades ahead.

The proponents of work structuring stress that, once earnings are above a subsistence level, workers become less interested in income than in other forms of satisfaction. The question remains, however, whether labor leaders and workers do, in fact, act in accordance with this idea or whether they are simply and constantly interested in fighting for more money. There is little hard evidence from the collective bargaining table to support the work structuring approach. This means that, although workers are definitely concerned about improving the conditions of the workplace, they are even more interested in higher wages, shorter hours, more paid vacations, and higher retirement benefits. Workers question, and probably rightly, the degree to which conditions on the factory floor can be improved. They do *not* question that they will be better off if they earn more and work less. Only the self-assured manager and the moralistic social scientist are certain that, if employees work fewer hours, they will not know what to do with their leisure. Workers themselves are not in the least beset by such worries. Hence if workers want more pay for less work and if managers want more work from them for the same pay but with altered work conditions, the confrontation that the sociotechnical theorists look forward to dissolving is likely to be with us for a long time. Work structuring is not likely to usher in the demise of the union.

There is talk in Western Europe, just as in the United States, that the day may not be far off when certain types of manufacturing will no longer be profitable. If this generation of young workers, and the next, really balk at accepting less desirable types of factory employment, if the countries involved run out of second-class citizens, such as workers from the south of Italy or blacks in the United States, and if these countries refuse to permit large numbers of foreigners to settle among them, then the outcome is clear. Certain manufacturing operations will move to other countries where workers have fewer options and lower expectations. To illustrate: In the United States, after the seasonal migration of Mexican farm laborers was prohibited in the mid-1960s, certain crops requiring laborers to stoop continuously could no longer be raised. In France, one of the oldest and most profitable radio manufacturing plants is seeking new production ideas in the Far East, as well as new markets!

Certain industrialists question whether they will still be able to manufacture at home a decade hence, or whether they will be forced to relocate to less developed countries where, regardless of working conditions, the opportunity to earn $1.50 to $2.00 an hour is welcomed. The rapid growth of low-wage manufacturing operations in developing countries is threatening the competitive advantages long held by more advanced European firms. Unless the latter can increase productivity, they may lose out in the competition involving the labor-intensive manufacture of goods ranging from clothing to radios.

In this perspective, experiments with work structuring are forced responses of management. The fact that only a small number of such experiments were initiated in countries with tight labor markets underscores management's preference for the conventional solution—tapping new sources of labor supply—rather than for major structural innovation.

However, the assumption that, in a struggle between management and labor over productivity, profits, wages, and working conditions, international competition will discipline labor to accept terms it would otherwise reject is wrong for two reasons. Labor bargains in the short run; international competition, to the extent that it operates, has an impact in the long run. Moreover, one of the interesting consequences of the greater degree of European economic hegemony is the increasing cooperation among national unions. All trade unions with agreements in Ford plants in Western Europe are coordinating their demands and aiming at a multinational settlement. Labor can play the multinational game about as easily as management.

Wide as the disparity is in the United States between most blue- and white-collar workers and between workers and managers, it is much wider in Europe. While the present gap is being narrowed in varying degrees in Scandinavia, France, and Italy by transferring blue-collar workers to the monthly payroll and equalizing their fringe benefits, it is difficult to see how work structuring efforts can effectively cancel out the differences between the man who uses his muscles eight hours a day and one who sits at a desk manipulating words, figures, or people. Someone once remarked that when he first became an office worker, he could not believe that what he was doing was "work," for it bore no resemblance to his earlier life in the factory. Some of the more reflective managers recognize this difference and see no way of eliminating it other than by rotating workers between the office and the factory—an experiment, I need hardly say, that has yet to be structured. They view problems with the labor supply as going beyond improvements in the immediate work environment, and beyond even adjustments in wages and benefits, because resistance to blue-collar work will continue as long as the dominant value systems assign it to the lowest rung of the social totem pole.

It is no accident that almost all the experiments in work structuring involve blue-collar workers. Only in Sweden are white-collar workers included in the experimental design, but these efforts smack more of work simplification than of work structuring. and nowhere is attention being paid to lower and middle management. Presumably, they are deemed to be highly productive and to be enjoying their work, presumptions without much supporting evidence. Every time a question was raised abroad about work dissatisfaction among middle management, employers were speechless.

Work Structuring and Political Reform

In attempting to analyze the relation between these two broad areas, we must distinguish between countries where the social democrats have long been in control (Sweden, Norway, and Israel) and the situation in France and Italy.

The long-term political ascendancy of the labor movement in both Scandinavia and Israel is under attack from within and without on a whole series of fronts—ideology, organizational structure, leadership. The dissidents include many members of the younger generation, the professional classes, disadvantaged minorities (and in fact, increasing numbers of the general public) who have begun to question whether the labor establishment can solve urgent national problems. Evidence of growing restiveness and disillusion can be read in wildcat strikes, alienation of youth, the growing hostility of unemployed intellectuals, the strident criticism from opinion leaders on the right and left, all of which indicates a loss of confidence in the institutions that labor built with so much loving care to usher in the new society. No one, other than the idealistic Thorsrud, sees work structuring as being responsive—or having the potential of becoming responsive—to the political malaise threatening social democracy.

The situation in France and Italy is different. The more progressive sectors of French management have not yet recovered from their nightmarish experience of 1968 when they were saved by the Communists, who refused to join the ranks of the revolutionary students. The wiser managers know that the discontents that fed the uprising are still present and that, next time, the rank and file may join the students. Hence a great many adjustments must be made as quickly as possible on many fronts—including improving the workplace, increasing the worker's share, and enlarging his role in the decision-making process. It is far from clear that the conservative political and business leadership in France will be able to make the long-delayed accommodations that are required to assure broad support for a system whose legitimacy is under serious attack. France needs not another Charles de Gaulle, but a Franklin Roosevelt. No one expects work structuring to provide more than an assist in the task of social reform.

The Italian scene is even more unstable. The economy is being radically transformed, while the political structure and class relations are changing very slowly. Work structuring has little to contribute to solving the urgent problems that demand attention: the swelling ranks of the educated unemployed; the abysmal poverty of the south; and the gap between workers' expectations and the ability of the economy to meet them.

Conclusions

Despite the substantial improvement in the lives of the working population of western European countries and of Israel during the past quarter-century—gains reflected in increased real income, higher educational attainment, improved social benefits, more leisure—a pervasive unease exists. European workers are increasingly bereft of the ideology, political organization, and leadership necessary to channel their discontents and formulate new goals.

Workers always welcome an opportunity to improve their conditions of work, just as they press for more wages and shorter hours. But when workers begin to question whether the good life consists only of more consumer goods, and when they are unclear about what they really want and are even less certain about how to realize whatever vision they have of a better future, adjustments at the workplace are a limited response at best. If workers direct a major effort to this new frontier, the issue that remains open is what lies beyond. Recent European experience tells us that management will explore a great many alternative ways of meeting its manpower needs before embarking upon large-scale experimentation. Management continues to prefer seeking solutions in the market.

11

Science Policy and Educated Manpower

A former president of the American Association for the Advancement of Science declared in 1972 that the United States must develop a "holding pattern" to preserve an excess of scientists and technologists who would be prepared to fill important demands in industry, government, and education in the decade after 1980. That is a long time to fix people in a holding pattern—and it indicates the rather desperate situation that presently confronts large segments of educated manpower.

The sharp decline in demand for highly trained manpower is affecting, to varying degrees, all recent college and university graduates who aspire to careers in business or academe. The 1972 annual meeting of the Modern Language Association had a funereal quality, so dismal were the employment prospects for people with newly acquired doctorates in the humanities. Historians, sociologists, and economists are having difficulty in obtaining attractive positions—and often cannot find even unattractive ones. Similarly, medical researchers, mathematicians, and physicists are keenly feeling the cutbacks in research funding, as well as the highly selective or no-hiring policy of business and educational institutions.

One hears Cassandra-like prophecies that the United States, like India, Indonesia, Egypt, France, and Argentina, has become a nation plagued by unemployed intellectuals. And some prophets of doom even see similarities between the United States today and the

Weimar Republic after 1929, when Germany was unable to absorb a relatively much smaller annual output of university graduates. What is the cause of this downturn in the demand for educated manpower? Is the future as desperate as many people think?

The Changing Role of Science

The current plight of educated manpower is, to a large extent, a function of changes in national science policy in the decades since World War II. During this period the relations between science and government underwent many alterations that initially were highly favorable to science, but more recently have been deeply distressing.

In the early 1930s, the total laboratory budget for the Department of Physics at Columbia University was about $10,000 annually, and the Navy's initial response to a request by Enrico Fermi for research support was negative. Even after the outbreak of World War II, Albert Einstein felt constrained to suggest to President Roosevelt that research into nuclear fission might be speeded if funds were sought from rich donors! It was not until the experiences of World War II convinced both the political and scientific leadership of the advantages of large-scale governmental support for defense research that the country moved toward massive support of science.

The government-science alliance was further strengthened by other political considerations, since Congress was interested in contributing to the financing of higher education and in supporting research into the causes and cures of life-threatening diseases. Also, the interests of powerful constituencies, such as the aerospace industry and the leading universities, were major influences on ever-larger governmental research appropriations. For the better part of two decades, the forces of expansion dominated.

To establish perspective, let us review what the scientific elite actively engaged in the shaping of science policy were able to accomplish. Their achievements were considerable.

They were able to ride piggyback on the large defense appropriations and see that a large amount of research money was made available for basic and applied research at universities and university-related organizations, such as the Jet Propulsion Laboratory of Caltech and Lincoln Laboratory of MIT, as well as in nonuniversity settings. These funds were large enough and were made available under sufficiently liberal conditions to enable the recipients to train a whole generation of young scientists. Moreover, the funds from defense and defense-related agencies, particularly the Atomic Energy Commission and the National

Aeronautics and Space Administration (NASA), provided the financial underpinnings for the science departments of most large universities. They enabled these departments to grow and prosper.

The National Institutes of Health, which received liberal support from Congress, stimulated a rapid expansion in the life sciences, specifically of biomedical research. Here too the major universities received important financial aid, particularly in bolstering the insecure financial underpinnings of their medical schools.

In addition, the scientific leadership found large numbers of able persons to fill critical positions inside and outside the government, thereby enabling them to influence significantly the deployment of growing research funds. By agreeing among themselves about high-priority goals, such as the construction of giant accelerators, the scientific establishment was usually able to convince the President and Congress about the next arena requiring large-scale support. It also succeeded in establishing peer review for judging scientific proposals, which kept subjective elements in evaluation within tolerable limits. And, most important, from time to time the voices of scientists could be heard above the din of the hardware-minded generals and admirals.

What then went wrong? During the years when the environment was propitious for expanding the role of science and research, the leaders of the scientific establishment were primarily concerned with obtaining congressional approval for ever-larger appropriations. In their view this was the best, and surely the quickest, way of building strength on strength. Time has proved that this policy was shortsighted, and that many of the present difficulties flow from an exclusive preoccupation with financing.

While there is merit to peer evaluation of research, the fact that the federal government was unconcerned about the repercussions on universities of large grants to individual professors undoubtedly led to excrescences in academe through the establishment of a new power center—the buccaneering research director. Only the uninformed would minimize the distortions brought about in the wake of these government contract relations.

Since the American Medical Association was opposed to federal support for medical education, the National Institutes of Health helped to keep medical schools afloat by making liberal grants through the back door of research. In the process they shifted the reward system of American medicine away from education and service in favor of research, so that there was greater incentive for physicians to work in the laboratory than to work with patients.

The heavy reliance on the project system also resulted in the concentration of more and more federal dollars at a relatively few institutions until these institutions reached or passed the point of optimal performance. Most of the time and energy of the senior staff was deflected to administration.

Admittedly, there is serious danger in a formula approach to the division of the federal research dollar, for instance in a formula that leads to a distribution based on geography rather than capability. Clearly, it is better that money go where competent scientists are. But an ongoing federal effort must be concerned not only with the present, but with the future. Consequently, it was appropriate for President Lyndon Johnson to stress the development of research capabilities in the less-favored sections of the country. It is amazing that the President, rather than the scientific community, had to force this issue.

In the benign environment of the late fifties and early sixties, the senior staff of the National Institutes of Health (NIH) began to play a rough game that could end only in reprisals, even if delayed. Year after year the NIH bureaucrats, with Senator Lister Hill and Congressman John Fogarty as their major allies, succeeded in getting Congress to appropriate more money than the Bureau of the Budget had requested. They did this by having their academic supporters—who were also their principal beneficiaries—testify about the need for more money before friendly congressional committees. Understandably, few reputable persons were asked or volunteered to testify in favor of lower appropriations for research into heart disease, cancer, and other unsolved scourges!

The scientific leadership and the senior governmental bureaucrats developed a good working relationship which, with the assistance of friendly congressional committee chairmen, enabled them to proceed from one victory to the next. The most that was submitted by way of caution or criticism in a decade of congressional hearings was the muted suggestion that perhaps too much money was chasing too few good people—a proposition that this writer advanced to the Joint Committee on Atomic Energy in the middle 1950s.

Trouble was building up, although it was slow to surface. Even before serious involvement in Vietnam and disenchantment with the military, the heavy dependence on Department of Defense appropriations for research funding introduced a major element of vulnerability. It was reasonably certain that defense expenditures would eventually level off and might even be cut back. At that point it should have been clear that the armed services might become a less enthusiastic and generous sponsor of basic research.

The rapidly rising total of congressional appropriations for basic and applied research was a certain prelude to disenchantment. During the four years (1959 to 1963) that I served on the Advisory Council of the National Institute of Mental Health (NIMH), its annual appropriations increased from about $50 million to $180 million. I warned my colleagues and the staff of the inevitability of intensified surveillance by Congress once we entered the big-money league. My warnings, which were coupled with a suggestion that we expand more slowly in order to expand more soundly, fell on deaf ears. Neither at the NIMH nor at the NIH would the senior staffs listen to any proposal advocating a slower rate of growth. The difficulties experienced in staffing and financing community mental health centers date from this euphoric period when key officials were accustomed only to large annual budgetary increases.

The men who played the leading role in the shaping of science policy during the 1950s and 1960s had been part of the forced growth that occurred during World War II. Having operated in an environment where neither voter nor legislator played a critical role in the decision-making process, and assuming that it would take a great amount of valuable time and scarce talent to educate the public and lawmakers to a level where their support would be freely forthcoming, the scientific leadership concentrated on persuading a small number of government leaders in order to get their programs accepted. This foreshadowed future trouble with both the Congress and the public. Sooner or later multibillion dollar appropriations would have to compete in the political arena. The scientific leadership outsmarted itself by getting so much, so quickly, from so few.

From one vantage, the scientific elite did extraordinarily well in gaining ever-expanding financial support for its work. However, the approaches that it favored were abortive: it had no broad congressional support; it could—and did—fall out of favor with the White House; the public had little or no understanding of the critical decisions that were being made by a handful of insiders; and most important, nobody was worrying about the impact of scientific policy on the career prospects of educated manpower.

As noted earlier, expanding research grants provided the money to train a much enlarged cohort and to subsidize students throughout their graduate and postgraduate studies. But the leadership paid little attention to their students' eventual employment, and less to their career prospects. No systematic and continuous analysis of the scientific manpower market was undertaken, either inside the government or out. The 1970 Folger report, *Human Resources and Higher Education,* was a one-time effort. A great amount of foresight was not necessary to recognize that any drop in the rate of increase of federal expenditures for research, and certainly a leveling-off or a reduction, in the face of rapid increases in the manpower supply, would result in turmoil. And that is exactly what has happened.

Why the Downturn?

When the economy slowed in the early 1970s, so did the demand for trained manpower. Industry cut its hiring drastically; federal expenditures declined for programs that had hitherto generated heavy demands for scientific and engineering manpower; the universities—emerging from their dream world of constantly expanding enrollments and access to "soft money" for research—were confronting dwindling entrance classes and fewer grants and contracts; the long-term shortage of teachers at the elementary and secondary level, which many had come to view as chronic, proved to be temporary.

Still, the economy had slowed down before, most notably in the late 1950s and early 1960s, and educated manpower was not badly hurt. The difference lay in the changing patterns of concentration of this type of manpower and the nature of its support. In the mid-1960s, my colleagues and I wrote *The Pluralistic Economy* in which we estimated that approximately two-thirds of all scientists and development engineers were employed in the not-for-profit sector—that is, their salaries came directly or indirectly from the government. Most of the work force of the large aerospace companies is paid for by federal money, even though the stock of these companies is traded on the New York Stock Exchange. In addition, many persons in academic employment and in the employ of nonprofit research organizations are dependent on the flow of federal dollars.

In the four fiscal years between 1965 and 1969, defense expenditures rose from under $50 billion to almost $81 billion. During the four subsequent years, defense outlays declined. The estimated outlay for fiscal 1973 was $74.8 billion—which, allowing for the erosion of the dollar, represents a sizable decline. Defense Secretary Melvin Laird pointed out that in terms of constant buying power the defense budget for 1972 was about equal to what it was in 1964. Total Defense Department-related employment increased from 6 to 8.3 million persons during the expansion, and declined to 5.7 million during the downswing.

Expenditures for space research and technology, another field that is a major employer of scientific and engineering manpower, rose from about $400 million in fiscal 1961 to a peak of $6 billion in 1966. Thereafter they declined, and the estimated expenditures for 1973 were $3.1 billion (this does not take into account the further erosion caused by inflation). Total employment in NASA programs increased from 47,000 to a peak of 410,000, and then declined sharply to 137,000.

A further complication was congressional passage of the Mansfield Amendment in 1970, which prohibited the Department of Defense from supporting basic research unless the armed forces could demonstrate that such research was defense related; this measure cut the flow of research dollars to universities.

The slope of decline in other areas has not been as precipitous as in defense and space, but the pattern is the same. The funds available for biomedical research increased for many years at a rate of more than 15 percent per year. But the prestige of the NIH began to slip in the middle 1960s, when both the President and Congress became increasingly concerned with the delivery of medical services. Since research had not succeeded in finding answers for cancer, heart disease, or stroke, the political leadership saw more votes in broadening the access of the poor and the middle class to medical care than in enlarging appropriations for research.

As far as federal expenditures for education, manpower training, and related services are concerned, from 1962 to 1967 the federal budget expanded fourfold—from about $1.5 billion to $6 billion; in the following five years the increase was more modest, particularly when allowance is made for inflation.

Fewer federal dollars meant fewer jobs for scientists, engineers, and other college-trained personnel. Southern California, with approximately a third of the nation's aerospace employment, had 486,000 persons on its aerospace payrolls in May 1968; in 1972 it had 340,000—a decline of roughly 30 percent. The reduced expenditures of Defense and NASA were also the principal influences upon the loss of employment opportunities for young scientists and mathematicians in research and development projects at universities and elsewhere. The National Science Foundation has estimated that, of the approximately 160,000 doctoral scientists and engineers in 1969, about 60 percent were based in universities, 26 percent in industry, and the remainder in government and other settings. Outside the universities, the predominant proportion of those holding doctorates (three out of four) was engaged in research and development activities. Hence, as the R&D funding declined, employment opportunities for young scientists were reduced both on and off the campus.

The educational system itself has long been a major user of educated manpower. This was particularly true during the 1950s and early 1960s as schools expanded to cope with booming enrollments; in addition, more and more young people were staying in school until they acquired a high school diploma. About three out of five holders of doctorates are employed in colleges and universities in teaching, research, or some combination of both. In *Human Resources and Higher Education*, Folger estimated that jobs in education at all levels have provided employment for approximately half of all new master's degree recipients. And elementary and secondary education has been the single largest employer of new college graduates; if sizable numbers of married women had not returned to teaching, the elementary and secondary schools would have absorbed one out of every three new recipients of the bachelor's degree.

Here too the situation took a radical turn for the worse. The shortage of teachers had been so severe and so prolonged that warning signs from changing demographic trends, reinforced by evidence of greater ease in recruitment, were largely ignored. One important reason for the present disequilibrium between demand and supply of educated manpower is now clear: the role of federal programming and financing in creating the booming market for trained people was not fully appreciated, and little consideration was given to the possibility of a radical shift in priorities in the federal budget.

To see the picture whole, it is necessary to review what was happening on the supply side. During the 1960s the number of baccalaureate and first professional degrees awarded annually increased from under 400,000 to over 700,000, and the expansion at the master's and doctoral levels was even more dramatic (from 75,000 to about 200,000 master's degrees per year, and from 10,000 to 29,000 doctorates). Paralleling this striking increase in the number of college and university graduates was the even more rapid expansion of community colleges. Enrollment in these two-year institutions increased about 200 percent in the 1960s, and by the end of the decade they were awarding about 180,000 associate degrees annually, or roughly one for every four baccalaureate degrees.

Further evidence of the explosive nature of the expansion of higher education can be found in the striking increase in the proportion of college graduates who entered graduate or professional school. In the fifteen years between 1950 and the mid-1960s the ratio jumped from one in six to one in two! Until 1971, 80 percent or more of the senior class at a number of select colleges was going on to graduate or professional school. The Selective Service system certainly helped to swell the ranks of both undergraduate and graduate students, as many young men took advantage of its liberal deferment policy. These youths may have had little interest in intellectual pursuits, but they preferred being bored in school to being shot in Vietnam.

A key element in the rapid increase in graduate enrollment was the substantial amount of money that had become available for the support of graduate students. Folger reports that in the mid-1960s, three out of five of the approximately quarter million full-time graduate students were receiving support in the form of fellowships or scholarships. In the natural sciences, four out of five graduate students received support; in nonscientific fields, the ratio approximated one in two. What we see then is a decade—in fact, two decades—during which the demand for educated manpower soared, while the supply struggled to keep pace.

The Blinding Optimism

How can one explain the fact that government officials with responsibility for manpower forecasting; professional societies with a concern for the career opportunities available to their members; education and manpower specialists engaged in monitoring changes in the training and employment of personnel, all failed to foresee the approach of the time when shortages would be replaced by surpluses?

First, most analysts ignored or failed to evaluate correctly a number of critical factors. Although there was no guarantee that the federal government would increase its appropriations for research and development by 16 percent annually, the fact that it had done so for almost a decade lulled many into assuming that such yearly increments would continue.

This basic miscalculation about changes in the level and direction of the federal budget was buttressed by two simplistic errors. Since education and research were clearly important undertakings, it was assumed that a rich society would want to invest more resources in them; the scientific and educational leadership did not contemplate that the American people might find other fields of investment more inviting. Second, the many lobbyists for basic science, defense, space, education, and health had developed considerable skill in marshalling their forces for the purpose of extracting ever-larger sums from both federal and state governments. They were expansionists by vocation. The occasional sign that might have led them to moderate their efforts was ignored, while they assembled new evidence to help justify higher appropriations.

The inflation that began in 1964-65 and gained momentum in the following years led to further distortions producing optimism, expansion, and more expansion, which in turn contributed to indiscriminate recruiting, stockpiling of talent, and rapid wage and salary advances.

The coincidence of a rapid increase in college and graduate enrollments characteristic of the 1960s and a relatively small number of new doctorates in the early 1960s led to the multiplication of doctoral programs and further helped obscure the future. Administrators who projected college enrollments foresaw many more years of continuing increases and ignored omens of an inevitable demographic leveling-off in the middle and later 1970s. They refused to give heed to Allen Cartter's warning in 1965 that a four- to five-fold increase in the annual output of doctorates—from about 10,000 in 1960 to between 40,000 and 45,000 in the late 1970s—would create a serious problem, since there was little or no prospect that the colleges and universities could continue to absorb the customary 50 percent of the new crop of doctorates.

The reasons for the plight of professional and technical manpower in the early 1970s may be summed up as follows: (1) a general slowdown in the economy; (2) a changeover from a defense-dependent economy to a quasi-peacetime economy; (3) a reduction in space expenditures; (4) a tapering-off of federal support for basic research and for education, particularly at the graduate level; and (5) the failure of colleges and universities to take account of demographic trends that signaled a reduction in the college-age cohort.

Overshadowing these many reasons for the present upheaval in the market for educated manpower is one startling fact: there was no organization, in or out of government, with a clear directive to monitor the situation and with a staff able to carry out such an assignment effectively. A group of this sort might also have been carried away by the euphoria of the times and erred seriously in its projections, but more probably it would have identified at least a few of the problems lurking beneath the surface.

The Near and Intermediate Term

Currently, educated manpower is in trouble. The critical question is whether the trouble is likely to be short-lived, or whether the distortions are so deeply ingrained that the oversupply of educated manpower is likely to continue throughout most or all of the 70s, as Wallace Brode and Allen Cartter anticipate.

There is no reason to believe that even a renewed economic expansion will result in absorption of all the educated unemployed as well as those who will be coming into the market. The federal government is the major source of the funds supporting the hiring of scientists and engineers and it is clear that, despite the cessation of hostilities in Vietnam, there will not be any significant amount of new money for civilian programs, such as research and development or education.

While we must not write off the possibility of a radical change in the level and direction of the federal budget, the odds are strongly against an increase in federal expenditures that would begin to right the manpower situation. The precarious financial position of most large private colleges and universities is forcing them to limit their staff recruitment severely (apart from the fact that the pace of new enrollment has slowed down). The large state universities also are in a period of trial and tribulation. For years state legislators appropriated large sums to expand the structure of higher education, since they had been assured by the educational leadership that there was a shortage of trained manpower and that a strong university system was a precondition for rapid economic growth. Now many of them are at odds with the educational leadership. In Illinois, the major state institutions requested approval of 280 new Ph.D. programs; the state board approved 6! In New York

State, the Commissioner of Education established a moratorium for a time on the approval of all new doctoral programs.

With the federal and many state governments in a tight budgetary bind, and with higher education no longer actively recruiting, the only remaining source of demand for high-level manpower is the private sector. In the short run, little relief can be expected here; in the face of marked uncertainty, most corporations are keeping a tight rein on new hiring. As new business expansion does take place, we can look forward to a more-than-proportional increase of professional and technical personnel on corporation payrolls. However, in the absence of forces that are not presently discernible, weaknesses in public demand will not be compensated for by a growth in private demand.

Although demand is likely to remain low, the supply of educated manpower will increase rapidly. While there is expected to be a 20 percent increase in the labor force between 1968 and 1980, there will be about a 50-percent increase in the number of workers with bachelor's degrees; a 100-percent rise in those with master's degrees; and those with doctorates will grow by over 115 percent. Seven out of ten new degree recipients are expected to enter the civilian labor force during these twelve years. The remaining three will continue in school, enter the armed forces, or marry and leave the labor force. The proportion of educated persons seeking employment will be far higher than in any previous decade.

Officially, the government is optimistic. In a 1970 publication, *College Educated Workers, 1968-80,* the United States Bureau of Labor Statistics concluded, "The supply and demand for college graduates as a whole is expected to be in relative balance during the 1970's." It foresaw trouble in only three occupations: mathematics, the life sciences, and teaching. In a 1971 study, *Occupational Manpower and Training Needs,* the bureau reaffirmed its earlier optimism: "The statistical analysis of supply and demand thus indicates the likelihood of a rough balance between the overall supply of and demand for college educated personnel for the 1970's as a whole."

But the Bureau of Labor Statistics, the National Science Foundation, and other agencies involved in manpower estimates still base their statistical predictions largely on projection of past trends. To the extent that their assumptions prove faulty, their forecasts must be revised. We may not be able at this time to discern the principal adjustments that will take place during the next decade, but we are able to call attention to some already under way and others that are likely to follow. We can state unequivocally that significant adjustments will occur; they always do in a decision-making environment that has feedback mechanisms.

Adjusting to Supply and Demand

The first pressure will be to reduce the supply itself—or at least new entrants. The federal government has cut back radically its support for students pursuing higher education. Several elite universities, including Harvard, Yale, and Princeton, are reducing the number of admissions to graduate study. Many graduate centers, while not adopting a cutback policy, are unable to offer financial assistance at previous levels, so fewer students enroll. There also has been a shift in student interest from graduate to professional study, especially to medicine and law.

It will be some time before we know how the changed outlook for scientific and technical employment will affect the numbers seeking to enter undergraduate and graduate schools. The short-term effect of a weakening in the job market is to encourage many to continue in school in order to improve their qualifications. However, if the market remains soft, and particularly if salary differentials in favor of degree holders narrow, the likelihood is that a significant minority of potential students may reassess their scholastic intentions. The large-scale increases in the college population since the end of World War II were stimulated by the attractive career prospects available to the degree holder. If these prospects worsen, the anticipated inflow of still larger numbers may not materialize.

While a continuing soft job market may reduce the number of applicants to college and graduate school and thereby help reestablish a balance between the supply of and the demand for educated manpower, the primary adaptive mechanism is the job market itself. Employers adjust their hiring requirements to the number and characteristics of job seekers. Since more college graduates are available for employment, they are likely to be offered jobs previously offered to high school graduates and college dropouts. The college graduate now risks being forced to lower his expectations. He may have to accept less challenging work, at a lower salary and with poorer career prospects than he had anticipated. To this personal frustration must be added the unrealized social investment of training people to the doctoral level ($50,000 to $100,000 per doctorate) and the potential social instability that may arise with the presence of a large number of disappointed and disgruntled, if not unemployed, intellectuals.

The market response of downgrading jobs to maintain a balance between the demand for and the supply of educated manpower is not the best equilibrating mechanism in a sophisticated technological society, however. The individual who has spent twenty or more years in school, and another decade or two working on a priority public program in space, defense, or health, cannot be declared surplus and told to fend for himself, even if he is assisted by a government grant for retraining or relocation.

In Search of Policy

There are at least two ways to view the present crisis with respect to educated manpower. The optimist can point to the fact that during the past thirty years our basic institutions—government, higher education, business—have been able to develop and employ the educated and trained personnel required for priority programs, both public and private. We are now in disequilibrium as the consequence of a concatenation of circumstances: a radical shift in the federal expenditure pattern; inflation; erratic business performance that has persisted longer than expected; the absence of a national policy for the support of higher education and science; the indifferent quality of educational planning; and the sorry state of manpower forecasting.

The optimist will argue that, as the foregoing deficiencies are remedied, the difficulties of the moment will recede. The pessimist holds that the present problems may be compounded in the years ahead: the demand for educated manpower will remain slack in the face of an ever-larger number of graduates coming into the labor market.

There is also a middle position. According to this view, the current large-scale unemployment of aerospace scientists and engineers, the difficulties of young Ph.D.'s in locating suitable positions, and the limited corporate hiring of college graduates are signs of trouble. An analysis of the short- and intermediate-term outlook for educated manpower suggests that the difficulties may worsen—at least for new doctorates who seek posts in academe or in research. Still, there is no necessity for the present crisis to develop into a full-blown, chronic disequilibrium between the output of institutions of higher learning and the ability of their graduates to find meaningful positions and careers.

It is not surprising that the United States has experienced marked instability in the markets for educated manpower, considering the instability of its support for science, once the darling of the federal decision-makers, now fallen from grace. Everything considered, the turmoil could have been much greater except for the inherent flexibility of the economy. Substantial as this flexibility is, it dare not be relied upon to assure a balance in the demand and supply for trained manpower. There is urgent need for specific action along the following lines:

(a) Development of a long-run policy for the federal support of science, with respect to both the level of funding and the rate of growth. Since the federal share has been 60 percent of a $28 billion total expenditure, erratic fluctuations are certain to cause serious manpower distortions.

(b) Institution of a long-run federal policy for the support of higher education that will provide support for graduate students through a judicious mixture of grants and loans, and that will help to keep solvent the hundred or so principal university centers.

(c) Consideration, in federal budget-making, of the manpower (particularly educated manpower) implications of the initiation, expansion, reduction, or elimination of large military and civilian programs.

These policies are urgently required. The earlier they come into being, the faster they are refined, and the better they are implemented, the more likely it is that we will be on the way to moderating the imbalances that have occurred and will continue to occur in the supply and flow of educated manpower.

12

Defense Manpower

Certain changes in a democracy are introduced after heated partisan political debate which generates such exaggerated promises that anticipated transformations cannot possibly be achieved, at least within a sensible time perspective. In other instances, a series of changes is introduced with relatively little prior public attention or controversy and, before long, important institutions have been radically modified or new ones have become deeply rooted. The "war on poverty" initiated in the mid-1960s exemplifies the first type of change; the all-volunteer force (AVF), introduced in the mid-1970s, is a prototype of the second. Admittedly, the end of the draft did not come about simply by administrative fiat or by the passage of legislation without prior debate. It is no overstatement, however, to say that there was relatively little public attention or argument focused on the multiple implications—military, social, economic—of suspending inductions under the Selective Service system, the principal agency for procuring manpower for the armed forces since 1940.

As a matter of fact, Congress and the public only rarely focused on the complex issues of efficiency and equity involved in the compulsory call-up of selectees throughout the more than three decades during which young men were subject to the draft. For the most part, defense manpower was viewed as the preserve of the Pentagon, the Selective Service system, and the Armed Services committees of the

House and Senate. Neither the press nor the professors paid much attention to an institution that impinged more directly on the lives and welfare of American families than any other intervention of the federal government. Once the American people decided that strong defense forces were essential, and Congress provided the authority and the funds required to support this goal, the details of implementation were left to the insiders apparently under the assumption that they alone had the competence to deal effectively with military matters.

It was not until 1968, when disillusionment with the Vietnam War had proceeded to a point where future funding was no longer assured, that Richard Nixon decided that he could win votes by promising that, if elected, he would explore the possibility of putting an end to the draft, a promise that he eventually carried out by appointing the Gates Commission and by translating its 1970 recommendations into a legislative proposal to phase out the draft by July 1973. Congress enthusiastically enacted the proposed legislation in 1971.

The thrust of the present analysis is to assess the state of defense manpower in the mid-1970s from the vantage of the AVF; to consider some of the larger issues connected with this radical change in the procurement of military manpower; and to speculate about some of the implication of this fundamental shift in the staffing of the armed forces.

Evaluation of the AVF

A great many Americans believed that the Navy (including the Marine Corps) and the Air Force, in contrast to the Army, were composed exclusively of volunteers, since this assertion had been made repeatedly for many years by spokesmen for the two services. Technically, these claims were correct; with only the most occasional exceptions, the Navy and Air Force had in fact filled their ranks with volunteers. But those in the know were fully aware that it was the Army's resort to the draft that had stimulated the flow of young men toward the Navy and the Air Force. Faced with the prospect of being inducted into the Army, many saw a distinct advantage, in terms of safety, comfort, and other conditions of service, to enlistment in one of the other branches, even if they had to remain on active duty for an additional year or so. While the Navy and the Air Force—and the Army as well—undoubtedly attracted a significant proportion of "true" volunteers, that is, young men who would have enlisted in the absence of pressure from the draft, it is questionable whether, at any time during the Vietnam conflict, they exceeded 50 percent of the total intake; often the proportion fell considerably below that figure.

The first consideration, therefore, in shifting from the draft involved an estimate of the prospective size of an all-volunteer force, since no informed person believed that a military force of 3.5 million (the approximate number of servicemen at the height of the Vietnam conflict) could be secured solely through enlistments. The planning for an AVF assumed a reduction in the size of the military force to slightly more than 2 million, to be accomplished by withdrawing from Vietnam, reducing future commitments, resorting to contracts to cover certain service responsibilities, and replacing military with civilian personnel.

It was recognized from the outset that the much smaller military force could be attracted and retained only if the pay and emoluments of service, especially for first-termers and for careerists with scarce skills, were substantially improved. The fact that, as early as 1967, the federal government had committed itself to tie the pay of federal personnel to prevailing wages in the private sector set the stage for a substantial increase in the pay of first-termers, even in the absence of the AVF. Had the draft continued, Congress might have dragged its feet to make this adjustment, which costs over $3 billion annually, but having already adopted the principle of pay comparability, it was more amenable to providing the financial support without which the AVF could not have been launched.

It is moot whether the more than $3 billion pay correction should be tied specifically to the suspension of the draft. However, two conclusions are clear. Even if conditions forced a return to the draft at some future date, it is unlikely that Congress would seek to reduce the current level of pay; and if military manpower requirements necessitated a return to the Vietnam level of about 3.5 million, it is well understood by both the Pentagon leadership and the Congress that even with pay comparability, it would probably be impossible to attract an additional 1.3 million enlistments. Moreover, the total cost of such a step (which has been estimated to be $40 billion or higher) would be beyond bounds.

If the issue of comparability in pay is put to one side, the other costs associated with the AVF, including additional recruiting expenses, improvements in the military environment, and related matters, have been estimated to be in the $700 million range at a maximum.

In light of procurement objectives and financial constraints the AVF could, at the end of 1974, be viewed as a success. It would be a mistake, however, to ignore several difficult problems that the transition process has brought to the fore and to assume that all problems are completely under control.

Some Critical Issues for the AVF

It is not generally appreciated that an annual procurement objective of around 400,000 new recruits—the approximate goal for the AVF in the mid-1970s—implies that the Department of Defense (DOD) must be able to attract about one out of three qualified young men in the eligible age group who are not college-bound. College youth who reach their junior year, it is presumed, will not be interested in enlisting except as potential commissioned officers. Since two out of five high school graduates continue their schooling, the total pool of eligible enlistees is very much reduced. There are further large reductions in the potential pool resulting from the inability of many youths to meet the physical, mental, emotional, or moral standards that Congress and the services have established on the basis of facts and beliefs about how those so handicapped perform in a military environment.

While there is considerable scope for argument about the correct cutoff point for acceptance, there are a great many studies that confirm that youths who are high school dropouts, who are at the lower end of the aptitude distribution, who have been convicted of a felony, who have health defects, or who have police records tend to experience difficulties in making successful adjustments to the military. Requirements for acceptance could be flexible when recruits were paid far below the competitive wage, but the armed forces are now under great pressure to have their personnel dollars stretch as far as possible. Accordingly, Congress recently took the initiative to raise standards for acceptance by passing legislation requiring at least 55 percent of all recruits to be high school graduates and 82 percent to be of or above average mental ability.

Although Congress was concerned about assuring that the quality of personnel available would enable the services to meet their commitments within the much-reduced ceiling, lurking in the background was a closely related concern. Members of Congress—and many members of the military—feared that in the absence of higher standards the Army and the Marine Corps would be staffed increasingly by blacks. Their apprehension was not without some foundation, because blacks increased from about 13 to 20 percent of total, active-duty Army enlisted strength during the year following the suspension of the draft, and it appeared that their proportion would rise further. The percentage of blacks in the Marine Corps increased from about 11 to 18 during the same period. The increase was more moderate in the armed forces as a whole: from 11.4 to 14.9 percent.

There was nothing new in the linkage between criteria for personnel recruitment and the racial issue. The long-term objective of the DOD was a ratio of blacks in military service approximately the same as the age group in the population, about 12.8 percent. Because of educational deficiencies, however, a disproportionate number of black recruits scored below the average on screening tests. The higher standards that Congress legislated not only ensured against a serious racial imbalance in the armed services but also against the enlistment of too many recruits, white and black, whose previous records suggested that they might not be able to meet performance requirements.

A related issue was whether there would be a regional distortion in enlistments in the AVF. Even in the absence of the draft, it is a matter of some importance that the services continue to recruit from all groups in the population and do not become unduly dependent on any particular region.

Monitoring of recruitment by geographic area has revealed that the shift to an AVF has not resulted in any serious regional imbalances: the distribution of enlistees is more or less proportionate to the distribution of the total population. The exceptions are above-average flows into the Army of blacks from the Southeast (where employment opportunities are relatively poor), and into the Navy of white recruits from the land-locked states of the Midwest, confirming the traditional belief in the attraction of the sea for those who have never been near it.

The primary and overwhelming challenge faced by the AVF in its first two years was to meet recruitment objectives not only for the regular force but also for the selective reserves who are subject to early call-up in an emergency. The regular forces met their objectives except for a slight shortfall in the Marine Corps; the record was less favorable in the case of the reserves which, with a requirement of slightly over 900,000, had an understrength of 60,000 in June 1973 and of 50,000 in June 1974.

The reserves are critical to implementation of the Total Force Concept developed by Secretary of Defense Laird, under which the selective reserve provides 30 percent of the total personnel immediately available in an emergency. The importance of increasing the recruitment of non-prior-service personnel into the active reserves is underscored by the fact that their net personnel cost is estimated to be only one-sixth that of regulars. As far as numbers are concerned, to increase recruitment of young men into the active reserves is the only real challenge that the AVF continues to face, and it is relatively minor.

The outlook is also favorable with respect to skills, although not completely free of problems. The most serious concern is the probability of a severe shortage of professional medical personnel, particularly physicians, because their civilian career prospects are extremely attractive. The response of the DOD to this problem has been to obtain congressional approval for a substantial fellowship program, which pays the medical school expenses of enrollees in exchange for a commitment to serve on active duty one year for each year of financial support. In addition, the DOD has secured congressional approval to establish a medical school in the District of Columbia area. The department also would like permission to offer a very large annual bonus to scarce medical specialists, up to $13,500 above a base monthly bonus of $350. In addition, the Secretary of Defense is exploring how to reduce medical requirements through new methods of providing health services to uniformed personnel and their families.

Although not so serious as the physician problem, the failure of certain enlisted specialists to reenlist has caused concern because of the very high costs of training—an estimated $45,000 for an electrical repairman in fire control and $20,000 for a sonar specialist, as examples. Accordingly, the DOD is seeking congressional approval to make more flexible use of re-enlistment bonuses so that they can be concentrated upon the retention of skilled specialists in short supply.

While recent rises in the unemployment rate should ease the recruitment and retention of the personnel and skills required for the AVF, the earlier manpower adjustments dictated by the suspension of the draft must be judged to have been more successful than most proponents, not to mention critics, had reason to believe. This major transition—and it is indeed major—was accomplished with relatively little turmoil.

Related Manpower Issues

The Department of Defense confronts other manpower issues, some of long standing, some of more recent date. Any effort to view defense manpower must consider, at least briefly, the more important of these concerns.

In addition to regulars and reserves, the DOD always has used large numbers of civilians, primarily within the continental limits of the United States. Civilians perform not only a large proportion of clerical functions, but also play a leading role in many service-supported activities, from hospital ward duties to ship repair. The cutback in civilian personnel after Vietnam was much more modest than the reduction in military personnel. About 250,000 civilians, roughly 20 percent, were dropped, compared to a decrease of 1.3 million, or 40 percent, in the military ranks. The ratio of the active military to civilians at the end of 1974 was slightly above 2:1, which indicates the numerical importance of the civilian in the total defense establishment.

Civilians in DOD are more numerous than they are influential, however. The effective leadership of the armed forces remains very much in the hands of the senior military, whose lives are devoted to competitive careers within the uniformed services. Such elements as special schooling; combat and noncombat assignments in a highly specialized environment; indoctrination as the principal protectors of the nation's security; and the desire to reserve the best positions for the in-group have served to keep most civilians at arm's length. Although a few civilians other than presidential appointees have succeeded in making their presence felt in key decision-making, they represent a small minority.

To complicate matters, congressional oversight of DOD personnel is divided among committees and subcommittees whose allegiance is either to the military or to the civilians. Hence the DOD is frequently pulled in opposite directions: one committee commends accelerating civilianization, while the other is critical of the heavy use of civilians.

The nub of the issue, however, is the absence of a total DOD personnel budget with strong incentives for top management to weave the disparate parts into an effective whole: that is, regular military, reservists, and civilians, to whom might be added consultants, indigenous labor, and employees of defense contractors. In the absence of incentives to make the most effective use of all DOD manpower resources, it is inevitable that considerable underutilization will continue. The senior military are determined to control most decision-making and to refrain from assigning major responsibilities to civilians, who are regarded as potentially ineffective because they are not subject to military discipline in an emergency.

Somewhat similar tensions have long existed and continue to exist between the regulars and the reservists. The regulars are convinced—often with justification—that a part-time serviceman cannot achieve and maintain the level of competence that will assure effective performance in an emergency. Therefore, the regular establishment has been reluctant to provide the officer personnel and equipment without which inadequate reserve performance is inevitable. Moreover, the tighter the personnel and equipment within the regular military, the less inclination there is to share with reservists. As a result, officers assigned to reserve units frequently have been mediocre, and the equipment provided to reservists has been secondhand. Although the senior DOD leadership is aware of the consequences of a policy of "shortchanging" the reserves, it is not likely to take substantial corrective action as long as the total resource situation remains taut. The long-standing struggle over resource allocation has led some observers both inside and outside the Pentagon (myself included) to advocate a smaller but properly staffed and equipped reserve force, rather than a much larger force that is far from combat-ready.

Until recently women have been permitted to volunteer for only a limited number of military assignments. There was no significant increase in their numbers or influence following World War II, although a small number of women officers who remained on active duty moved up in rank and one or two exceptional women earned a star. The combination of the women's liberation movement and the AVF has served as an impetus for very vigorous efforts by the services to increase the proportion of women in uniform, and to provide them with more diversified career opportunities. As a result, women are now eligible for almost every position in the military except combat. Moreover, the target rates established for female enlistees in the mid-1970s is 8 percent, or one in

12—a rise from 2.5 percent, or one in 40, at the beginning of the decade. The Air Force, taking the lead, has set a late-1970s goal of one woman out of about every five enlistees! It is difficult to identify any military personnel change with more pervasive implications for the long term. A battle now is being fought over the admission of women to the service academies. It is hard to believe that this next-to-last bastion (combat arrangements being the last) will not soon fall.

There remain three interrelated manpower problems that bear directly on utilization: the ratio of officers to enlisted personnel; the combat support troop ratio; and the size of the training establishment.

From the viewpoint of costs, Congress is concerned not only with total numbers but also with grade distribution; it recently has shown considerable restiveness about the marked upward drift in the proportion of officers in the top ranks—generals and flag officers. At the end of World War II, the ratio was one general or admiral per 6,000 enlisted personnel; it now is less than one per 2,000, a 300-percent increase in the proportion of general officers. When forced to justify this very substantial increase, the DOD cites the increasing complexity of military technology, which requires more highly qualified individuals, and the necessity of assigning a large number of general officers to other agencies of the federal government and to the staffs of international organizations.

These justifications, however, do not fully explain the substantial inflation in the higher ranks. There are other reasons as well: the difficulty of achieving a proportional decrease in the higher grades as radical demobilization occurred after World War II and to a lesser extent after Korea and Vietnam; the multiplication of headquarters after the amalgamation of the War and Navy Departments into the Department of Defense with its Army, Navy, and Air Force components, and the upgrading of the Marine Corps; promotions to compensate for lagging military salaries in the 1950s and the first half of the 1960s; and the failure of the Bureau of the Budget and of congressional committees to prevent the upward drift.

Any force reduction tends to be at the relative expense of junior rather than senior officers. From the acceleration of hostilities in Vietnam in the mid-1960s to the cessation of hostilities in the mid-1970s, there was a reduction of 32 percent in the number of lieutenants and captains; of 24 percent among majors, lieutenant colonels, and commanders; of 14 percent in colonels and captains; and of only 8 percent in generals and admirals. The relatively large number of officers in the higher ranks led the DOD leadership in 1974 to ask Congress to grant permission for the immediate retirement of a considerable number of lieutenant colonels and colonels. This would provide room for the advancement of junior officers in a total force that has been substantially reduced and, in the absence of an international confrontation, is unlikely to expand.

The high ratio of support to combat troops has been a matter of increasing concern both to personnel managers in the Pentagon and to various committees of the Congress that deal with the armed services. In 1971 Dr. John Foster, then Director of Defense Research and Engineering, the third man in the Pentagon hierarchy, claimed that the DOD budget was being eroded by the high personnel costs of maintaining and repairing complex weapons systems. He estimated that 1.5 million persons were then engaged in this one activity and placed much of the blame upon the manufacturers of equipment, who grossly overestimate the reliability and durability of advanced weapons.

The apparently ineluctable tendency of headquarters personnel to multiply and the continuing efforts of the services to improve the level of amenities—housing, mess, hospitals, recreation—result in the availability of fewer men for assignment to combat units. In testimony before the Senate Subcommittee on Manpower and Personnel in the summer of 1974, Secretary of Defense James Schlesinger took pride in pointing out that the DOD had succeeded in increasing the numbers assigned to general purpose forces, despite the reduction of more than 100,000 military personnel. Moreover, he anticipated an increase from fourteen to sixteen in the number of Army divisions within present personnel strengths. Nevertheless, the problem of keeping overhead under control remains a major challenge to the military, just as it does to the civilian sector.

The effective utilization of military manpower is also a function of the number of trainees and the length of time spent on individual training to acquire the basic skills to perform subsequent assignments. As many as one out of every six men is in individual training at any one time, and the combined cost of such training amounts to over $6 billion annually.

The Secretary of Defense has pointed to the potential gains that might be achieved from improved coordination of the services' training missions. Certainly, at the basic and intermediate levels there cannot be much difference in training goals. More significant economies may come about as a result of the AVF, which has reduction of turnover as one of its primary objectives. Additional gains may also be possible through shifting from heavy reliance on classroom instruction to training on the job.

Some Larger Considerations

Now that the draft has been suspended and the armed forces are moving rapidly to a career personnel system, the issues involved in defense manpower have assumed a somewhat more prominent place on the nation's agenda than in earlier times. The principal reason for this is financial: while federal civilian manpower programs are estimated to total approximately $4 billion annually, the DOD personnel budget is ten times as large. The magnitude of the financial costs is such that, unless the trend is contained, there will soon be less and less money available for new weapons systems. The country will be spending more dollars for defense, but will be obtaining less security.

There are additional critical issues involved in the shaping of a military manpower policy, however, that transcend the dollar expenditures. One is the possible risks arising from reliance upon the AVF. A career military service may lead to less than an optimal response to emergencies owing to the aging of the regular forces, and it will take the most careful management to avoid this threat. The fact that the AVF has not been tested in battle is another crucial concern. Since there is widespread agreement that an additional million volunteers could not be mobilized even if Congress would tolerate the cost, in an emergency would the public agree that fighting should be the sole responsibility of the regulars and the active reservists? If hostilities continued for any length of time, would the citizenry find exclusive use of these units tolerable, and would the careerists feel bound by the bargain they had made earlier?

Even if these hurdles were surmounted, preferably by avoidance of armed hostilities, a democracy must still monitor a career force that is largely cut off from the rest of the country, heedful of President Eisenhower's warning about the potential dangers of a strongly organized military-industrial bloc. A career force that becomes conscious of its potential bargaining power might not go as far as Professor William McNeil has suggested and solicit the nation for a ransom of $100,000 a year per serviceman, but it might succeed in forcing a great many concessions, especially if it were able to achieve effective alliances with ambitious politicians.

With the AVF in place it behooves the American public not only to continue to press the military to make more effective use of its manpower, but also to be alert to insure that the services perform their important missions with due regard for the primacy of civilian control.

13

Blue-Collar Workers:
A Search for Perspective

Roswell C. McCrea, dean of the School of Business at Columbia University in the 1930s, once called attention to an interesting transformation that had occurred in his youth. In McCrea's earliest years in Norristown, Pennsylvania, the town clerk was at the top of the middle sector of the occupational hierarchy—below the lawyer, the minister, and the physician; above the skilled worker and the farmer. Only a small minority of the population had learned to read and write well enough to be trusted with public records. Before McCrea was out of his teens, however, the relative pay and prestige of the clerk had dropped several notches as a result of the widespread increase in literacy. By the time he left home to go to college, the craftsman had displaced the clerk in rank and was receiving equivalent pay.

This anecdote serves to introduce the subject of this chapter: the changing position of the blue-collar worker in American society. It presents an analysis that seeks perspective by examining past history, current developments, and future prospects.

Traditionally, the appellation "blue collar" has referred to manual workers in nonagricultural jobs who earn wages rather than salaries—craftsmen, foremen, and kindred workers; operatives; and nonfarm laborers. For the purposes of this discussion, however, holders of nonhousehold service jobs are considered blue-collar workers because the two groups tend to have similar educational preparation, working conditions, values, and life-styles.

Their points of resemblance indicate not only a broad identity of interest but also generally serve to distinguish manual and service workers from white-collar workers. Workers in this broadened blue-collar classification presently account for nearly half of the nonagricultural labor force.

Major Transformations

The work options of the millions of immigrants who entered the United States in this century were at the bottom of the occupational scale. As a consequence, the immigrants pushed the native born up the occupational ladder. Immigration was restricted, however, in 1924, and some years later a leading industrialist suggested that the rising aggressiveness of the trade union movement was a direct reflection of the growing dissatisfaction of many native-born workers who, in the absence of immigrants, were confined to the lowest-level jobs. Since the early 1930s, many native-born Americans, who have been taught from birth that opportunity is open to everybody and that hard work entitles everyone to the good things in life, have been able to find only low-paid blue-collar work.

Over the same period, the United States has been making increasing investments in education. The typical young person used to be an elementary school graduate; now he is a high school graduate. The image of the college man no longer is the raccoon-coated, playboy son of an upper-income family; today he is often a commuting student from a modest home.

The vast rise in educational attainment has become associated with occupational and career potential. At the turn of the century, a man who got a job in a steel mill or on the railroad could hope to outdistance his competitors and move several rungs up the ladder. That is no longer the case. Occupational placement is often predetermined by educational credentials. Even an able man is unlikely to obtain a preferred job unless he has a college degree; he is unlikely to make the jump from the factory floor to the ranks of management.

Another change has been a substantial decline in agricultural employment with concurrent pressures for the rural population to obtain alternative employment. A great many people who lost their farms, left them voluntarily, or drifted away sought employment in an urban environment. Most of them ended up in the blue-collar ranks.

As we said in Chapter 8, there has also been a radical change in the role of women in employment. Prior to World War II, it was customary for women to work until they married or until they had a child. They then withdrew from the labor market and, unless their husbands were injured or died, they were not likely to return to work. Since the war, more and more married women have been working on a continuing or intermittent basis, often in blue-collar jobs.

The disproportionate number of blacks in the blue-collar ranks is another notable change. Between 1910 and 1960, the total black labor force increased from about 4.7 million to 6.9 million, or by approximately 70 percent, but the number employed as blue-collar workers more than doubled, from about 2.2 to over 4.7 million. During the same period, the number of blacks in farming declined from 2.3 million to about 750,000.

Following the curtailment of immigration in 1924, it was not immediately clear who the new recruits for blue-collar employment would be. In addition to native-born white males, usually from rural areas, the pool that filled blue-collar job openings turned out to be married white women and Southern-born blacks who had migrated to the North and West.

Another pervasive influence upon the lives of Americans during this century has been the steady and pronounced trend toward smaller families, although there was significant variability in the speed with which birth control techniques were adopted by different groups. Since a high proportion of blue-collar workers are Catholic, their acceptance of the new techniques was delayed. Moreover, forces beyond Catholic dogma operated to produce larger families among blue-collar workers than white-collar workers. The inflow to blue-collar ranks of many former farmers and farm laborers from a background where large families were the norm served to retard the use of birth control measures. However, recent data suggest that increasing numbers of blue-collar workers are utilizing family planning techniques.

The number of children in a family has a significant influence on its standard of living. Not only does it determine the use and division of the family's income, it also affects the ability of the wife to make a contribution to family income. Moreover, the prospects for children of blue-collar workers to pursue extended education are reduced when there are many children in the family because higher education, even when supported by government, always involves considerable out-of-pocket expenditure.

This brings us to a final major transformation in American society: the marked advance in mass communications. While we know less than we need to know about the ways in which movies, radio, and television have affected both the expectations and the behavior of different social groups, we can postulate that they have had a deep and lasting impact on the value structure of Americans, and have generated and reinforced a mass desire for high-level consumption. For many blue-collar workers, this means that there is a substantial gap between their current standard of living and that to which they aspire.

Any valid assessment of the position of blue-collar workers must be sensitive to these transformations. But first we shall consider changes in blue-collar work and how these impinge on the lives of workers.

Changes in Blue-Collar Work

A person's job is one of the best clues to the life he leads and to the opinions he holds. Significant changes in the conditions of employment have occurred during recent decades. In the earlier part of the century, employment was characterized by a considerable degree of seasonality. It was the exceptional blue-collar worker who worked full-time, full-year. In the 1920s, a group of forward-looking large companies, such as Kodak, Procter & Gamble, and General Electric, and smaller ones, such as Hormel, Hickey-Freeman, and Dennison, experimented with ways of reducing and eliminating the seasonality of employment. Their efforts were washed away in the turbulence of the Great Depression.

Although seasonality has not been eliminated—even a strong union like the United Automobile Workers has not been able to win a guarantee of annual hours of work—a significant proportion of *male* blue-collar workers are employed full-time, full-year. This was true for seven out of ten of the more than 10 million craftsmen and foremen, and three out of five of a similar number of operatives and kindred workers, who worked during 1970. Among the other 9 million male laborers and service workers, the proportion who worked regularly varied from almost two-fifths to more than half. During the present century, blue-collar workers have experienced significantly reduced vulnerability to layoffs resulting from seasonal fluctuations.

A second important change on the employment front has been the substantial reduction in the average number of hours worked per week. One of the causes of the major steel strike at the end of World War I was that men had to work 84 hours a week when they changed shifts! A 60-hour week was widespread. For the last quarter-century, the weekly norm has been around 40 hours, although a few blue-collar unions have succeeded in negotiating a much shorter workweek. For example, the contract of the electrical workers in New York City sets 25 hours a week as the norm.

In contrast to the industrial nations of Western Europe, the United States moved slowly to enact labor legislation aimed at controlling occupational accidents and disease, both because the dominant ideology sought to keep the government out of employment relations and because immigrants, who had to accept the least desirable jobs, were considered expendable. Among railroad crews at the turn of this century, about one of every hundred men suffered fatal injuries each year! The passage of time has brought governmental reforms which, together with preventive actions by management, have led to a marked reduction in fatalities and injuries in the workplace. Although we still lose over 14,000 workers annually through fatal accidents, and another 800,000 are injured seriously enough to lose time from work, much of the risk to limb and life has been removed from the work setting during recent decades.

A related development had been the marked improvement in other aspects of the work environment. For instance, advances have occurred in temperature control, which have contributed greatly to speeding the industrial development of the South. Similarly, the cleanliness and orderliness of the areas where employees work, eat, and rest have been substantially improved. However, there remains considerable room for further improvement.

The first half of this century saw a rapid increase in unionization among blue-collar workers, with the result that today about half belong to a trade union, in contrast to a quarter of the labor force as a whole. Unions have helped to reduce the powerlessness of the workers. First and foremost, union workers are no longer subject to arbitrary dismissal. As they acquire seniority, they come to "own" their jobs and to exercise more control over the rules that govern their work.

In a great many ways, unions have been able to reduce or eliminate vulnerabilities. Many blue-collar workers are no longer industrial slaves but are participants in an employment relation that gives them job security, enables them to play a part in determining how they work, and provides them with considerable freedom to engage in off-the-job activities. These changes are of extraordinary importance and their reach goes beyond union members. Many large employers have matched and even exceeded the benefits that unions have secured for their members in the hope of keeping their employees from organizing.

Another development of importance to blue-collar workers for which unions can take considerable, but not exclusive, credit is the vast expansion of fringe benefits. Currently, only slightly more than three-quarters of gross payroll costs for blue-collar workers in manufacturing consists of straight-time pay. Another 5 to 6 percent represents legally required employer contributions for social security, unemployment insurance, and workmen's compensation. The remainder, approximately 15 to 20 percent of gross payrolls, is accounted for by pay for overtime, vacations, holidays, sick leave, and by employer contributions to private pension plans.

This bundle of benefits has gone far to remove some of the worst insecurities that used to confront blue-collar workers: the uncertainty about what would happen when they, or members of their family, required hospitalization; became unemployed or disabled; or became too old to work. Although the blue-collar worker and his family are not protected against all exigencies resulting from loss of earnings, the importance of the changes that have been introduced should not be minimized.

The best-protected blue-collar workers are eligible for supplemental unemployment benefits that enable them to receive up to 90 percent of their regular wages for a period up to one year; they are entitled to three or four weeks of vacation a year; they are eligible for three months of vacation after fifteen years of employment; and they can retire with three-quarters pay at the end of twenty-five or thirty years of service or when they reach the age of 65. So far, these benefits accrue to only a minority of all blue-collar workers, but they indicate a trend.

Although it is not likely that any one blue-collar worker has benefited from all the foregoing advances—the decrease in seasonality of employment, reduction in hours of work, protection against industrial accidents and disease, improved conditions of work, greater control over the job, and enlarged fringe benefits—almost every blue-collar worker enjoys some of them. If he compares conditions in the past with those that govern his present employment, he cannot fail to note that in almost every respect he has made significant gains.

A Typology of Blue-Collar Workers

Now that we have set out the major transformations in the conditions of life in the United States and have noted substantial changes in the world of work that have affected blue-collar workers to varying degrees, we shall seek further perspective by shifting our focus to the blue-collar worker himself.

The blue-collar group embraces workers with different backgrounds, achievements, and aspirations. Some of them carry memories of the Great Depression, when no jobs were available no matter how hard they tried to feed themselves and their families. The great majority, however, has known only the conditions of post-World War II prosperity; the youngest among them entered the labor market during the longest expansionary period in the recorded history of the American economy (1961 to 1969).

Some blue-collar workers are at the top of a seniority list. This means that, short of an economic catastrophe, their jobs are secure and they can look forward to better assignments in the years ahead. Many others hold low-paying nonunion jobs; they cannot feel optimistic about their future work, income, or deferred benefits.

Some blue-collar workers have limited the size of their families, whereas others are struggling to earn enough to give their many children a reasonable start in life. People with different family responsibilities see the present and the future differently.

The family background of blue-collar workers is an important element in a consideration of their present status. For example, the basic wage rate in the repair shops of American Airlines in Tulsa in 1972 averaged

$5.25 per hour, for a 40-hour week. This comes to a gross pay of $210 weekly, without additions for seniority, lead job, or overtime. To a worker who was born and brought up on a neighboring marginal farm and whose father never cleared more than $2,000 a year, such a job is a big forward step. The same job means something different, however, to a Tulsa-born man whose father was a fireman on the Southern Railway. At best, this job enables him to maintain a family standard of living comparable to that of his father. To the son of a professional who began college, dropped out, and, after moving from job to job, finally settled into the job of airline mechanic, the position represents a move downward.

As has been implicit in these remarks, how a person feels about his current position depends upon how he measures himself: he can look backward; he can look around; he can look forward. By looking backward, he assesses his present position from the vantage of his father. Has he moved upward in terms of the work he does, the income he earns, and the way he lives—from the standards that prevailed in his parents' home? In this assessment, he is likely to make allowance for the fact that over the period of a generation there has been an upward trend in the occupational and income structure. By looking around, a worker evaluates his opportunities to move up the occupational and income scale during the course of his working life. By looking forward, he considers the prospects that lie ahead for his children.

In order to demonstrate the variability that exists within the broad blue-collar classification with respect to the past, present, and future, I have devised a typology that encapsulates background, present circumstances, and expectations. Although no schema can be responsive to the entire range of diversity that exists within so large a population, it is hoped that a simplified outline may prove to be a useful tool for social analysis. The typology is predicated on the existence of three basic types of blue-collar worker: the upward bound, the immobile, and the vulnerable.

The upward bound.   Using the criterion of generational improvement, a significant proportion of blue-collar workers, particularly craftsmen and foremen who are the offspring of native-born white American farmers or laborers must see themselves as having moved several notches up the occupational-income scale. The same must be the case for the vast majority of blue-collar workers who are of foreign birth or parentage, most of whom come from deprived rural or urban backgrounds.

Perhaps the clearest instance of upward mobility is that of the blacks. Gunnar Myrdal, writing in the early 1940s, was deeply concerned about the economic future of the black population. He noted that most of them were marginal farmers in the Southeast, a region where agriculture was declining. The route up for the Southern black in the 1930s was to get on the public assistance rolls, preferably in the North. Yet by 1971 almost one of every three black male workers was either a craftsman or an operative. During the 1960s, the rate of increase for blacks in the preferred craftsman category was four times the white rate. In 1971, blacks were no longer underrepresented in the operative category and, among craftsmen and foremen, the difference between whites and blacks had been narrowed to 6 percentage points (14 versus 8 percent). Unquestionably, discrimination against blacks continues to be embedded in every sector of American life—in education, health, housing, and employment—but the foregoing figures suggest, and other data and analyses confirm, that powerful forces are working to improve their occupational status.

Except for the relatively few female craftsmen and foremen, the average current earnings of full-time, full-year female blue-collar workers are under $5,000. Nevertheless, where these women are supplemental earners, their contribution to their families' income is often substantial and in such cases it is likely that their current socioeconomic status is an improvement over that of their parental family.

In general, a comparison between the present socioeconomic status of blue-collar workers with that of their parents suggests that a high proportion can be classified as upwardly mobile. This is particularly so in the cases of children of white native-born low-income farm families; most workers of foreign birth or parentage; some working wives; and, above all, the vast majority of black male blue-collar workers.

How extensive are a blue-collar worker's opportunities to move up the occupational and income scale during the course of his working life? In the absence of adequate longitudinal studies, a gap that Herbert Parnes is beginning to close, only qualitative judgments can be made.

A high proportion of the workers who complete apprenticeships eventually leave the blue-collar ranks for management or to enter business for themselves. This has long been the pattern in the building trades. A second road to advancement that has often been used by blue-collar workers is the direct transition from worker to employer status: the waiter who opens his own restaurant; the mechanic who becomes the owner of a repair shop; the truck driver who becomes a small fleet owner; or the taxi driver who buys his own cab. Although there is no certainty that such a shift will result in a net improvement for the ambitious blue-collar worker—the mortality rate for small business is high—the fact remains that this route enables many to raise themselves by their own bootstraps (often with financial assistance from their relatives).

Another approach coming increasingly to the fore involves the considerable number of blue-collar workers—mechanics, drivers, protective service workers, cooks, repairmen—who, after twenty years' employment, are able to retire on pensions, often representing three-quarters of their most recent earnings. With substantial retirement pay, and often with additional benefits, these blue-collar workers are able to do quite well either by taking a similar job in a new environment or by shifting into a new occupational category.

Gaining access to a high-paid blue-collar job, such as skilled construction work or long-distance truck driving, is still another upward route.

This brings us to the last and by far the most widespread method of upward mobility: the progression provided in the internal labor market of a large corporation. A worker is hired at the bottom, usually as a laborer or semiskilled worker. With time and seniority, he has the opportunity to move up by bidding for training and a better job. In the steel industry a beginner may earn no more than $7,000; the top men in the mill who are responsible for determining when the furnaces are to be tapped can earn as much as three times that sum.

The diverse routes available to blue-collar workers, particularly white males, demonstrate that there are many opportunities open to them to improve upon their starting position. Of the current total of about 39 million blue-collar workers, approximately 28 million are males. Some 10 million are classified as craftsmen and foremen, and for the most part these jobs carry above-average income and status. In addition, there are two major subgroups with above-average income and status: high-earning operatives (long-distance truck drivers), and those who have left blue-collar employment for managerial or entrepreneurial status. Conventional wisdom notwithstanding, blue-collar work does permit occupational advancement.

Definitive data are scarce regarding the prospect of improvement for the children of blue-collar workers. Nevertheless, there are a few facts and figures that provide at least a basis for speculation and extrapolation.

There are two routes along which the offspring of blue-collar workers can move ahead. The first is through the help they receive in gaining access to preferred employment opportunities. The classic illustration is the craftsman who facilitates the entrance of his son into the apprenticeship program operated by his union. Moreover, parental help is not limited to the fields where formal apprenticeship prevails. A young man whose father is a foreman, a lead man, or simply a respected long-term employee will definitely be preferred as a "hiree." If the firm practices promotion from within, he is off to a good start.

The other way up the mobility ladder is through education. Since parental income is a major determinant of educational attainment, the sons and daughters of more affluent blue-collar families are in a preferred position to go to junior or senior college, especially if the family is not large. Unfortunately, many blue-collar families who are able to support their children while in college, especially if they live at home, fail to encourage them to attend, a pattern more characteristic of white than black families.

So we see that many blue-collar workers are upwardly mobile in the sense that they are relatively better off than their fathers; they themselves have had opportunities to advance; and many have reason to believe that their children will be able to continue to move up the socioeconomic ladder.

The immobile. A large percentage of blue-collar workers are themselves the offspring of blue-collar workers, which establishes an initial presumption that they have not improved upon their parents' status. Whether they are immobile, in fact, depends on their position within the blue-collar hierarchy relative to that of their fathers. If a man's father was a laborer and he himself has become a foreman in a major company, we can classify him as upwardly mobile, even though the generational shift has been within, rather than beyond, the blue-collar category. But where there is no intra-occupational improvement, such persons must be classified as immobile. (The relatively few blue-collar workers who have slipped below their fathers' job level are downwardly mobile, or vulnerable.)

It is impossible on the basis of currently available statistics to estimate the proportion of all blue-collar workers who should be classified as immobile, but the number must be sizable. Included are large numbers of second-generation workers in the North and South who are employed in the manufacturing plants of companies that are the principal source of a community's employment. There are also many first- and second-generation blue-collar workers in heavy industry whose fathers held similar jobs, and numerous journeymen sons of construction workers and of other craftsmen.

Because the fathers of relatively few blue-collar workers were in white-collar occupations, practically all blue-collar workers today (except for those who came from farms) are the sons, and in many cases the grandsons, of blue-collar workers. If intra blue-collar upward mobility is disregarded and the focus is on remaining within the blue-collar ranks, a significant proportion of present-day blue-collar workers must be considered immobile in generational terms.

Some younger workers may eventually move up in the job hierarchy, either to a higher-level blue-collar occupation or to a white-collar position. However, many of these workers are likely to remain fixed in a status similar to their fathers', to a large extent because they are unwilling to risk losing the security and shelter attached to their jobs.

Whether the children of the immobile have the opportunity to advance beyond their parents depends upon their family incomes, which often may inhibit extended schooling. In addition, while a father's job may not represent generational improvement in social status, it may still offer financial inducements that attract his children, especially if there is no family encouragement toward higher education.

The low earnings of female blue-collar workers have already been noted. Where these women are heads of households, they are usually in the immobile group, at best. If more information about their backgrounds were available, a few might be reclassified as upwardly mobile; this would apply, for example, to an operative earning $4,000 annually whose parents had been migrant workers. However, it is probably correct to conclude that most blue-collar female household heads have not moved beyond their parents' positions.

The vulnerable.   Most people seek to achieve a level of work and income at least comparable to that of their parents and feel uncomfortable, unhappy, or frustrated if they fail in the attempt. Individuals whose achievements do not measure up to the standard attained by their parental family are defined as "vulnerable." Included within this category, as we have seen, are blue-collar offspring of white-collar workers. Some blue-collar workers may not be in a worse position than their white-collar fathers, if the sole criterion is income; in fact, they may be better off. But income is not the whole of the matter. Take, for instance, a worker on a Detroit assembly line whose father was the pastor of a church in a small southern community or the principal of a small rural school. In terms of income, the automotive worker is relatively better off; and yet he is likely to feel that he has slipped on the social scale.

Also among the vulnerable are full-time, full-year blue-collar workers who do not earn $5,000—a modest figure indeed for someone who must support a family. Among males in 1971, about 8 percent of all craftsmen and foremen, 5 percent of operatives, 24 percent of service workers, and 27 percent of laborers fell below this earnings level. Among women, over half of the operatives who worked full-time, full-year earned under $5,000, as did 58 percent of the laborers and two-thirds of the service workers. Of all fully employed male blue-collar workers, 14 percent were unable to earn $5,000 or more; and among women who worked regularly, three of five failed to meet the $5,000 level.

The foregoing data do not begin to reveal the full range of vulnerability and failure. There are many other male and female blue-collar workers who are heads of households and who are *not* employed full-time, full-year; most of them fall below the poverty line. Any person who is unable to support himself and his dependents at a reasonable level above the poverty line is likely to be dissatisfied and to consider himself a failure.

Another insight into the vulnerability of blue-collar workers can be gained by assessing the prospects that face their children. Young people who do not finish high school will be in a poor competitive position, and a high proportion of all dropouts come from blue-collar families. This means that even some blue-collar workers who have done quite well—and who would be ranked as mobile in terms of their own achievements—would be classified as vulnerable in terms of what is likely to happen to their children.

In summary, considerable numbers of blue-collar workers must be classified as vulnerable either because they are lower on the occupational scale than their fathers, because they are unable to earn enough to enable their families to live above the poverty level, or because their offspring are unlikely to make a satisfactory advancement. A man can be classified as upward bound using his father's status as one criterion; the same man can be immobile in terms of the progress he himself has been able to achieve; and he can be assessed as vulnerable in terms of the potential achievement of his children. There are several other possible intergenerational combinations, so that judgments about the progress of blue-collar workers as a group must be made with caution.

A Look Back and a Look Ahead

This analysis has been highly selective. No reference has been made to rapid changes in technology that have eroded the livelihoods of many blue-collar workers; to compulsory military service that resulted in death or injury to large numbers of young men from blue-collar families; to the racial revolution that has impinged so directly on blue-collar workers and their families by altering the environments in which they work and live; to the erosion of the national self-image and power that has called so many verities into question, thereby adding to the unease and discontent of many blue-collar families.

What then should one conclude from this search for perspective? First, American society continues to be characterized by considerable flexibility, which enables many children to move to a higher occupational class than their parents and permits others to improve their economic position considerably, even if they remain in the class into which they were born.

Second, during the last three decades a high proportion of blacks have made striking advances in their occupational and income status, both absolutely and relatively, by moving into, through, and out of the blue-collar category.

Third, many families in the blue-collar category have been able to move into the upper quartile of the income distribution as a result of wives' ability to supplement their husbands' earnings.

Fourth, because of the low wage scales typical of the fields in which most women are employed, it is difficult for blue-collar female heads of households to earn an income adequate to support their dependents.

Fifth, a significant number of blue-collar male heads of households, even when they work full time, and particularly when they work part time, are not able to lift their families out of poverty.

Sixth, whether or not the children of blue-collar workers will be able to improve their status will depend in large measure on whether they earn a college degree.

It must be recalled that blue-collar workers account for almost half of all nonagricultural workers. It is almost as difficult to generalize about them as about the employed population as a whole. If we limit ourselves to one cautious conclusion about the past, it is that during the first seven decades of this century the transformations in American society and the economy have enabled most blue-collar workers to achieve a position that is relatively better than that of their fathers.

Admittedly, the type of perspective from which blue-collar workers have been viewed may also be utilized for all other groups in American society. The reason for concentrating upon this occupational group has been to demonstrate the error of treating blue-collar workers as a monolithic class. As we have seen, they are not a homogeneous group, and this analysis of their differences is presented to indicate that it is a mistake to treat them as an undifferentiated social entity. Instead, they are more likely to reflect the same uncertainties, tensions, and conflicts that beset us all.

14

Paycheck or Apron: Revolution in Womanpower

The tradition that the place of a married woman, particularly a mother, is in the home was shattered under the hammer blows of World War II when women were told that it was their patriotic duty to take a job. As frequently happens when major social changes occur, neither men nor women realized that the move of married women into paid employment would be not only for the war's duration, but would represent a revolution in the American way of life. While many women gave up their jobs when the war ended, they had tasted the apple: they liked the money they earned; they liked getting out of the house; they liked the independence and esteem associated with paid work; they liked the cooperation from their husbands and children in the housework; they liked, above all, the wider horizons that work creates.

To put the record straight, we must remember that there always were married women who worked out of the home. For the most part, these were either women whose husbands were unable to support their families, or middle-class female professionals. The dominant pattern, however, was for a working woman to give up her job *permanently* when she married or during her first pregnancy. In the absence of family misfortune, it was the rare women who sought paid employment in middle age.

The Situation Today

In 1970, 38.7 million women of a total of over 93.6 million workers held a job at some time during the course of the year. An additional million did not work, but looked for work. Almost three out of four females between the ages of 18 and 25 worked, as did almost three out of five of those between 25 and 60. In the 45- to 54-year-old group, 60 percent worked, the highest proportion of any group of women over the age of 24. Since approximately 95 out of every 100 women marry, those who work overwhelmingly represent women who are or have been married. In fact, if we disregard women who are 65 or older, we find that more than half of all women who were married and living with their spouses in 1970 had worked during the year; if they had been married, but were widowed, divorced, or separated, the chances were 7 out of 10 that they worked; if they were single, the probability of their working was 4 out of 5.

It is not generally understood, either by the American public or, for that matter, by most labor economists, that the prototype of the full-time, full-year worker barely comprises a majority. Of the 93.6 million men and women who worked or looked for work in 1970, only 52.4 million or 56 percent fell into this category. The other 44 percent represented two major subgroups: those who desired full-time employment but were unable to find it; and those who preferred to work less than full-time, a high proportion of whom were women. Of the 38.7 million women who worked, 16 million or about 41 percent worked full-time, full-year. About 11 million women worked full-time for less than a full year, and the other 12 million worked part-time throughout or for part of the year.

A critical question about individuals who work during part of the year is whether they do so from preference or necessity. Of the women who fell into this category, almost half (48 percent) indicated that they were out of the labor force for part of the year in order to take care of their homes. The second largest group, about 20 percent, were attending school. Of the remaining 32 percent, most could not find jobs for the full year and the remainder were kept from working some of the time because of illness, disability, or other reasons.

It would be easy to conclude that a weakness in the demand for labor is a factor of relatively minor importance in explaining why women work less than full-year. But before making this deduction, we must note that for 2.9 million women lack of jobs was identified as the key variable, and that another million females looked for work but could not find jobs. Some part of the 2.7 million who worked less than full-year because of disability or for other reasons might have worked full-year had the demand for labor been stronger. The proof of the sensitive relation between the strength of demand for labor and the full-year employment of women is found in the following six-year trend. From 1965 through 1970 the total number of women who worked increased by 4.9 million. The increase in the number of those working full-time, full-year was 2.9

million. The proportion of women who worked full-time increased from 38.8 percent to 41 percent, which suggests that many women will respond to the opportunity to shift from part- to full-time employment.

While most women who hold jobs work less than full-time, in any week about one in ten women who is employed works not only full-time, but overtime. In May 1970 there were 2.5 million females who worked overtime, over one-third of whom received premium pay. Over 40 percent of the women who worked overtime were married and living with their husbands.

Other important dimensions of the role of women in the world of work are the kinds of job they hold and the amount of income they earn. Of the women who were employed in 1970, those in white-collar occupations accounted for more than half. Approximately one out of every three employed women was a clerical worker. About two out of five were blue-collar or service workers in establishments other than private households. The remainder were private household workers or farm laborers.

Women workers are concentrated in a relatively few occupations and are often overrepresented within those occupations. Over 97 percent of all stenographers and typists are women, as are private household workers. Women account for six or seven out of every ten workers in the following areas: health; teaching, except college; waitresses and cooks; clerical other than secretarial; and typing. In contrast, women represent a relatively small minority in such occupations as craftsmen, farmers, managers and officials, and professional and technical workers, other than those in health or teaching. The concentration of women workers can also be demonstrated by reference to the industries in which they are employed: they account for approximately half or more of all employees in banking, insurance, local government, apparel manufacturing, general merchandise retail stores, eating and drinking establishments, apparel and accessory stores, medical and health services, personal services, and communications.

In 1969, the median annual earnings of women workers who were regularly and fully employed throughout the year were three-fifths of those of men—$4,977 and $8,227, respectively. Marked discrepancies between the salaries of males and females who work full-time full-year are found in each major occupational field. The greatest absolute and relative discrepancies are found among sales workers: the median annual salary of women was $3,704, or 41 percent of the male median. Among managers, the women's median was $6,091 or 53 percent of the men's. Among professionals and clerical workers, women's salaries were 65 percent of the male median and they were 59 percent of the medians of both operatives and nonhousehold service workers.

There are several factors that help to explain the marked differences in earnings between men and women in the same occupational category. Within each category, women are likely to be employed in the less remunerative branches—for example, nursing, rather than medicine; apparel manufacturing, rather than chemical manufacturing operatives; tearoom waitresses, rather than hotel waiters. Since women are more likely to have had a discontinuous work experience than men, they are normally concentrated at the lower end of the job ladder; moreover, they are less likely to work overtime than are men. Nonetheless, much of the explanation for sex differentials in earnings lies in the reluctance of many employers to assign and promote women to the more prestigious and higher-paying positions in their organizations. Despite antidiscrimination legislation and executive orders, there has been no significant change in the relative position of women's wages in recent years.

Other factors affect the substantial wage and salary differential in favor of men; an example is the lag in the number and proportion of women who have pursued their studies to the doctoral level, a factor that has precluded their sharing fully in the employment and income opportunities that have opened up for professional workers since the end of World War II. Furthermore, many women are unable to respond to job opportunities that require more time than the regular workweek, and many women cannot accept jobs that are not near their homes. All these facts hamper their progess in the labor market.

A Backward and a Forward Look

Between 1947 and 1970, the civilian labor force increased by 24 million, from slightly over 59 million to almost 83 million, or close to 41 percent. Of this increase, the expansion of the male labor force accounted for approximately 9 million; the female labor force almost doubled—it increased by about 15 million, from 16.6 million to 31.6 million.

These figures indicate that had it not been for the much heavier involvement of women in the world of work, the sustained growth that characterized the American economy during this period would not have occurred. The small additions to the civilian male labor force in the fifties and sixties reflected the depressed birth rates of the thirties and the buildup of the armed forces during the Korean and Vietnam wars. The elongation of the educational cycle was a third factor that reduced the numbers of young male entrants into the labor force. During the twenty-three-year period, the civilian male labor force grew by only about 20 percent. In sharp contrast, the female labor force participation rate increased by 88 percent.

In each of the strategic age groups, the labor force participation rates for women increased substantially. The biggest gains were scored in the older age groups. By the middle sixties, more than one out of every two women between 45 and 54 years of age was working or looking for work.

The post-World War II decades provided a conducive environment for women to find employment out of the home, not only because of reduced competition from males but also because the service sector of the economy, which traditionally makes heavy use of part-time workers and of women, was expanding rapidly. Between 1950 and 1965, the average annual increase of part-time female workers was almost 300,000, only slightly below the average increase of full-time male workers. In the four years following the Korean hostilities, there were eleven new part-time workers for every additional full-time worker, and two-thirds of the former were women. In the sixties the increase slowed, but by 1970 increases in employment again were largely in part-time jobs. Over the twenty-year period 1950 to 1970 the proportion of all workers who were employed at part-time jobs rose from 16 to 20 percent.

The increasing proportion of female workers both full- and part-time has reflected the influx of middle-aged women into the labor force. Between 1950 and 1964, the most significant increase was among women aged 45 to 64 years, whose proportion of the labor force rose from 27 to 40 percent. However, since 1965, the greatest female labor force increase has comprised women below 45. By 1970, the peak labor force participation rate among women had shifted to the 20-to-24-year age group (58 percent), although the 45-to-54-year group ran a close second (54 percent).

What has been the labor force participation of younger married women who are living with their husbands and usually have young children? In 1948, about a quarter of those in the 20-to-24-year-old bracket were in the labor force; two decades later the proportion was more than two of five. The next age group, 25 to 34, showed a parallel increase— from about one-fifth in 1948 to over one-third in 1968. One of the major determinants of whether a woman seeks employment is whether she has children, particularly of preschool age. For instance, among women under 35 who lived with their husbands and had one or more children under the age of 6, 30 percent worked in 1970; of those who had children between the ages of 6 and 18, 50 percent worked.

The total number of children a woman has, as well as the age of the youngest, influences her work pattern. The more children a woman has, the less likely she is to work. Since 1957, important changes have been occurring in the birth rate or—to use a preferred measure—the general fertility rate, which indicates the number of births per 1,000 women between the ages of 15 and 44. In 1957, this rate reached a high of 123.0.

By 1970, it had declined to 87.4, and by 1972 it had dropped to the lowest level in American history, 73.4.

The 1972 Report of the Commission on Population Growth and the American Future noted that an important element in the decline in the birth rate is that today's young people expect to have far fewer children than people a few years their senior. According to a 1971 census survey, married women in the 18-to-24 group expect to have an average of 2.4 children. While the report cautions that the past tendency has been to underestimate ultimate family size, the trend is certainly downward.

Such radical reductions in the birth rate during a period of continuing high-level employment and income are not easy to assess. They unquestionably reflect a multitude of influences, including the growing perception among the middle class that, while the marginal cost of a third or fourth child may be small in the early years, contingent expenses loom large, since tuition at good private colleges is now in excess of $3,000 annually. The dissemination and use of improved birth control methods is a factor, as is the availability of abortion. The declining attractiveness of the suburbs, as a consequence of increasing population pressures, may also be a factor. But it is a reasonable assumption that part of the decline must be the result of the growing recognition by many women that their ability to work will be significantly affected by the number of children they have. If a woman limits her children to one or two and spaces them closely together, she has much less difficulty in returning to work than if she waits to return until the youngest of four or five children is in school.

The Department of Labor estimates that women will contribute 43 percent of the labor force growth between 1968 and 1980; their proportion of the total labor force will thus expand from 35.5 to almost 37 percent. The rate at which women enter the labor force is expected to continue to account for a disproportionate share of its growth. However, because the big population increase in the 1970s will be in the group aged 25 to 34, an age when women are less likely to work because of family responsibilities, the increase in the number of women workers is not expected to exceed that of men as it did in the 1960s, when the greatest population increases were in the age group under 25 and in the 45-to-64 group, ages in which large proportions of women enter or return to the labor force. If mothers of young children continue to increase their rate of labor force participation and if the size of their families is as small as is now anticipated, there may be a larger involvement of young mothers in paid employment. Of course, the participation rates of women will be greatly influenced by the availability of jobs and by competition from men. And in the years ahead, because of changing demographic trends, there will be many more young men entering the labor force than in the preceding decade.

Education and Income

Whether a woman works regularly, periodically, or not at all is greatly affected by her educational level. In turn, the income her husband earns influences her decision to seek a job, just as her own earnings may have a significant effect on her family's standard of living. These three variables, a wife's education, her husband's income, and her own earnings, warrant consideration.

The most important single finding about women's education and their labor force participation is that the more education a woman has had, the more likely she is to work. In 1970, about 71 percent of those with five or more years of college and graduate school were in the labor force, compared with about 56 percent of college graduates, 50 percent of high school graduates, 31 percent of those who graduated from elementary school, and 23 percent of those with less than eight years of schooling. Among women younger than 65 who have had at least one year of graduate study, the proportion in the labor force never drops below two-thirds and in the age group 45 to 54 the proportion reaches the astonishingly high rate of 82 percent. Among college graduates, half or more work at every age.

Since there have been many changes which have affected all women in the labor force, the data presented above do not disclose the full force of education in pulling women into work. This influence is better seen when labor force participation rates of women in the strategic age group 25 to 34 are compared according to their education in 1952 and 1970. There was an overall increase of over 9 percentage points during those years— from 36.3 to 45.6; high school graduates and college dropouts showed an increase close to the average, while the group composed of those with four years or more of college and graduate school showed a rise of more than 17 percentage points—twice the average.

A significant relation between level of education and participation in work is hardly surprising. Many women, like men, undertake additional education for occupational reasons. Hence the achievement of a career goal is a strong force in their planning and action. Moreover, once they have made the investment of time, money, and energy in attaining a college or higher degree, their interests in a particular field are likely to be awakened or strengthened so that they will seek to gratify them through work.

The relation between working and family income runs in two directions. On the one hand, the level of family income influences whether women seek jobs. And the income that women earn from work affects the level at which the family is able to live. We noted earlier that single women and women whose marriages have been broken by death, divorce, or separation are likely to be employed unless they have young children. We shall therefore focus on wives living with their husbands.

In 1970 the median family income of white men whose wives did not work was $9,206; families in which both men and their wives worked had a higher median income—$11,800. Of the white women who worked, 18 percent were married to men whose earnings were between $5,000 and $7,000, 31 percent were married to men who made between $7,000 and $10,000, and 30 percent had husbands with earnings of $10,000 and over. Of the white women who were *not* in the labor force, 14 percent were married to men who earned between $5,000 and $7,000, 25 percent to men earning between $7,000 and $10,000, and 37 percent to men making $10,000 or more. We see that as far as these gross income categories are concerned, it is only when men earn $10,000 or more that their wives are somewhat less likely to seek outside employment.

An interesting facet of the problem is the effect of women's working on family income. In families with a total annual income of under $3,000 in 1970, only about one out of five wives worked and those who did tended to be employed part-time or part-year. In families with income of $10,000 or over, more than half of all the wives worked, and in those with incomes of $15,000 or more, most working wives are employed full-time. Another finding is that there were significant differences in family income depending on whether wives worked relatively few hours (1 to 26 weeks full-time or 1 to 52 weeks part-time), a moderate length of time (27 to 49 weeks full-time), or regularly. Median family income reflects this variable as follows: $9,770, $10,886, $13,357, respectively.

In 1970 the median annual wage or salary of all women who worked was $2,237. However, those who were regularly employed year-round earned a median of $5,440. The median income of families with both husband and wife in the labor force in 1970 was $8,052, indicating that if both husband and wife work, it can make a significant difference to the family's income level.

What These Data Reveal

These are the contours of the revolution revealed by the data:

(a) Except for those with very young children, women are now likely to be employed outside the home for some time during the year.

(b) Most women who work do not hold full-time year-round jobs; they work part-time or part-year.

(c) The more education a woman has, the more likely she is to be employed.

(d) Although women with husbands at the upper end of the earnings distribution are less likely to work than those in the middle, a significant proportion of the former are in the labor force.

(e) A large number of families are in the middle-income bracket as the result of the supplementary earnings of wives.

(f) Mature women in the age group 45 to 54 are more likely to be employed than any age group over the age of 24.

(g) An increasing proportion of women in the major childbearing years (25 to 35) are finding it possible to hold a job.

(h) The employment of women has been facilitated since the end of World War II by the reduction in the percentage of young men entering the labor market and by the growth of the service sector.

(i) Government forecasts anticipate a continuing rise in the labor force participation rates of women in all age groups.

(j) Women continue to be highly concentrated in certain occupational and industrial fields, particularly clerical work and service occupations.

The Challenges That Remain

In the early days of the revolution in womanpower, many observers were afraid that the increasing participation of women in the labor force would result in a rise in male unemployment. There was also widespread concern that the children of many working mothers would be neglected and become delinquent. Some critics worried about psychological upsets that might result if a wife had a better job and earned more than her husband. Many other fears and apprehensions were expressed. Most of these have now been stilled, although some people continue to believe that working mothers are a major contributory cause of juvenile delinquency. If children of working mothers are neglected, these critics are probably right; but the fact is that many women who do not hold jobs neglect their children, and that most of those who work do not. At least, there is no reliable evidence of a significant correlation between a mother's work status and the current or future delinquency of her children.

Although the problems that held the center of the stage early in the revolution—the impact on the employment of men, the unsettlement of sex roles in the home, the delinquency of youth—are now receding into history, there are other issues that warrant public attention and action.

One of the characteristics of every society is the failure of its institutions to adjust to new circumstances and conditions. Many important institutional changes and adjustments are overdue if our society is to take greater advantage of the potential and developed skill of its women. First, our educational and training systems require adjustment. For instance girls still shy away from the study of mathematics and the sciences in favor of foreign languages and the arts, although there is no justification for this choice in terms of what we know about the sex distribution of aptitudes or about the needs of the marketplace. To a certain extent, they are diverted from certain fields because of the inadequacy of educational and occupational guidance and counseling in the home, school, and community. Many girls and young women do not yet realize that they will spend most of their adult years at work, and they do not know how to prepare themselves to take advantage of work opportunities. Few are aware of the different ways in which it is possible to balance career and home. On these fronts, our society is deficient. We have permitted old models and stereotypes to remain entrenched in the face of a vastly altered reality.

Many colleges and universities continue to favor men over women in their admissions policies and in granting financial aid. Many educational institutions continue to ignore the fact that many women will interrupt their education in their early twenties, but will seek to complete it later. Some institutions are beginning to recognize this problem and to make adjustments. However, in most cases this has been done because of a slowdown in younger college entrants, rather than because of a new commitment to older women. Little imagination has been shown with regard to maintaining the skills and interests of the many women who interrupt their education or their careers but who continue a few years later.

A great deal of career development takes place in institutions other than colleges and universities, and these institutions have likewise been negligent. For example, it is rare indeed for administrators of medical residencies to arrange programs to enable mothers to train part-time. And only the most alert corporations have recognized the advantages of part-time training programs for attracting able women back into employment. Most employers are disinclined to make their in-service and extramural educational and training opportunities available to women, because they believe that their investment will be wasted on many women who will soon leave the labor market. Their reasoning, however, ignores the fact that many women with high occupational status remain in the labor market (or if they leave, will return shortly), as well as the fact that a large number of young men also quit their jobs.

With respect to utilization, there is unequivocal evidence that many employers prefer stupid males to smart females. They are usually unwilling to make even modest adjustments in hours, vacations, and other scheduling to attract able women. Of course it is easier to run a large organization according to a single set of rules, but one set of rules is never adequate for all employees, regardless of sex.

Conclusions

Let us touch briefly on three areas where the opportunities that have been opened up for women remain to be more fully exploited.

The family as a unit of employment. Economists have long postulated that the individual earns income, but the family is the strategic consumption unit. Now, however, we are witnessing a trend that is making the family the effective unit of employment. Increasingly, a job transfer or job change for a man requires a satisfactory situation for his working wife. The implications of this new type of constraint on labor mobility warrants more systematic exploration.

Child care centers. For the past several decades the American people have been slow in establishing and expanding good child care facilities, thus giving expression to their ambivalence about the desirability of mothers of young children working. We have seen that, despite this cautionary attitude, more and more young mothers are working. Congress has become concerned about the possible adverse effect of a shortage of suitable child care facilities on the work potential of mothers who are on the Aid-to-Dependent Children rolls, since the legislature is seeking to promote their employability. While its primary goal is to reduce relief expenditures, it is also worried about the shortcomings of a welfare system that enables many women to eschew work. Many of these women would prefer to work, especially if their children were looked after competently. Since Congress has started addressing this problem, and since certain organizations, such as hospitals and trade unions, are beginning to be concerned about working mothers, we may be entering a period of accelerated development of child care centers. If we do, the forecasters had better restudy their earlier calculations because the labor force participation of young women is likely to move up even more sharply than has been anticipated.

Unions and wages. A third area involves the unionization and wage levels of low-paying service jobs, a high proportion of which have been filled by women. Since more and more women are entering, reentering, and remaining in the labor force, the quality of jobs available to them becomes a matter of greater interest and concern. The willingness of legislators to bring more and more previously exempt jobs under labor standards, the increasing success that trade unions have begun to experience in organizing hospital workers, the upward drift of wages for unskilled service jobs—all bespeak new, if belated, adjustments to the more permanent effects of the revolution in womanpower.

A revolution that alters the relation of one sex to the world of work will inevitably impinge on a great many social institutions and mechanisms. We have addressed only three. No aspect of life will be untouched by the revolution in womanpower, and there is reason to believe that the changes that result will improve the lives of both sexes.

15

Women's Challenge to Management

We all know that increasing numbers of women are demanding equal consideration in competing for the better jobs in the economy. However, this challenge is approached from different vantages, generally either that of the challengers (women who seek high-level employment) or that of the challenged (employers of managerial personnel). The challengers' approach centers primarily upon the forces that have shaped women's life-styles and that have led to increasing female dissatisfaction with the status quo. The employers' approach examines the managerial function and employer attitudes toward upgrading the female labor force. These approaches are of course complementary, and it must be recognized that underlying women's actions and employers' reactions is the value system of the larger society.

Cultural and economic factors have produced differential expectations for the sexes. An interplay of social forces has given ascendancy to the female role of full-time homemaker, which has had the dual effect of lowering females' work expectations and of deterring employers from considering women as serious competitors for high-status employment.

Attitudes are shaped early in life and, when girls become aware that primacy is given to male work goals, they learn to act accordingly. Since all discriminatory systems have a built-in dynamic that leads the victims to supply a rationale for bias, female conformance to societal norms has served as justification for differential treatment of the sexes. Because its roots go deep into every facet of our society and women as well as men reinforce existing preconceptions about proper female roles, sex discrimination is exceptionally difficult to eliminate. However, despite prior conditioning and the continuing pervasiveness of the "feminine mystique," significant changes are occurring that will slowly but surely result in modifications in women's traditional role.

The question of family size is a key determinant of the career opportunities available to women. As explained in Chapter 14, we appear to be in a period when small families increasingly will be the norm as a result of personal preference, the availability of improved birth control techniques, and the legalization of abortion. Hence fewer and fewer women will leave the labor force, and those who do will leave it for a shorter time. In the future women workers will represent a less distinctive and differentiated labor supply than in the past.

The greatest danger in considering a rapidly changing situation involving minorities—and in this context women may be viewed as a minority—is to project past experience. In a rapidly changing situation, such projections are certain to be wrong. To continue to postulate a high rate of female withdrawal from the labor force would probably turn out to be erroneous.

A related point concerns the future educational achievements of women. The dip in the curve of women with higher degrees has been reversed: many more women are in medical school; more are in law school; and female recipients of Ph.D.'s are increasing, although the proportion relative to men is still below the peak of the 1920s. The rationalization that women hold poor jobs because of their failure to invest in higher education is becoming untenable. The more education they acquire, the more formidable competitors they will be for the limited number of superior job openings that are available.

However, there is some question about the number of women who are oriented to management. There is no real tradition of women in leadership roles in the business world. Even in predominantly female occupations, executive positions are held largely by males. While there is little doubt that many women qualify for managerial employment, it is an open question whether large numbers will gravitate to managerial careers without special encouragement and support.

Some women are undoubtedly moving under their own momentum, much more than in the past. Our society is an amalgam of special interest groups. Everybody fights with everybody else for a bigger piece of the action. Historically, women have not been sufficiently organized to wage successful battles, but now they have begun to organize themselves far more effectively. Their cooperative efforts have created an effective pressure group, and it is likely that their joint actions will intensify.

The general egalitarian thrust, heavily influenced by the racial revolution and reinforced by the youth revolution, can have only positive effects upon the women's revolution. We live in a society where strong forces for change are at work, and the women's movement is part of these larger social adjustments.

Nevertheless, pervasive discrimination against women in large organizations—private, nonprofit, and public—has existed, presently exists, and will probably continue to exist for a long time. What happens to women in the marketplace reflects not competitive realities but employer discrimination. No longer can it be claimed that women "get what they deserve" because they lack requisite education, skill, or motivation. While role differentiation can account for the relative scarcity of female aspirants for high-level positions, considerable evidence has been adduced that women with proper credentials have been unable to move into preferred employment in business, government, or universities to the same extent as men.

Certainly personnel policies affecting women are influenced by social attitudes, but there appears to be a significant time lag between changes in the status of women and management's recognition of female interest in and competence to perform leadership functions. The fact that the executive's wife has been touted as a full-time helpmate may deflect many executives from appointing women to other than subsidiary positions. However, the crux of the matter is whether most employers who believe that they have been doing very well without female managerial personnel can be persuaded to change their attitudes and accept this unknown, untried, and upsetting innovation.

An assault upon male-dominated strongholds will undoubtedly meet a great deal of resistance, but the female assailants are showing increasing strength and it is generally agreed that they will eventually prevail. Moreover, it is believed that a successful challenge to management by women will result in widespread changes that will affect all employees. Significant changes in a manpower system cannot be made without influencing and transforming its many subcomponents. For example, in the comparable movement to open up more opportunities for blacks, considerable reevaluation and revision has taken place in selection procedures, recruitment policies, personnel support systems, marketing tactics, and community strategies. The same turbulence is likely to ensue as progress is made in improving the position of women.

Furthermore, a positive response to women's challenge to management will result in societal repercussions, since alterations in traditional employment relationships will certainly have large-scale reverberations beyond the labor market.

Directions for Women's Action

Those who have the most to gain must assume the primary responsibility for action. Women must become more knowledgeable and more sophisticated in manipulating the various systems for their own benefit. One cannot realize opportunities for other people. One can help them, support them, show them the way, encourage them, even train them, but finally, the responsibility for change rests with the party of primary interest. And because women have been on the periphery for so long, the magnitude of change involved in this case presents many difficulties.

One striking difference between women and other minorities is that women, particularly white middle-class women, have more opportunity to learn how the system operates from their fathers and husbands. Poor blacks and other outsiders do not know people high in the system to whom they can turn for help. But many white women have male relatives and friends who can supply them with critically useful information. Informal communications networks serve as important information and hiring channels. Many women who seek managerial-level jobs have access to such a network; those who are reluctant to utilize personal contacts need to be reminded that men have always done so.

It is well to remember that the men who are prejudiced against women and discriminate against them are the sons of women. Therefore women must do a better job of raising their sons, not only as potential employers of women, but as future husbands who will encourage and support their wives' work aspirations. Moreover, mothers carry much of the responsibility for the low career aspirations of their daughters. Thus they have a wide area for constructive action. Since women are the major nurturing agents in our society, they must take the lead in breaking down sex stereotypes. Although ours is a society pervaded with sex prejudice and discrimination, of which women are the victims, as the society begins to lower discriminatory barriers, mothers must be prepared to encourage their children to respond positively to the new forces.

Women must also make greater efforts to get into positions of influence in organizations that have a high potential for accelerating change. While women have been voting for many years, they have a poor record as elected and appointed public officials. They have not pressed hard enough for their share of the limited, and therefore highly valued, political plums. Since political action can be a force for social change, women must organize and fight for larger representation in government if they wish to speed their progress.

Women are members of trade unions, and yet they have made limited progress as members of the union hierarchy. They comprise the majority of workers in large governmental bureaucracies such as school systems, yet they have seldom if ever challenged the sex discrimination that has systematically prevented them from moving into the highest positions. Women must work to reshape the organizations of which they are a part, so that these institutions will be more responsive to their needs.

In these several efforts it is desirable that they seek and find allies with whom they can form coalitions. There are some men in positions of power who now appear willing to cooperate with women in breaking down sex barriers. The male peers of women students in professional and graduate schools can also be useful. Often people in a position to help will do so, but only if they are prodded.

However, reminders and prodding will not be sufficient to move many men from their rigidly fixed positions. Then stronger actions, such as sit-ins, picketing, boycotts, and other harassment techniques, may be in order. Women who are serious about moving aggressively against discrimination must be willing on occasion to adopt unladylike tactics.

One must not minimize the hard work that is involved in collecting money, building staffs, and constructing an organization. Here is one instance where the efforts of blacks can serve as models. Our racial problem would be much farther from solution were it not for the National Association for the Advancement of Colored People, the National Urban League, the Southern Christian Leadership Conference, and similar groups. They took the lead to create an environment predisposed for change and they did the hard work of fighting cases through the courts. If more and more women become interested in their own progress, they must do more than rely on the American Association of University Women or the Business and Professional Women's clubs, useful as these organizations have been. There must be more organization, more staff, more money, and more programs.

Directions for Management Action

Management will move faster or slower, depending upon the amount of pressure to which it is subjected. Management has the primary task of keeping an organization going—to treat patients, educate students, make a profit—depending on its mission or goal. It will respond to new demands only when it is forced to deal with them. Yet good management tries to stay one step ahead of the changing environment. If it sees changes occurring on the equal opportunity front, it will try to put more women into middle and top management. It will recognize that it must make an effort. A smart management does not want to be a straggler.

Moreover, management is highly imitative. If one large organization discovers that another is following a new approach, it will probably follow suit and soon most managements will fall in line. Managers like company; they crowd into the same boat. No management likes to go too far out ahead or lag too far behind.

In seeking women for higher-level positions, management should, in the first instance, look at its own pool of female talent, which is often considerable. Of course, it may hesitate to do this, fearing that if it finds many talented women in the pool, it will be branded as having been incompetent. It would not be easy for employers to acknowledge that women whom they refused repeatedly to consider for promotion suddenly are promotable.

Nonetheless, management may find it easier than not to follow this road because the best device for selecting people for promotion, perhaps the only reliable one, is the quality of their performance in the specific work environment. If sex is no longer a barrier, then women within the organization deserve to be carefully considered.

Employers must also improve their external recruitment. First they will have to decide on the criteria to use in selecting women to assure equality of opportunity. They must locate pools of candidates who are oriented to management. Women with baccalaureate degrees, business school graduates, as well as certain key professionals such as lawyers, should be sought for executive positions. It may even be in the employer's interest to subsidize the education of young women interested in entering male fields. In any event, university placement offices can prove to be a major referral source, but only if management is serious about changing its policies, convinces the placement staff that it is reforming, and proves by its hiring and promotion policies that it is in fact no longer discriminating against women. College and university staffs are too sophisticated to play along with the employer who has a fine line of talk but whose actions belie his words.

Management faces a difficult task in breaking down conventional male-female job classifications. According to law, almost every job should be open to members of either sex. This does not mean that most production managers in the future will be women; it does mean that an occasional production manager may be a woman.

Considerable corporate education must be undertaken if the new policy toward women is to be effective. It is not enough that the president of the company is interested in promoting women. He is interested in a thousand issues—that is, if he is an effective top executive. And increasing opportunities for women is not likely to be near the top of his agenda. For example, given the complex problems facing a cabinet officer, he cannot be expected to spend more than a half-hour twice a year on the problem of expanding opportunities for women under his jurisdiction. The most one can ask of him is to delegate this task to a senior administrator and direct him to push this policy and to persuade middle management, which is often indifferent or hostile, that he means what he says.

Antinepotism rules can safely be discarded, even while the integrity of the organization is protected. One way in which a conflict of interest can be avoided is to see that neither spouse is directly responsible for evaluating the work of the other.

A strong effort should be to facilitate leaves of absence for women without loss of benefits. Some women will want or need to take considerable time off to raise their children, but many will return within a short time, and they should be encouraged to do so.

Another issue relates to the actions that corporations take when they relocate managers. They should seek to work out reciprocal relations with other firms that face similar problems of finding a job for a second family member when they want to relocate a spouse. Increasingly, organizations that want to reassign a male executive will have to find a position for his working wife and vice versa. We have seen the beginnings of this trend to family placement in the armed forces and in the State Department. And a few corporations and universities are exploring solutions to the problem.

Corporations have long cooperated with one another in hiring the sons of senior executives. Now they will be asked to do the same for daughters and wives. In general, it is not considered cricket to bring one's son into one's own organization. It creates too many problems. But it is customary to ask the head of another corporation to take one's boy in, and to reciprocate.

It is interesting that during the years of substantial employment and income gains, from 1940 to the present, there has been so little effort to shorten the workweek. That is not to say that there has been no change in the amount of free time. We have had more leisure because of longer vacations and more paid holidays. Nevertheless, we shall probably not have to wait much longer for the workweek to be reduced. When that happens, it will mean a redesigning of the working calendar that will have direct and significant implications for women. They, in particular, would profit from a somewhat shorter workweek or fewer hours of work per day.

A European invention called "floating hours" is also worth consideration. Floating hours implies that employees may come in for a stipulated number of hours at any time during the course of the week as long as they interface with other employees for certain periods. Sometimes, when interfacing is unnecessary, they can work any time they prefer as long as it adds up to the stipulated total.

Directions for Government

The affirmative action program is probably the single most significant development in speeding the employment of women at high occupational levels. Increasing public concern with this problem bespeaks a growing awareness of the potential impact of this regulation. The pressures that women have exerted to achieve equal employment opportunity have borne fruit in various legislative and administrative developments that foreshadow ratification of the equal rights amendment. For the near future, the actions of the Office of Federal Contract Compliance will exercise the principal leverage by pressing federal contractors, who include the country's largest employers, to produce affirmative action goals and to live up to the prescribed guidelines.

The manner of implementation of the program remains to be revealed: no one can be sure how much pressure the government will exert, which goals it will accept as reasonable, or the time it will allow to reach the goals. Government will probably move cautiously in response to conflicting political pressures. As it acquires experience in enforcing affirmative action, it will probably become more strict: when it finds that one company can meet the requirements, the next firm will not be permitted to plead hardship. It will be years before the situation will be clarified, but it is certain that the employment picture will never again be the same. The pressure is on, and it can go in only one direction—up!

Most people probably do not know that the inclusion of women in the Civil Rights Act of 1964 was meant as a joke by Judge Howard W. Smith, chairman of the Rules Committee of the House of Representatives. He believed that to add sex discrimination to other types prohibited by the proposed law would certainly kill the legislation and thereby avoid the necessity to expand employment opportunity for blacks. He thought that his colleagues would never agree to add women to the statute. But he misjudged them, and the amendment was passed. Judge Smith's "joke" has had serious results. For example, AT&T has had to pay millions of dollars because of noncompliance with the legislation. This company, and others as well, have had to pay substantial restitution to female workers who have been subjected to sex discrimination.

Another arena of public action relates to day care facilities for children of working mothers. The relevance of public child care facilities for managerial and executive personnel is unclear, since these mothers' incomes are likely to permit them to make private arrangements for their offspring. However, a small number of corporations and nonprofit institutions may find it relatively easy to operate facilities on their premises for employees' children. If employers have no alternative but to establish child care facilities to attract and retain their female work force, they will do so. While employees do not usually attain managerial rank when they are young, women who aim for high-level posts may require day care assistance during their early periods of employment. For these women, publicly financed centers may make the difference between a continuing employment relationship leading to better jobs or involuntary (if temporary) withdrawal from the labor force.

The educational system is an important mechanism for effecting changes in female attitudes and expectations. Schools have tended to reinforce differential expectations for boys and girls. From their earliest years, girls are encouraged to engage in "feminine" pursuits and discouraged from enrolling in "male" courses. Guidance counselors have been notorious purveyors of sex-typed information that presents restricted options to girls. Pressures for change in occupational patterning cannot be effective unless young girls early become aware of their available options and are encouraged to pursue their preferences.

Problematics

There are a number of uncertainties about issues that remain to be resolved. First we must remember that the number of good jobs in every organization is limited, that the competition for these jobs is severe, and that even most white males lose out. There are many disgruntled males in business, unhappy because they did not make it.

Many people do not enjoy working for a large organization. It becomes even less attractive when a man realizes that he is going nowhere. We have to remember that business is highly competitive and that there is not much room at the top. With many competing for the few most desirable jobs, it is not easy to work out reasonable targets for women in higher management. That is an assignment still to be met.

What does progress mean in terms of increasing the number and proportion of women in the middle and higher echelons? What are realistic goals? The answers are complicated by the fact that many veterans and many black male college graduates are active competitors for the same few jobs near the top.

Black women must also be filtered into this complex, competitive situation. It would be a mistake for black women to withdraw from the competition in order to make it easier for black men to move up the executive ladder. This would be poor strategy, since no one who withdraws from the race can assure who the winner will be. No group controls the job market. Everybody who is interested in competing should compete. We must move as quickly as possible toward becoming a society that is color-blind, sex-blind, age-blind—in short, a society that has eliminated discrimination.

In some situations, community groups have acquired control over a block of jobs. If the blacks in New York or Detroit secure control over hospitals, school boards, and welfare centers, they may decide on a policy that gives preference to men. However, it is questionable whether and for how long such a policy would be effective.

Youths are sometimes considered allies of women in the workplace. This is true from one point of view, but not from another. If the employment level remains unsatisfactory, not many young men will go out of their way to help women. It is easier to cooperate in a world in which there is lots of opportunity. The outlook for educated manpower in the near future is unclear. The supply and demand relationships, especially for those holding a doctorate, are seriously awry. If the outlook is ominous for males, it is difficult to be optimistic about the prospects for women.

Another confused issue is the antimaterialistic bias on the part of many upper-income, well-educated youths, which is associated with a reluctance to devote all their energies to maximizing income. They do not want to kill themselves for their employers. If this is true of males from upper-income homes, we must ask whether it also reflects the attitudes of females from the same group. If so, we had better be cautious about the strength of their career drives.

Technology can work for both good and ill. Women may be able to work at home with the aid of new communications devices, and technology may facilitate flexibility in work scheduling. On the other hand, technology threatens to eliminate many clerical and middle-management jobs, from which women might otherwise gain access to higher-level jobs.

Historical Perspectives

In the mid-1950s a study of womanpower was placed on the agenda of the National Manpower Council by a single vote, since the minority did not consider it worthwhile to probe the subject in depth. There are two ways of looking at the subsequent fifteen years. One is to bemoan the slow progress that has been made to reduce and eliminate discrimination against women. The other is to recognize the big leap forward from the council's study of womanpower to the affirmative action program.

We should not minimize the support that the sex revolution has received from the race revolution. It is inevitable that, as the American people begin to eliminate the pathology long present in white-black relations, this sanitizing will have a carry-over effect on male-female relations in the world of work. The black and female revolutions will be mutually supportive, although they may find themselves in competition with each other from time to time. For the long pull, the women's revolution will be accelerated by the institutional changes precipitated by black progress.

Powerful constraints pervade the family, school, church, university, philanthropy, business organizations, government; it cannot be assumed that these complex institutions can be turned around overnight. However, women are reaching new levels of consciousness, and this is critical; for unless victims of discrimination become aware, they will be unable to alter matters. Women's consciousness of sex discrimination has reached a point that can lead only to further change. This will be a function largely of the pressure women exert and the degree of resistance they meet. We may be overestimating both forces. Women may not push as hard as some anticipate, just as the critical institutions may not be as resistant as others predict.

One point in conclusion. We have addressed ourselves to the problems of women as a group and in the process have discussed the problems of racial and ethnic minorities. While we must think and act in terms of groups, we must never lose sight of the fact that the real challenge that our democratic society faces is to broaden opportunity for every individual.

Part Three

MANPOWER

This last section speaks directly to policy issues both within and beyond the manpower arena and to the broad role of government in shaping a democratic society.

Specifically, the first three chapters address certain critical manpower themes: the first decade of manpower training programs; the potentialities of public employment programs within the context of a broadened national manpower effort; and the extent to which adjustments in manpower policies and programs can contribute to increased productivity.

The following two chapters are also concerned with manpower issues but in an enlarged framework. They consider the extent to which diverse federal programs and policies have a major impact on the development and utilization of manpower resources; and how the problems of the American metropolis can be approached from a manpower research perspective.

The last two chapters look at the serious consequences that flow from the economist's neglect of the pervasive role of government in transforming our pluralistic economy, and the results of the large-scale interventions of the "Great Society." This entire section is an effort to precipitate lessons for the future.

16

Manpower Programs: Boon, not Boondoggle

In the United States, no government policy seems to take hold of the public's attention for long. Witness the evanescent appeal of foreign aid, urban renewal, and civil rights. This phenomenon is especially noticeable in the case of government programs for manpower training.

The Manpower Development and Training Act (MDTA) was first passed by Congress in 1962 with full-scale bipartisan support, and three years later the act was amended with a unanimous vote in the House. For ten years, Congress cheerfully appropriated funds to expand the various programs authorized by this legislation.

By December 1971, however, the euphoria over manpower training had evaporated. President Nixon's veto of a manpower bill, drafted by the Democrats under the leadership of Senator Gaylord Nelson, was based on his opposition to the use of federal funds to create jobs for the unemployed. The President based his objections on his belief that such a measure could lead to the re-creation of a make-work program like the WPA. After a decade of close cooperation between the executive branch and the Congress, the manpower coalition had begun to come apart. Aside from discernible political and ideological shifts, there were other signs of strain with manpower programs. The country was confronted with the question, were these programs actually working and were they paying their way?

Appraisals were undertaken by the Comptroller General, by academicians applying cost-benefit analysis, by the Department of Labor, and by Congress. While many findings were favorable, certain weaknesses in both conception and execution were uncovered.

In August 1972, the Deputy Secretary of the Treasury told the executive committee of the American Bankers Association that an expenditure of $40 billion on manpower training over the preceding decade had resulted in a decline in the unemployment rate of only one-half of one percent. At about the same time, senior officials in and out of the Department of Labor began to quote an in-house study based on social security data, which purportedly proved that the employment and income records of persons who had been enrolled in training programs were not better than those of workers who had not had such assistance.

The point is less whether such indictments were accurate—there was reason to doubt them—but rather that critics of manpower programs avidly seized upon this new "evidence" to support their position. Such critics included the chairman of the Council of Economic Advisers and business executives who had cooperated with the federal government in training and employing the disadvantaged. In addition to these members of the "establishment," other expressions of disaffection came from certain militant civil rights groups who proclaimed that government efforts at manpower training were nothing more than attempts to keep the poor in their place.

For a long time supporters of manpower programs had felt no need to buttress their position with data and studies. How could anyone doubt the good sense of rehabilitating the unemployed by offering them allowances, basic education, and training in specific skills, plus such additional supports as counseling and placement? As a result, proponents of the programs found themselves unarmed in the face of sudden attack. For instance, no one contradicted the supposed failure of a $40-billion program, despite the fact that both the Comptroller General and the Joint Economic Committee had estimated its cost at $7 to $8 billion, and responsible officials in the Department of Labor were using a figure of $13 billion.

Ultimately the only way to beat a path through the claims and counterclaims of those who see manpower programs as a boon and those who insist that they are a boondoggle is to sort out the objectives of each of the programs and to determine the actual number of people who have been and are being served by them, relative to the costs involved.

How the Money is Allocated

The budget for the fiscal year 1973 amounted to about $1.5 billion for manpower training and $1.2 billion for emergency employment. In addition, a considerable portion of the Federal-State Employment Service and related labor market services, funded at about $575 million, was directed to the same clientele.

The simplest figure to explain is the $1.2 billion for public service employment: about 140,000 man-years of employment were funded at an average cost of $8,000 per job. The $1.5 billion for manpower training is a bit more complex to define. The principal institutional and on-the-job training programs (MDTA institutional training, JOBS, New Careers, and certain public service on-the-job training efforts) were funded at about $550 million and provided opportunities for approximately 320,000 enrollees. Since most of those enrolled in institutional programs receive allowances, the amount of federal money actually spent on their *training* was approximately $350 million.

The remaining $950 million can be divided into two broad categories: preemployment assistance for youth, primarily monies appropriated under the Neighborhood Youth Corps (NYC), which provides earning opportunities for low-income youth in school, out of school, and during the summer; and preemployment assistance for adults under two major programs—the Work Incentive Program (WIN), aimed at moving welfare clients off relief and into employment, and the Concentrated Employment Program (CEP), which enrolls seriously disadvantaged men and women, primarily in slum areas, in an effort to prepare them for productive work. While occupational training is provided by both WIN and CEP, the larger proportion of the monies is spent on making people employment-ready through providing access to health services, basic education, job orientation, and counseling—that is, services they require, or are thought to require, *before* they can begin a training program or a job.

Thus we see that the federal government was not spending $1.5 billion annually to teach people skills, but at most about one-third that sum. Another third represented wage payments to young people who, in the absence of NYC, would have been hard pressed to acquire spending money. Some of the youngsters did useful work such as cleaning their classrooms, supervising play groups of younger children, or helping at local hospitals. Some received a little training; but all received money—and it is the money they most want and need.

Many of the adult enrollees in CEP and some in WIN have also benefited from the increases in income that accompany training; but when people fail to achieve other gains, such as improving their general education or acquiring specific skills that enhance their employability, they are unlikely to consider their enrollment a success.

Evaluating the Major Programs

An alternate approach to assessment would be to look at the type of program. Of the approximately 1.1 million persons enrolled in training programs in fiscal 1973, about 45 percent were young people, most of whom were employed part-time at the minimum wage for a limited number of weeks by government or nonprofit organizations—that is, in jobs that enabled them to earn between $750 and $800 in the course of the year. Another 320,000 were in institutional or on-the-job training; and 260,000, or 25 percent, were in preemployment programs for welfare clients and the seriously disadvantaged.

Each of these major manpower programs must be examined more closely before we can begin to judge its effectiveness. As far as institutional training is concerned, it has been heavily concentrated in a relatively few occupations, and the typical program runs six months or less. At its best, this training has had highly favorable results: a poorly educated woman who completes a year's training as a licensed practical nurse will be able to earn over $6,000 a year; a man who goes through a good course in refrigeration repair should find a job paying $130 a week, excluding overtime. But many fare less well. For instance, a considerable number of women who have studied typing are unable to find an employer willing to hire them at the end of their course. After four months of electronic assembly training, others are hired at a minimum wage for jobs they could have obtained without training. About three of every ten persons who complete institutional training have serious difficulty in finding jobs.

On the other hand, for those who receive on-the-job training, the slippage between training and employment is slight (10 percent), since the person is hired first and then trained. On-the-job training (OJT) is often successful: people unable to find suitable jobs are hired, meet performance standards, and become regular members of the firm's work force. A former trainee may acquire sufficient seniority to gain a relatively secure berth. Because of their low seniority, however, the recession of 1969-70 resulted in layoffs for many who had completed OJT.

Another problem with OJT is the use, or rather the nonuse, by certain employers of the governmental subsidies instituted for the purpose of training disadvantaged workers. While many employers abide by their contractual obligations—in fact, some large employers hire the disadvantaged without federal subsidy—many others provide little in the way of real training and even less in the way of supportive services. It has also been charged that a significant proportion of OJT contracts go to employers who on their own had been hiring disadvantaged workers. They therefore receive government subsidies for doing what they would be doing anyway.

The most serious drawback to on-the-job training is that it is inevitably caught up in cyclical shifts. In bad times, when employers are laying off workers, they are obviously not going to take on new ones for training; in boom times, they are apt to hire the untrained without government subsidies.

It is impossible to make any blanket judgment about these training programs. It can be said that good training, which is genuinely geared to labor-market trends, focused on people with the capability of completing the course, and linked to an effective placement service, can be very helpful to the disadvantaged. No one knows how much of the total training effort under MDTA met these criteria, but surely some of the efforts of the last decade can provide the basis for a useful federal program.

When it comes to a program like the Neighborhood Youth Corps, degrees of success or failure are even more difficult to determine. Although job training has been a relatively unimportant feature, studies of postenrollment employment and income seem to suggest that NYC has done well in these areas. Unfortunately, these studies have dealt with only a tiny fraction of a vast program (over half a million enrollees in 1973) and must be construed cautiously.

Jobs and income are not the only—not even the major—criteria for assessing the Neighborhood Youth Corps. Annual congressional debates indicate that the legislators view the summer program as "riot insurance," and in this they have been strongly supported by the big-city mayors. Since the unemployment rates for minority teenagers in slum areas fluctuate between 33 and 50 percent, the congressional attitude is understandable.

Congresswoman Edith Green, however, insists that the money is being put into the wrong hands (it should go to parents). Since the in-school program does not contribute to reducing the dropout rate, refunneling the money into a year-round program combining work and school might be more beneficial. However, this is no response to the demands for insurance against summer rioting.

The other major effort in the area of manpower training has been unsuccessful. The majority of those who entered the Concentrated Employment Program (CEP) dropped out; some of the few who finished had great difficulty finding jobs; and others who did find jobs quit soon thereafter because of low pay, poor working conditions, or transportation problems. In other words, the number who acquired permanent jobs is small.

Even here, whether or not this proves failure is moot. The people CEP has tried to help are the most alienated members of the ghetto community. Many of them have never held regular jobs. Perhaps, as the National Manpower Advisory Committee suggested to Secretary of

Labor Willard Wirtz in 1968, it was a misplaced allocation of effort and resources to pick out the most seriously handicapped for training; it might have been more useful, and in the end more helpful to the community, to concentrate on those with a reasonable chance of success. Wirtz's reply was one that his advisers could not but appreciate: it is unconscionable for the richest country in the world to turn its back on those most in need of assistance. Despite the merit of such a view in a booming economy, it may lose strength in the face of an unemployment rate that has risen from 4 to 8 percent.

The Work Incentive Program (WIN), aimed at moving potential employables off the welfare rolls and into productive employment, produced a mixed result. The program was voluntary at first and provided a range of manpower services for female heads of households and for husbands and teenage children. In 1967 Congress established an income set-aside (participants could retain the first $80 of earnings per month) as an incentive to welfare recipients who were willing to attempt to become self-supporting.

Many of the potentially eligible were poorly educated and unskilled and therefore could not look forward to earning much above the minimum wage. The number of people who entered the program remained small, and the number who completed it was even smaller. Late in 1971, the Talmadge amendments to the Social Security Act put the program on a new footing. The federal government assumed more responsibility, and an element of coercion was added insofar as many welfare clients had to register and participate if they wanted to retain their benefits. Although WIN is at a substantially higher level of activity than in its formative years, it remains to be seen whether the program can, to any significant extent, achieve its aim. The odds are against it, particularly in the big cities of the North and the West where women with limited skills seldom can earn more than $80 to $90 weekly, a paltry sum on which to support an urban family. Without adequate jobs at adequate wages, the determination to reduce the welfare rolls will, by itself, yield few results.

Finally, there is the last manpower program category, public service employment. Direct government employment of the unemployed has to be viewed from two angles, its effect on the participants and its effect on the economy as a whole. Andrew F. Brimmer, former governor of the Federal Reserve Board, believes that public service employment is a valuable antirecession device, since it can put money quickly into the hands of the jobless consumer. The principal beneficiaries of this program have been relatively well-educated veterans who returned from military service and encountered difficulty finding jobs. On the other hand, it has done relatively little for the seriously disadvantaged.

A Mixed Tally

It would be gratifying if one could report that manpower programs were distinctly successful in improving the employability and income of the participants and that experience speaks for a substantial increase in such efforts. Or if the evidence of failure were unequivocal, that too would be useful as a guide for public policy. However, neither conclusion is warranted.

The authors of the most carefully constructed analysis of MDTA (Garth L. Mangum and John Walsh, *A Decade of Manpower Development and Training,* Olympus, 1973) concluded after an intensive evaluation of all available studies: "The fact is that after 10 years, there is no *definitive* evidence one way or the other about MDTA outcomes" (p. 47). They point out that no large-scale, controlled study was ever undertaken, and that some experts question whether it would be feasible to design and carry out such an inquiry. The studies that are available, they note, point to a substantial increase in earnings for those who participated in either institutional or OJT training.

There is a broader perspective within which these training efforts can be assessed. While the United States was entering upon a new effort in the manpower arena, it was also pursuing a host of related programs directed toward eliminating poverty, improving race relations, and expanding educational opportunities. Since the manpower effort interacted with these other programs, a determination of its value may be viewed in relation to results in these other areas.

The staffs of manpower programs involved about 47,000 persons in 1970 and carried an annual price tag of approximately $250 million. A survey by the Bureau of Social Science Research revealed that the representation of blacks on these staffs was twice their proportion in the total population. This was also the case with respect to the staffs of Community Action Programs and other "Great Society" agencies. Clearly, these efforts provided new opportunities for the indigenous leadership. One contribution of the sums that the federal government invested in manpower and related programs therefore was to create openings that enabled representatives from severely deprived groups to find new roles and to acquire new skills.

Brimmer has noted that blacks accounted for half or more of all enrollees in the following: Job Opportunities in the Business Sector; Neighborhood Youth Corps; Job Corps; Concentrated Employment Program (*The Great Society,* Basic Books, 1974). While he is careful not to interpret enrollment in manpower programs as a guarantee of later regular employment at a satisfactory wage, Brimmer concludes that the new federal initiative made a contribution to helping the black minority.

Further evidence of the linkage between manpower programs and civil rights is the substantial increase in minority group representation in apprenticeship programs, rising from 6 to 12 percent in the late 1960s, in large measure stimulated by specifically designed preapprenticeship programs funded by the U. S. Department of Labor.

While difficulties have long existed at every level in dovetailing educational and manpower programs, the new departures in manpower in the 1960s unquestionably stimulated a corresponding interest in strengthening vocational and technical education. In the second half of the 1960s, there was a 60-percent increase in federally aided vocational-technical enrollments, from 5.4 to 8.8 million, and the Comprehensive Employment and Training Act of 1973 provides a financial incentive to states that place the educational and manpower efforts within the same planning structure. In addition, former Commissioner of Education Marland's advocacy of career education (discussed in Chapter 2) has stimulated growing concern for the difficulties revealed by the manpower programs.

The numerous and vocal spokesmen who promised that a $13-billion manpower program would significantly reduce the national unemployment rate, or would slow inflationary pressures by adding to the pool of scarce skills, were advocates, not realists. Still, it is not unrealistic to say that hundreds of thousands of people profited to some extent from training; that millions of youths were given an otherwise unavailable opportunity to earn wages through the intervention of the federal government; and that more than 200,000 people were placed in public service jobs.

We get what we pay for. At a cost of 1 percent of the federal budget and 0.25 percent of the GNP we have experimented with manpower programs. Some of them have proved sound; others have not. Critics notwithstanding, our option is not to discard manpower programming, but to strengthen and enlarge the existing structure. Certainly no advanced economy can afford to operate without effective manpower programs.

17

Perspectives on a Public Employment Program

This chapter will delineate the issues we should analyze and evaluate before we assess the desirability of a substantial expansion of federally financed public employment programs (PEP).

As background, we shall consider the evolution of this approach to manpower problems. Because Franklin Roosevelt believed in work relief rather than the dole in the 1930s, the United States embarked upon two large, sustained public employment programs: the Work Progress Administration (WPA) and the Public Works Administration (PWA). No definitive studies have been made of the effectiveness of the WPA, which was much the larger program. Although many of its projects consisted primarily in leaf-raking and other maintenance efforts, others resulted in a good deal of useful output, from the production of state guidebooks to the construction of airports.

It is clear, however, that despite its large expenditures over many years, the WPA did not have a pronounced contracylic effect. It was mobilization for war that was finally responsible for lowering the excessively high unemployment rates that prevailed after the depression. Nevertheless, a WPA job represented a marked improvement in living standards for many members of disadvantaged groups, who had never previously enjoyed comparable wages and whose employment experience had been spasmodic at best. Writing in the early 1940s, Gunnar Myrdal pointed to the gains made by many blacks who were able to obtain WPA jobs.

Since World War II, there have been only a few limited efforts to reestablish work relief as a major component in manpower programming. For the most part, advocates of this approach have been conservative legislators who believe that able-bodied persons on welfare should work for the dollars they receive, unless they have overriding family responsibilities. The Senate Finance Committee's rewriting of President Nixon's welfare reform proposal in 1972 was infused with this attitude. Manpower legislation over the years has included some small programs based upon a work relief philosophy. These are directed primarily to limited constituencies of older unemployed men who live in areas where the employment base is eroding and who otherwise would be unable to get jobs.

There has been some support for developing PEP as an adjunct to a more comprehensive manpower training program. This approach would provide public employment for a year or two for persons unable to find jobs in the private sector after they have completed a course of training. During the transitional period, it is hoped that they might be able to find "regular" jobs. This type of program was advocated in the mid-1960s by the President's Task Force on the Inner City.

For most of the period since the passage of the Manpower Development and Training Act (MDTA) in 1962, despite occasional prodding by Senators Joseph S. Clark, Winston L. Prouty, and others, Congress has apparently been unwilling to undertake any large-scale federally financed employment program. When such legislation was finally passed by the Congress in 1970, President Nixon vetoed it, warning against the reinstitution of a nonproductive public employment program. However, in 1971, in the face of a persisting, relatively high unemployment rate, Congress approved a two-year Emergency Employment Act (EEA), with an authorization of $2.25 billion. A presidential veto was avoided by including the proviso that public service jobs would be "transitional" and that at the end of two years persons slotted into them would be transferred into permanent private or public jobs. Congress recommended that veterans and the disadvantaged be given special consideration in filling these positions.

The EEA was a breach in the theretofore almost exclusive concern with training as the core element in manpower programming. In dollar terms, the size of its two-year appropriation was only slightly less than the first ten-year expenditures for the MDTA. However, when EEA authorization expired in 1973, new manpower legislation, the Comprehensive Employment and Training Act (CETA), provided under a special title only modest sums for public service employment—$250 and $350 million for the first two years—although the act gave the prime contractors discretion to spend all, some, or none of their regular allocations on public service jobs.

Nevertheless, pressure for expanded public service employment continues. Competing proposals for welfare reform stress employability and look to the transfer of able-bodied relief recipients to some form of employment, including public service. Many analysts believe that a substantially enlarged public employment program could contribute to improving the quality of urban life, since most large cities are financially strapped and therefore are unable to provide an adequate range of basic services, from police protection to health care. Hence, despite recently decreased federal appropriations for PEP, it seems likely that public employment programs will continue to be in the center of the manpower stage and that strong pressures will be operating to increase their scale.

Since the EEA program is our most recent large-scale public employment program, it may be useful to review its experience. The Department of Labor was able to launch the program expeditiously and the states and localities were able to move quickly to hire people, thereby demonstrating a flexibility in placing the unemployed in public service positions.

The average cost per person hired was approximately $7,200 per year. Because of congressional insistence that most of the money be used for wages, local programs were often handicapped by the lack of suitable equipment or lack of training opportunities, which had adverse effects on productivity. Additional sanitation workers without sanitation trucks are not able to contribute much to improving the cleanliness of a city.

Although, together with veterans, the disadvantaged were to be given priority in placement, only a minority of the jobs, about one in four, were filled by nonhigh-school graduates, the best single indicator of disadvantage.

A prime objective of EEA was to move those holding federally funded jobs into regular positions on civil service or into the private economy. While a minority were able to make the transition, this critical objective of the program had only modest success.

The arguments of the proponents of a vastly expanded PEP are many and varied. Some believe the federal government should move energetically and directly to provide a job for every person who is able and willing to work. This implied commitment has been waiting to be fulfilled since passage of the Employment Act in 1946.

To others, the continuing high rates of unemployment among specific groups, such as youth, minorities, and older persons, even during the longest boom in the nation's history (the 1960s) are proof that the private economy cannot provide jobs for all who want to work. Consequently, they feel, the federal government should step in, especially since the experience of the EEA proves that state and local governments can, if funded, quickly put the unemployed to useful work.

Some observers note that state and local governments have been and continue to be the fastest growing job sector, but one in which minorities have encountered difficulty in obtaining jobs and, especially, in being promoted. Therefore they would like to see more federal government inducements and pressures in the form of money and more effective anti-discrimination efforts to open more civil service jobs for minorities.

The fact that the average EEA job "cost" over $7,000, and that 90 percent of all EEA funds had to be spent for wages, led some to look to public service employment to improve the number of better-paying jobs in low-wage communities, since EEA jobs paid much above the minimum wage.

Other students of the manpower scene are convinced, on the basis of the nation's experience during the 1960s, that a strengthened national manpower program must add a significant employment dimension to its previously almost exclusive preoccupation with training and income transfers. They see greater potential for training programs, particularly those directed to the disadvantaged, if the training were more effectively linked to work opportunities, especially to jobs in the public sector.

There is also a growing consensus that, for older persons who require assistance because they cannot easily be relocated from declining to expanding labor markets, it is preferable to provide support via work rather than via the dole.

As we have seen, the substantial increase in unemployment among scientists and engineers after 1969 was largely a result of the vagaries of the federal budget. This has led various professional and governmental leaders to contend that it is the responsibility of the federal government to assist these displaced workers. Putting them to work on socially useful projects financed by federal dollars is one recommended type of assistance.

Although the arguments cited above do not represent an exhaustive list of reasons offered for favoring a much enlarged PEP, they do include those with the widest appeal.

The National Manpower Advisory Committee (NMAC) considered federal job creation and related types of programs on repeated occasions from 1965 through 1971. Several conclusions emerged from these discussions. The committee looked with favor on the establishment of programs of direct employment as a major step toward fulfilling the promise of the Employment Act of 1946. It warned, however, that such programs should be directed primarily to assisting persons with persistent difficulties in finding and holding jobs rather than to the short-term unemployed who have lost their jobs because of a decline in the general level of economic activity. It also recommended that training be built into such programs and that wages, fringe benefits, and supervision be structured to encourage the relocation of people from public service jobs into the regular economy.

The NMAC countered arguments against federal involvement in job creation efforts by pointing out the extent of the government's underwriting of jobs for various groups such as workers on highways, in defense plants, and in the maritime industry. Furthermore, the committee noted that the existence of several government programs for out-of-school youth and for those on summer vacation represent at least halfway steps toward sponsorship of a public employment program for new labor force entrants. The committee's consensus was that the issue of federal involvement has less to do with principle, and more with scope, scale, and clientele.

Cognizant of the shortfall in jobs for many who successfully completed manpower training, the committee suggested that the availability of public employment opportunities would result in making training investments more productive. In addition it noted that those who could not find jobs in the private sector and who were hired for public service jobs would be able to proceed simultaneously with additional training while performing useful work. There is suggestive evidence that a combined work-training pattern might prove effective in helping to rehabilitate those like ex-prisoners and former drug addicts, who have been outside the mainstream of employment. The committee insisted, however, that a program of governmentally sponsored jobs should not be initiated unless the jobs are "real" and not created simply to make work.

Public employment programs provide a way of ascertaining whether the pathology with respect to work which is ascribed to the disadvantaged reflects shortcomings in the labor market or in the individuals themselves. Unless one who cannot find a job in the private sector can obtain one through government auspices, it is difficult to test whether his unemployability reflects weaknesses in the market or in himself.

Nevertheless, the committee recognized certain problems presented by a governmentally sponsored job program: potential disruptions in a labor market where large numbers of people are employed at or below the federal minimum wage; the high dollar costs of a large-scale program; difficulties in dovetailing the job program with existing welfare programs that provide income transfers without a work requirement; and the difficulty of moving people from government to private jobs, many of which pay less and offer less security.

At its meeting in the fall of 1968, the committee's discussion was informed by a background paper prepared by Professor Garth Mangum of the University of Utah. At that time the following additional points emerged.

As in many programs, certain groups require special attention in job creation. For example, older rural residents with limited education and skill should not be pressured to relocate in urban centers where their employment prospects are poor at best, but should be enabled to do useful public work at home. Likewise, urban residents who cannot find jobs, although they are willing to work at minimum wages before or after completing manpower training, represent another group for whom the federal government might consider creating public service jobs which would be considered as interim, not permanent, positions.

The largest categories of economically handicapped people are those who work full-time full-year, yet whose earnings are not sufficient to raise their families out of poverty, and those who have become so discouraged that they no longer seek employment. The adverse circumstances affecting these two groups reflect race and sex discrimination, population concentration in low-income areas, low productivity, and low wages. While even a large-scale federal job creation program cannot compensate for all of these disabilities, it can assure every American an opportunity to work and to earn a living wage.

To what extent would a job creation program affect the unemployment rates of youth, particularly ghetto youth? The committee concluded that, although an increase in job opportunities would result in a considerable reduction in the present levels of teenage unemployment, many young blacks would not be responsive to jobs that pay only a minimum wage and lack opportunities for advancement. Even a massive government program of job creation would not be a panacea for the alienation and frustration of large numbers of ghetto youngsters whose willingness and ability to accept and respond to conventional work incentives and goals depend on whether they believe they will be dealt with equitably by society.

We have seen that years ago the National Manpower Advisory Committee realized the importance of a public employment program as part of a comprehensive national manpower program and recognized the many difficulties of fitting such an effort into the existing structure. At no point did the NMAC view PEP primarily as a countercyclic mechanism; rather it looked to public service employment as a potent device in removing employment barriers from the path of disadvantaged groups.

The impact of a significantly new job creation effort must be assessed in terms of the problems it is expected to ameliorate. Let us consider the following shortcomings in the nation's manpower markets:

(a) A chronic tendency for employment to grow less rapidly than the numbers of persons seeking full-time or part-time jobs.
(b) The mismatch between workers looking for jobs and employers seeking specific skills.

(c) The substantial numbers of workers living in areas of the country where the long-term outlook for employment is unfavorable and where there is little likelihood of rapid change for the better.

(d) The considerable numbers of low-skilled workers who are employed full-time or part-time throughout the year but who nevertheless are unable to support their families adequately.

(e) The substantial difficulties encountered by many young people, high-school dropouts and members of minority groups in particular, in making the transition from school to work. And the corresponding difficulties faced by older people when they seek full- or part-time employment.

(f) Large numbers of workers who are unable to make more than a peripheral attachment to the labor force, which means that they have little prospect of acquiring job security, a decent income, and promotion.

(g) The pervasive discrimination, based upon race, ethnicity, sex, credentials, age, and other arbitrary factors unrelated to performance, that continues to characterize most sectors of the labor market.

(h) The large numbers of young people, both high school dropouts and graduates, who have not acquired useful skills, which increases the probability that they will become peripheral workers.

(i) A serious and continuing imbalance between the demand for and supply of college and university graduates.

(j) The inadequacy of available child care facilities to meet the needs of mothers who desire full-time or part-time jobs.

(k) The inability of the federal government to assure a level of economic activity close to full utilization of its resources, which results in excessive unemployment.

(l) Geographic concentration of industries, which means that pools of unemployed persons are formed whenever there are sudden and large-scale reductions in demand.

(m) The restricted opportunities for handicapped persons to work under sheltered conditions.

We shall now consider some critical questions about the extent to which PEP may be able to provide a constructive response to the most important of these issues.

In 1972 there were approximately 2.5 million more people unemployed than three years earlier. In an arsenal of antirecessional policies how ·much weight should be given to PEP, which would cost about $3.5 billion annually for each 500,000 new jobs?

How do the unemployed support themselves during a recession? Would PEP retard their effective reabsorption into the economy? What gains, individual and social, might result from a much larger PEP program?

Would there be serious difficulties if there were prior planning for the quick absorption of between 500,000 and 1.5 million people into PEP jobs as an antirecession measure?

If large numbers of "peripheral" workers are put into public jobs, would they exert organized pressure to remain in these jobs after the economy begins to recover? What stimulus would they need to find jobs in the private sector?

Can a dynamic economy require certain types of workers to relocate if their source of employment evaporates? For example, would it have been sensible if a large number of scientists and engineers in Seattle or Huntsville had been given PEP jobs in the early 1970s?

Will the federal government be able and willing to provide public jobs for the millions of persons who would welcome the opportunity to earn $7,000 a year? Such a commitment would unquestionably draw additional large numbers of married women into the work force and would retard the withdrawal of older workers.

To what extent will it be possible to organize meaningful work at locations accessible to the homes of all eligible persons? Many people, including some of the most disadvantaged, cannot be served by a vastly expanded public employment program because they have special needs, such as sheltered employment, training, and child care facilities. A governmental commitment to provide jobs for all must go beyond the mere provision of jobs: it requires the concomitant commitment to provide a range of supporting services, which may well bring the $7,000 average cost per job to $9,000 or $10,000.

Will it be possible to move any significant number of temporary public job holders into regular civil service employment? If not, what are the implications of having two groups of public workers, one composed of regular employees, the other of specially subsidized labor?

How can we operate a large public employment program that pays a living wage in low-wage areas, such as the rural South, without creating serious strains on the local economy? What is to stop low-wage earners, even those in high-wage areas, from trying to leave private employment to secure a public job?

Since a high proportion of low-income workers belong to disadvantaged groups, is there any likelihood that local politicians will give them priority in filling better-paying PEP jobs? Is it not more likely that most federally funded jobs, especially in low-wage areas, will be reserved for those with political influence?

If disproportionate numbers of minority groups secure PEP jobs, what will be the effect upon discrimination in the rest of the labor market? Will PEP provide employers, trade unions, and white workers with a rationale for avoiding the basic changes necessary to eliminate discrimination in other sectors of the economy?

What consideration should be given to the implications on productivity of vastly expanded public service employment? There is disturbing evidence that the addition of large numbers of workers to governmental payrolls has not resulted in corresponding increases in either the quantity or quality of services received by the public.

The thrust of the foregoing questions and observations has been to point out some of the problems associated with the use of PEP as a contracyclic device and/or as a major approach to providing suitable jobs for all who have the ability and desire to work.

These cautionary observations are not meant to imply, however, that there may not be significant, although more limited, roles that PEP might play in meeting selected manpower goals. For instance, the principle underlying Operation Mainstream—providing work and income for older unemployed men in Appalachia—could be broadened to provide public service employment for older, low-skilled persons in urban areas who have minimal prospects of securing private employment. In addition, PEP jobs could well be provided for a period not exceeding two years for all people who complete a government-sponsored training program but who cannot find work in the private sector because of a shortage of jobs.

Other reasonable uses of a public employment program include establishing part-time and full-time jobs in or close to low-income areas, where many female heads of households need training and work. Public jobs can also be used in a major effort to expand work study programs to increase the employability of large numbers of young people who are not being properly prepared by the present formal educational system. In rural areas, where older adults are being dislocated as a result of economic and technological changes (as in the tobacco industry in the Southeast), an expanded public employment program might be helpful.

The burden of this analysis has been to demonstrate that a public employment program can be an effective part of an expanded and improved manpower system, but that it cannot in itself be a major instrument for promoting economic growth, redistributing income, eliminating discrimination, shifting consumer demand to public services, or eliminating substandard jobs.

18

Private and Public Manpower Policies to Stimulate Productivity

The principal thrust of this chapter is evaluative, not descriptive. The objective is to explore various manpower approaches that might lead to improved productivity in a dynamic economy and society characterized by a variety of interacting forces that contribute to change, by marked differences in entrepreneurial and industrial relations structures, and by a steady expansion of public and private measures aimed at enhancing the efficiency of the labor market without increasing the vulnerability of workers to technological and related changes.

Several constraints should be noted: the emphasis is on the sector of the economy where trade unions are strongly ensconced, and the macrodeterminants that largely determine the total level of output and employment are not considered.

The Nature of Change

Since productivity is affected by such diverse factors as technology, management, market position, demand, structure of the economy, attitudes and behavior of workers, governmental regulations, business fluctuations, as well as a host of other elements, it is difficult to outline a set of manpower policies that can be clearly related to enhancing productivity.

There are two potential resolutions. One approach frankly acknowledges the tangled skein and proceeds on the assumption that any alternative that adds to the efficiency of the labor market will contribute, at least indirectly, to the improvement of productivity. Hence an exploration of any and all manpower policies to determine which of them might contribute to the minimal efficiency of the labor market would also demonstrate which of them might contribute to gains in productivity.

The second approach recognizes that institutional changes in both the public and private domain in the United States ordinarily are responses to specific, not general, challenges. While there are difficulties in designing manpower policies that hold promise of contributing to productivity gains, this approach sets more precise bounds than an open-ended attempt to consider improvements in the operations of the labor market per se.

There may, however, be a third position, one that defines the subject area broadly without removing all constraints or boundaries. It starts with the recognition that productivity changes are always the outcome of multiple interacting forces. At the same time, it acknowledges that the rate at which desired changes can be introduced will depend in considerable measure on the reactions of the workers who will be or who believe that they will be *directly* affected by such changes. Therefore manpower policies should be concerned with the attitudes and behavior of the workers who will be directly involved in changes that are expected to lead to productivity gains.

It would be possible to broaden this focus further and include a combination of manpower policies that would be responsive also to workers who are *indirectly* affected by productivity changes. Such a broadened focus could still stop short of encompassing all members of the labor force. For instance, if a major plant that dominates a local labor market closes as a result of technological or market changes, all the workers in that community can be said to be affected and might require different types of manpower assistance. This would not make it necessary, however, for manpower programs to be equally responsive to workers in distant communities, even though their employment might be indirectly affected by the plant closure.

The principal purpose of the foregoing discussion is to underscore that the wider the net is cast to deal with the impact of productivity changes, the greater the difficulty of designing specific manpower policies that will be responsive—and the more reliance that must be placed on general manpower remedies. The narrower the focus, the greater the potentiality for specific measures.

Historical Perspectives

In 1962 Congress passed the Manpower Development and Training Act

(MDTA) in the mistaken belief that a large number of skilled workers were becoming redundant as a result of automation and that governmental intervention and assistance were required if these workers were to be retrained for profitable employment. Within twelve months it became clear that the widespread unemployment of skilled workers in 1962 did not represent dislocations caused by automation but rather was cyclic unemployment. As the economy recovered, almost all of these skilled workers were reabsorbed without retraining. At that point, Congress modified the thrust of the MDTA in the direction of improving the employability of the hard-to-employ. Through later amendments the legislation was further broadened to be more responsive to the needs of young entrants into the labor force.

Against the background of this recent history, it would be well to consider briefly the concerns of the National Commission on Productivity, a special initiative of Secretary of Labor George Shultz. One strong impetus for its establishment was the belief that gains in productivity might retard inflationary price rises. Another was the disappointing reversal in the late 1960s when, at the height of a boom, the American economy showed only modest gains in productivity. Since the establishment of the Productivity Commission, there has been growing concern with the intensified competition that the United States faces in international trade. Imports in several critical industries such as steel, autos, shoes, and textiles are commanding an ever-larger share of our domestic market, and questions have been raised about the ability of our export industries to maintain their position in the international market. Hence there has been intensified concern with productivity.

These contemporary preoccupations must be put into context, more particularly into the framework of the American economy's long-term adjustment to change, which has often been remarked upon by European observers. We have been heavily future-oriented. With a large continental market at their command, American businessmen have envisioned gains from large-scale capital investments predicated on improved technology, and American workers for the most part have been willing to accept new processes and new techniques as long as part of the gains would accrue to them in the form of higher wages and better working conditions. Moreover, American workers have been more willing than workers in Western Europe to follow the job. They have been willing to pull up roots and move to where opportunities are greater.

This openness to change has been reinforced by the fact that, except for the depressed 1930s, the thrust of the American economy has been toward steady expansion, a fact that has helped moderate worker opposition to productivity changes associated with labor-saving devices.

Workers had reason to believe that change would lead to more, not fewer, jobs. Moreover, the strong emphasis of American trade unions on job security has contributed to an openness toward change on the part of workers with seniority who believed that their jobs would not be jeopardized, even if future hires were reduced.

It is worth stressing that, with relatively few exceptions, alert management has been able to introduce new machines and new processes aimed at lessening costs without running into headlong opposition from organized labor. The classic illustrations of noncooperation exemplified by printers' setting bogus type, reductions in the size of painters' brushes, extra men in the cab or the cockpit, are conspicuous exceptions. However, beyond these cases of deliberate barriers to the reduction of labor costs, one must take note of the pervasiveness of work rules that set the pace of work and the quantity of output far below a level consistent with the health and well-being of the work force.

But work rules must be seen in context. Management is—or should be—constantly concerned with bringing about changes in the production process that will result in a reduction of labor costs. Employees are determined that they be recompensed for any changes in their accustomed ways of working, since the gains that management will achieve depend in part on workers' cooperation. Unless they are recompensed in terms of higher earnings, workers will seek to profit from the changes by shortening work time, by working less energetically, or by deriving some other benefit from the innovation. Since work rules come about as a result of an implicit or explicit agreement between management and its employees, it follows that workers will not agree to changes in the rules unless they receive some form of compensation. In their view, management's agreement to existing work rules is always in lieu of some other benefit. Thus they believe they are entitled to some form of compensation if they agree to a change in the rules at management's behest.

Because management tends to make new capital investments when it seeks to strengthen and expand its share of the market, it seldom runs afoul of labor's principal concern, which is protection of jobs and income. If these are not in jeopardy, management can usually work out an arrangement with its labor force enabling it to introduce new machines and processes. Conflicts are likely to arise only under the following conditions:

(*a*) If the work force sees a threat to its jobs or earnings from the innovations;

(*b*) If management refuses to pay a proper price for alterations in work rules required by the innovations;

(c) If the innovations threaten to alter the relative position and power of the different groups of workers (and the unions) in the plant;

(d) If the process of innovation is initiated in an atmosphere of suspicion and distrust.

There are several other observations that can be extracted from a broad review of American experience. Poor management, incremental work rules, and lagging productivity are strongly correlated. Unless the leading firms in an industry are able to compete successfully at home and abroad, they will be unable to earn the profits and attract the funds required to modernize and expand their plants. In a dynamic economy, failure to keep abreast of changes in technology, markets, and other parameters sooner or later will lead to shrinking sales, profits, and employment. Once a company or an industry loses momentum, the work force is likely to become less open to change, fearing that contemplated innovations may speed the erosion of their jobs. Moreover, firms under severe competitive pressure are less able to pay the price that labor may insist upon if it is to agree to changes that management desires to introduce.

Another aspect of productivity change is the role that business fluctuations play in effecting adjustments in the work force. Workers acknowledge the right of management to reduce the work force in the face of marked decline in the level of business. What frequently ensues, especially during a recession that lasts for a year or two, is that management makes numerous reductions in staff in its efforts to cut costs and rehires a smaller number of workers when expansion sets in.

Another classic method that facilitates the introduction of new technology occurs in multibranch firms. In this case, management expands in new plants with new machines and new methods and closes out its operations in old locations where its labor and other costs are much higher.

A further aspect of the American experience is the marked variation in the strength of organized labor in different sectors of the economy. This feature is reflected in the degree of success achieved in negotiations relating to wages and to other contract provisions, including supplemental unemployment benefits, pensions, and early retirement. In the face of such differences, it follows that public manpower policy is likely to be geared to standards that are at the middle or lower ranges, rather than at the top. Because there is such a wide spread in wages and benefits, it is desirable that any new manpower efforts directed toward stimulating gains in productivity provide maximum opportunity for labor and management to work out mutually suitable arrangements, and that government restrict itself to establishing a conducive environment and standards that are applicable to the broad array of firms. The fact that state governments play a role in setting the levels of some benefits—unemployment insurance, for example—is a further basis for recommending elasticity in bargaining positions, rather than federally prescribed approaches and standards.

As will be clear subsequently, while this approach places primary responsibility on the partners to collective bargaining to find apposite solutions, it still leaves considerable scope for governmental policy.

Private Arrangements

There is a marked parallel between the approaches used by the principals in collective bargaining on both sides of the Atlantic when dealing with the facilitation of productivity changes. While differences in terminology or emphasis can be noted—for instance, the much-touted "productivity bargaining" in Great Britain at the beginning of the 1960s had long been described in the United States as "sharing the gains from increasing productivity"—the striking finding is the degree of similarity in the treatment of the problem. In short, a review of the European experience does not uncover principles and techniques that have not been tried in this country. What one can derive from such a review, however, is knowledge about the value of various approaches—at least to the countries examined.

One of the most important findings from a comparative analysis is the extent to which the countries of Western Europe still see the issue of adjustments to productivity change as lying primarily within the private domain. Although government does play a role, the principal actors are labor and management; the principal instrument is collective bargaining. For the purposes of this section, we shall deal with two private approaches: ongoing adjustments and compensatory assistance.

Manpower planning.   If there is one arena in which the Europeans may be said to have the jump on the United States, it is manpower planning. There has been a general reluctance on the part of American management to take labor into its confidence with respect to any large-scale changes that carry with them the threat of serious reductions in the work force. Management has feared that such discussions would result in severe losses such as alerting competitors to impending changes, inducing the departure of key workers, and other untoward consequences. Hence it has tended to play its cards close to its chest.

Moreover, American trade unions generally have not bid for a role in broad decision-making affecting investment, markets, and product lines.

They have been willing to leave these matters to management, believing that their increased strength depends upon restricting themselves to bargaining about wages and the conditions of work. This stance has prevented them from assuming a major role in decisions about important technological and related changes. It is worth observing that the two outstanding instances of formal advance manpower planning for major technological changes—telephone dialing in the Bell System and computerization in the Internal Revenue Service—both involved noncompetitive situations. There are signs that American trade unions are becoming increasingly interested in contractual stipulations that provide them with prior information about company decisions that are likely to result in major disruptions or declines in employment, such as those that accompany the closure of a plant.

European trade unions have gone much further than their American counterparts in seeking an active role in the decision-making process within the firm; witness the codetermination structure in Germany. Even when trade union representatives are a part of management, however, there is no assurance that the work force will readily accept changes that will bring significant alterations in employment, wages, or other conditions of work.

In Sweden, arrangements have been worked out between management and labor for regular consultation aimed at improving productivity by providing the work force with technical and planning information. Employees are informed about the position of the firm and the actions that it wishes to take to strengthen and improve its competitive position. The usual devices for such consultation are joint study committees or work councils. The presumption is that workers who know the alternatives that management faces and the actions necessary to maintain or improve productivity will be less resistant to the proposed changes. To the extent that workers have confidence and trust in the competence and integrity of the management, to that extent will their cooperation in accepting innovations be forthcoming.

The effectiveness of such manpower planning depends, in considerable measure, on the extent to which management is open and responsive to workers' counterproposals concerning the best ways of adjusting to the contemplated changes. If management limits itself to providing advance information, it may smooth its way. But the critical issue is whether management is willing to sit down and engage in a give-and-take with representatives of the workers so that the final decisions represent a balancing of the employer's need to introduce innovations and of the union's desire to obtain a share of the benefits and to avoid undue hardship for individual workers. Union leaders in most instances, are under severe pressure to reject arrangements that will adversely affect any significant minority of workers; because of this, American management is loath to let them share in decision-making about innovations that may reduce labor inputs.

There are additional difficulties with respect to manpower planning at the corporate level. Business leaders have more know-how in devising new ways of producing goods and services than in assessing the manpower implications of such innovations, particularly in terms of the adverse effects on particular groups of workers. Manpower planning is a new technique, and corporate manpower planning can at best make only a minor contribution to rasing productivity. Nevertheless, manpower planning efforts in large companies, paralleling their technical efforts to improve productivity, hold promise that some of the preexistent difficulties stemming from ignorance or neglect of the manpower consequences of new technology and other managerial innovations eventually will be lessened, if not eliminated.

An active corporate manpower policy can, in fact, contribute to facilitating productivity changes. Reference was made earlier to the experience of the telephone industry and of the Internal Revenue Service. To a marked degree, they relied on attrition to resolve manpower disturbances incident to the introduction of a radically new technology. In addition, they used such techniques as transfers, special assistance with placements within and outside the company, opportunities for workers to be retrained in order to meet new skill requirements, and other devices to lessen dislocation.

Another dimension of manpower planning is typified by the efforts of unions representing plumbers and typographers. In recognition of the major changes occurring in the technology of their respective industries, these unions have invested sizable sums to train journeymen to cope with the new machines and processes. In the case of plumbers and pipefitters, the sums required to finance the program—of the order of $1 million annually—are raised from union contractors; the training program is administered jointly with Purdue University, which provides special instruction for the training staff. In slightly more than a decade 80,000 journeymen have been retrained. The printers' training and retraining effort is financed by the International Typographical Union, which spent aobut $2 million in the early 1960s to establish and equip a thoroughly modern school in Colorado Springs. One of the interesting aspects of the program is that union members usually attend on their own time—during vacations—and must pay for room and board either out of their own pockets or with the assistance of their local unions.

These two examples from the American scene have much in common with the experience in various European coutries, where management and labor have cooperated to establish training and retraining opportunities so that the work force can stay abreast of rapidly changing technology.

One might call attention to the original British law providing for industry training through joint employer efforts, financed by a training tax. In exceptional cases the government undertakes to provide the required instruction. The British approach recognizes the need for substantial and continuing training and upgrading if Great Britain is to remain competitive in the markets of the world. It should be observed that after this legislation was passed in 1965, the British hardly proceeded with "all deliberate speed." With the exception of a few industries, the efforts were still in the take-off stage more than five years later.

We are forced to conclude that manpower planning in the private sector on both sides of the Atlantic is still embryonic, although there has been a recent emergence of the art of corporate manpower planning. Otherwise, action has been limited by the lack of experience of most industries with management- labor consultation regarding productivity and related changes; the reluctance of American management to include these issues within the scope of collective bargaining; and the time and costs involved in building responsive institutions, such as new training structures. Within these limitations it is worth noting that most efforts that have been launched have relied largely on cooperation within the private sector. The government is pretty well out of the picture.

Adjustments affecting productivity. Every industrialized economy is subject to change. Every alert management seeks to anticipate and respond to new developments—technological and market—to improve its efficiency and to control, if not reduce, its costs. Every trade union strives continuously to get a greater share of increased productivity for its members. These forces in a modern economy lead to the conclusion that issues of productivity are a major concern of all collective bargaining, directly or indirectly. Management is striving for ways to gain worker approval so that productivity can be increased; all workers are striving to obtain a quid pro quo for acceptance of the changes that management desires. The process of negotiation and settlement is a never-ending one, for no sooner is one arrangement reached than the negotiated situation is buffeted by fresh forces. Management is constantly on the lookout for changes that may contribute to further gains in productivity, and workers will not cooperate unless they are offered something of value in return.

To the extent that the foregoing is a reasonable facsimile of what goes on in the arena of labor-management relations, it follows that many solutions that have developed as a result of collective bargaining are intertwined with efforts to stimulate productivity. For productivity gains—broadly defined—are the key to management's goal. Without such gains, profits will erode and markets disappear; the firm cannot survive.

Brief consideration should be paid, therefore, to a range of approaches that are part and parcel of collective bargaining arrangements, in order to assess their relevance to stimulating improvements in productivity. Among the most important are union-management cooperation, group incentives, and work-rule settlements. Others involve training and retraining, job design and redesign, adjustment of hours and work schedules, elimination of seasonal fluctuations, and the policing of worker behavior. Additional devices might be considered as potential contributors to enhancing productivity, but we shall limit our attention to what we believe to be the three most important.

For the most part, organized workers in industrialized settings look upon management from an adversary point of view, that is to say, they are generally unwilling to offer suggestions about how things could be done better—more quickly and with less waste—unless there is something in it for them. They believe that if they are not careful they run the risk of becoming victimized in the very act of seeking to help management improve its productivity, since certain workers may become redundant as a result. Despite this conventional adversary or bargaining relation whereby suggestions are offered by workers only if they lead to potential rewards, there have been occasional successful efforts by management to elicit worker cooperation without immediate and direct recompense. An American case frequently cited in this respect is consultation in the Tennessee Valley Authority, where representatives of management and workers at different levels in the organization review monthly suggested improvements originating from either group.

A second case relates to union-management attempts to improve plant safety in the West Coast pulp and paper industry. Since there are many small employers in the industry, the union plays the dominant role in this effort, which has proved highly successful since World War II. The injury-frequency rate has dropped by about seven-eighths and is now far below the rates prevailing in comparable plants in other parts of the country.

A third related approach is that carried on by the Industrial Engineering Department of the International Ladies Garment Workers Union where, in response to requests by both small and large employers, union technicians make their skills available to assist management in improving the scheduling, subdivision, and allocation of work. Having developed substantial expertise in connection with its wage negotiations, the union believes that it is to the benefit of its members to make these skills available to employers who are struggling to survive in a highly competitive environment in which many will fail unless they can improve their productivity. The union recognizes the close links between improved productivity for the employer and job security and higher wages for its members.

The Joint Study Committees of Works Councils in Sweden, and some of the arrangements worked out as part of the codetermination model in West Germany, are similarly directed toward finding a common ground on which management and labor can cooperate to improve a firm's productivity.

However, it is in Japan where such efforts have proved most successful, especially in some of its best managed firms. I recall seeing plant engineers hold regular sessions with semiskilled workers to elicit their recommendations about materials, adjustment of the machines, and other details aimed at increasing the firm's productivity. Inquiry disclosed that in one firm, a leading manufacturer and exporter of electronic equipment, such supervisor-worker sessions were held at the work site twice weekly, each lasting an average of thirty minutes. It is interesting to speculate how much longer cooperation rather than confrontation will be characteristic of Japanese industry.

The increasing importance of continuous processing in modern manufacturing has led to a lessened reliance on piece-work systems of wage payment. Correspondingly, management has had less opportunity to make use of individual bonus payments as a spur to higher productivity. Instead, it has begun to experiment with group bonus schemes. Even after many years of experimentation, particularly with the Scanlon Plan and its variations, the fact remains that the group bonus approach has not taken deep root in the United States. The essence of the plan is a bonus based on a ratio of total payroll to product sales. Through joint committees with management, workers present suggestions for increasing productivity and, if the payroll ratio declines, part of the gain is distributed as a group bonus. Many workers evinced only limited interest in the plan because of the small amount of money available for distribution; and many managements are dubious that workers are really entitled to a bonus, since a decline in payroll costs need not reflect worker contribution.

A large-scale move in the direction of a group bonus plan was the Kaiser Steel Workers' Long-Range Sharing Plan. The principal objectives, worked out with the assistance of outside experts, were two-fold: basic elimination of individual bonuses, and more flexibility for management to introduce new machinery or to modify existing production processes. The outcome is equivocal. Many workers, given the option, refused to shift from an individual to a group bonus; in certain years the fluctuating group bonus was disturbingly small; and workers did not agree to give management the wide latitude it sought for the introduction of cost survey approaches. The plan has not been replicated in any other steel plant. On balance, use of the bonus route to speed worker acceptance of changes leading to increased productivity has not progressed very far.

The essence of the confrontation between management and labor over the initiation of such changes is nowhere better illustrated than in cases where long-established work rules must be altered if new productivity gains are to be made. As indicated earlier, work rules represent a form of settlement negotiated by management and labor in lieu of adjustments in wages, hours, or other benefits. Hence, once in place, they cannot be removed by unilateral action of management but must be bargained away. Often the price is high in dollar or other terms. In the case of West Coast longshoremen, the original dollar cost of attempts to rationalize the handling of cargo came to $27 million of benefits to union members. Later studies revealed that the employers were well satisfied with the bargain they had made because of still greater savings in labor costs and in time spent in handling freight movements. More recently, the threat of containerization and progressive methods of off-dock loading and unloading has created new frictions between management and the union, underscoring that even a highly successful arrangement is likely to become unsettled as new issues come to the fore.

Much concern has been expressed over the years about "bogus work" in the printing industry, although an inquiry in the 1960s revealed that only about 2 to 5 percent of all locals were still engaged in such make-work activity. Most locals had bargained away their rights for coffee breaks, overtime, time off, sick leaves, and other types of paid leave. A management that must deal with costly, featherbedding printers is a management that probably slipped twice: when it first agreed to the practice, and when it later failed to buy itself out.

What we have then—at least in the United States—are collective bargaining arrangements that occasionally make use of consultative devices for exploring new approaches to work as a way of improving productivity; that more often resort to group bonus plans to serve the same end; and that even more frequently involve bargaining procedures that force management to pay a price (often a substantial price) to get rid of particular work rules that stand in the way of greater productivity.

Compensatory assistance. Even if manpower planning were more effective than it actually is, and even if adjustments through collective bargaining arrangements were able to remove obstacles to productivity gains to a greater extent than they can, the incontrovertible fact is that in a fair number of situations, the survival of a firm or industry may require a scale of adjustment that will have widespread and deleterious effects on the welfare and well-being of a significant part of its work force.

In such situations the basic challenge is to determine a range of compensatory devices to assure the workers affected that they will not be forced to bear the burden in the form of loss of job, loss of income, or loss of other benefits. This is an imperfect world, and it is probably not possible to assure that the affected workers suffer no losses whatever, but the quality of a society can be assessed in part by the efforts it is willing to make to prevent the costs of progress from being borne by those whom fate has placed in the path of the juggernaut. At a minimum, a civilized society—especially one that is affluent—should provide a range of benefits and protections for the innocent victims of change. Here we are concerned only with measures that fall within the province of the private sector, recognizing that additional actions of a remedial nature can be initiated and carried out within the public domain, either exclusively or in cooperation with the private sector.

The well-publicized history of the plant closings of Armour and Company in the early and middle 1960s can serve as background to the different types of arrangements that moderate the dislocations suffered by long-term employees as the result of a company's actions to improve its competitive position by modernizing and relocating its plants.

One of the simplest approaches is to give notice of the change. At first Armour limited itself to ninety days; later, it agreed to a six-month lead time. The longer the lead time, the better the opportunities for workers to find alternative local employment, to enter training programs, or to explore opportunities in other labor markets.

The company also made an offer to transfer workers to another plant, but only a minority took advantage of this possibility. Many were reluctant to uproot themselves from the communities where they had been born or had lived for many years; others were uncertain whether they could adjust to a new working and residential environment. Hence, they preferred to accept lump-sum severance pay instead.

Later on, the company broadened its transfer offer to include the opportunity to try out a new job in a new locale. If a worker didn't like it—or couldn't make it—he had "flow-back rights," which meant that he could return to his old location without loss of benefits, including moving expenses and separation pay. Far more workers were willing to accept a transfer under these conditions.

Many of the older long-term workers were unable to find new jobs. They received monthly retirement payments, eventually pegged at a minimum of $150. Other workers found jobs, but earned considerably less than previously. The most helpful adjustment in their case probably would have been the provision of higher early-retirement benefits.

Railpax built on this and related experience with respect to workers on interurban passenger railroads who are released or downgraded. The Secretary of Labor approved a guarantee that, for a period of six years, such workers would receive the full wage of their former jobs, including increases. In addition, provision was made for the maintenance of full fringe benefits, moving expenses for relocation, separation allowances, and compensation for losses involved in the sale of homes and cancellation of leases.

These liberal arrangements do not apply to the bulk of the work force in the freight end of the railroads. The principal relief for most railroad workers threatened by technological change has been in the form of agreements to reduce the work force primarily through attrition accompanied by varying types of wage guarantees, rather than through precipitous forced separation. While such arrangements often have been difficult to achieve and have led to conflicts in implementation, the fact remains that during the last three decades large numbers of workers were removed from the railroad work rolls in a more or less orderly fashion, and in a manner that offered most of them considerable protection until they could find other jobs or until they reached retirement age.

In most respects the European experience parallels the approaches that have been delineated above—particularly the use of attrition, early notification of closure, severance pay, retraining and relocation allowances, supplemental payments to assure previous earning levels, and early retirement.

Increasingly, long advance notice is being given. In some European countries monetary compensation is preferred in lieu of notice. Some employers fear that reliance upon attrition results in a distorted age structure among the remaining work force and that, in one-industry towns, new firms are discouraged from entering.

In Sweden trade unions urge that the amount of severance pay be geared to the difficulties workers face in finding alternative employment, rather than only on work experience and earnings, as is the rule in most European plans. There is awareness in some European countries that the value of early retirement schemes depends on the adequacy of the money involved. If the sum is too small, it will fail to provide the alternative adjustment that a redundant older worker requires.

An additional method that has won varying degrees of favor among the countries of Western Europe is adjustment of the workweek in order to apportion the reduced workload among a larger group of workers. It is recognized that this device has severe limitations because it may lead to inefficient operations and the retention of an excess work force. Thus many potential gains from the introduction of technological or related improvements would be eroded.

The timing of work force adjustments is less equivocal. Spacing separations, or gearing them to an expansion in local and neighborhood employment, has proved successful. Time off with no loss of pay is a device that some European firms have used to facilitate the job search of potentially redundant workers.

Large corporations that are closing down or moving away may make special efforts to facilitate the location of new firms in the area in the hope and expectation that they will provide employment opportunities for workers who are being left behind. A related device used by firms that face a sudden surplus of workers is to make special efforts to arrange placements with other companies in the immediate vicinity or even some distance away.

While it is not easy to quantify the extent to which these various devices have become accepted practices in different European countries, it is fair to say that the most responsive countries, among which Sweden appears to be the leader, have been experimenting and institutionalizing a wider range of mechanisms to smooth worker readjustment than has the United States.

Public Policies

As noted earlier, in both Europe and the United States the major effort to cope with the manpower dimensions of productivity changes has taken place in the private domain, primarily through collective bargaining. But there is a series of public programs which, although addressed to other social and economic needs, has a potential to contribute to solving the problems of workers affected by productivity changes. These programs include social security, particularly the opportunity to receive benefits at the 80-percent level at age 62; unemployment insurance, sometimes reinforced by privately bargained supplemental benefits; public training and retraining programs, particularly those of the Manpower Development and Training Act; and Federal-State Employment Service counseling, placement, mobility allowances, and related forms of assistance. These and other public manpower and manpower-related programs are available to workers who meet stipulated criteria, including many who have suffered a loss of employment or income consequent to productivity changes in the enterprise where they had been employed.

The important points to note in this connection are that the aforementioned benefits were developed without consideration for the special disabilities that workers are likely to experience as a result of productivity adjustments; and that such national or federal-state programs are likely to pay relatively low benefits—far below what is needed to ensure that workers displaced by productivity changes can continue to enjoy their accustomed standard of living, or anything close to it.

In addition to this basic structure of support and assistance, brief reference should be made to Trade Readjustment Allowances which, under a complex of safeguards, provide special assistance to workers who lose their jobs as a result of import competition resulting from tariff concessions. Workers may receive up to 65 percent of their average weekly wage, or of the average weekly manufacturing wage, whichever is less, for a maximum period of 52 weeks unless they are in training, in which case they may receive pay for 26 additional weeks (13 weeks for those over 60 years of age). If they cannot find suitable employment in their normal place of residence, they may receive relocation allowances equivalent to two and one-half times the average weekly manufacturing wage plus reasonable expenses incurred in moving their families and household effects to the new employment location. Despite the fact that the legislation has been on the books for the better part of a decade, by 1971, Department of Labor certifications had affected only about 10,000 workers at a total cost of about $7 million. Most of the assistance has been in the form of allowances. Few workers have been retrained, and fewer relocated.

A related program has been Adjustment Assistance under the Automotive Products Trade Act of 1965. In the three years prior to its expiration, certificates were issued to 2,500 workers in six states. About 1,950 workers received weekly payments totaling $4.1 million. Only 100 workers received training, at a cost of $61,000. Despite the restricted use of these adjustment procedures, it must be acknowledged that the provision of special benefits to workers who have lost jobs and income as a result of national trade policy represents a significant departure.

Against this background of domestic experience, it is worth observing the more ambitious efforts and experiments that have been undertaken in the public domain in Western Europe and Canada to ease the adjustment problems of workers adversely affected by technological and related changes.

Europeans favor legislating minimum standards to which the private sector must adhere. Specifically, such legislation requires employers to provide the following: severance pay to redundant workers; portability of private pensions; advance notice to the Employment Service; and obligatory consultation with representatives of the workers.

In the view of Europeans, such legislative standards help to ensure at least minimum performance; assure benefits to all workers, rather than only those who belong to strong unions; help to equalize labor costs among a large number of firms; reduce barriers to mobility resulting from private pension programs; and generally stimulate manpower and personnel planning and management.

There are additional dimensions of the European experience relevant to the problem at hand. A relatively high level of employment has been conducive to the reabsorption of redundant workers, except those nearing retirement age. When older workers lose their jobs, they face major problems in finding work and many retire. To assist disemployed older workers, several European countries have experimented with subsidized training and employment within industry, with sheltered work, and with income maintenance. Without elaboration, one can say that none of these efforts has been particularly successful. The Swedes, who have again been the most active in this regard, are increasingly worried about the growing numbers of older workers being cast upon the public sector for employment and support. Several countries are seeking ways of facilitating the early transition of older workers to the pension system if they lose their regular employment several years before they would normally qualify.

A final aspect of foreign experience that should be noted relates to the efforts of several countries to establish closer coordination between private and public adjustment policies. The earlier reference to legislative standards is relevant here. Also germane is the establishment of the Canadian Consultation Service, in which governmental experts use their good auspices to facilitate agreements between management and workers. In Great Britain, public sector enterprises (such as the British railways) were requested to adapt their employment reduction program to the government's regional employment objectives. In France, a major steel producer who was closing down a plant was able to secure government cooperation in building an industrial park and inducing new firms to hire the dismissed steel workers.

Foreign governments have also moved to make public facilities available to private companies for the retraining of their work force. And in several countries governmental agencies provide special manpower services for small companies faced with difficult adjustment problems, such as testing employees and facilitating their job hunt and transfer. The commitment of all sectors to a policy of high employment makes such collaboration between the public and private sectors easier, as does a consensus that it is important for people not to be victimized by change and to be afforded every assistance to remain employed and self-supporting.

It will be difficult, unless and until we succeed in achieving a much lower level of unemployment, for the United States to borrow liberally from the elaborate panoply of measures devised by Europeans, either in the public arena alone or in collaboration with the private sector, in order to ease the adjustment of redundant workers.

New Directions

This discussion has reviewed different private and public manpower policies that might be introduced or strengthened to facilitate improved productivity in the American economy. The following brief checklist indicates the principal directions where new initiatives hold promise of constructive advances.

——A declaration of public policy stressing the twin objectives of speeding productivity changes and of assuring that the workers adversely affected will receive due compensation for injuries suffered as a consequence.

——Acknowledgment by key leadership groups that there is broad scope for the creation of a more conducive environment for speeding productivity changes through improving both private and public manpower policies.

——Establishment of a technical assistance service, panel, or group of consultants to work with management and labor in facilitating manpower adjustments to productivity change.

——New or improved private, public, and joint manpower programs:

(a) Compulsory vesting of private pensions after a qualifying period of ten years or so. (In 1974 Congress passed the Employee Retirement Income Security Act with full vesting after ten years as one option.)

(b) Liberalization of the Social Security system to permit earlier receipt of pensions by displaced workers.

(c) More liberal mobility allowances for workers seeking employment in new locations.

——A higher degree of coordination among government procurement policies, regional development policies, and manpower policies to moderate adverse effects of productivity changes and to facilitate the reemployment of displaced workers.

——Improvement of the interstate clearance system of the Employment Service and introduction of other efforts to strengthen its services to displaced workers.

Above all, the federal government must recognize that the sine qua non for an environment that is conducive to the stimulation of productivity is a continuing high level of employment. Otherwise there is little prospect of success for private or public manpower policies directed toward facilitating the adjustment of workers affected by productivity changes.

19

The Manpower Reach of Federal Policies

Federal programs specifically designed to influence the supply, demand, or utilization of manpower represent a relatively small proportion of all governmental actions that have an impact upon the nation's human resources and requirements. The principal focus of national manpower policy has been upon the provision of training and work experience for the unemployed and underemployed. There are, however, large numbers of other federal policies that have direct and indirect manpower implications. In fact, most federal expenditures, as well as a wide variety of federally imposed standards and controls, have major impacts upon manpower.

In order to illustrate the manpower reach of diverse governmental policies, this chapter will discuss a variety of federal programs that impinge directly or indirectly upon manpower. Although there are many instances where a particular policy produces multiple types of repercussions, for schematic purposes this analysis will deal sequentially with governmental actions primarily affecting the supply, demand, or utilization of manpower.

Policies Affecting Manpower Supply

The federal government has a long history of involvement in activities affecting both the quality and quantity of the country's human resources. Its principal influence upon quality has been through selective support of education and training. Immigration regulations have affected both the numbers and nature of the manpower supply, and social security legislation has had an impact upon the size and age composition of the labor force.

Education and training.   The basic goal of education in the United States has been to produce an informed citizenry. While the acquisition of occupational skills is an important by-product of the educational process, and is often a specific objective of educational efforts, few persons regard it as the primary goal. Nevertheless, many federal programs designed to improve education have directly affected the character of the nation's labor force. The federal government's support of education began as early as 1862, when land grant colleges were authorized by the Morrill Act. These institutions, initially directed at strengthening agricultural and technical expertise, eventually provided broad access to higher education for significant numbers of the nation's youth. There is little doubt that the availability of public higher education has made a substantial contribution to raising the quality of the nation's manpower.

The federal government has been involved in the support of vocational education since World War I. Such programs by their very nature have direct manpower effects, insofar as they are designed to facilitate the acquisition of skills by members of the work force. They differ from the more recently inaugurated manpower programs by virtue of the fact that they were not designed primarily to serve disadvantaged population groups, but are basic components of the secondary school and community college systems.

The federal-state program of vocational education has been a principal source of formal training for occupations that do not require a senior college education. Over the years the program has been repeatedly modified and expanded. Federal expenditures—a small part of the total—increased more than sixfold during the 1960 decade, from $45 million to $300 million. Although there have been serious criticisms of the effectiveness of vocational education in general, and of certain programs in pa.ticular, there is little question that many young people have received occupational orientation and basic skill training through vocational courses.

In response to the Sputnik trauma, the National Defense Education Act (NDEA) was passed in 1958 as a major step in widening the involvement of the federal government in the production of an increased supply of scientific and professional manpower. By the mid-1960s, 40 percent of all graduate students in science, engineering, and mathematics were being supported by federally financed fellowships or traineeships.

These NDEA programs together with other types of federal support contributed to the very rapid growth of highly specialized manpower during the 1960s. But, as noted in Chapter 11, with the shift in the federal budget in the late 1960s and early 1970s, the number of graduates of doctoral programs began to exceed the current and prospective demand, as a result of which federal support for graduate education was cut back substantially or eliminated in most fields.

The major exception has been support for the training of additional medical manpower. Federal dollars were used to encourage medical schools to expand enrollment, to reduce the training period, and to convert two-year institutions of basic sciences to four-year medical schools. These efforts, together with other forces favoring expansion (mostly new state schools), will result in an estimated doubling of physician output by the end of the 1970s.

In addition, the federal government is attempting to increase the supply of other types of health manpower—dentists, nurses, and health professionals of various sorts. One possible consequence of these energetic efforts is a likely oversupply of health manpower in the not-distant future, similar to that engendered in other fields by the NDEA. Clearly, federal involvement in the training of high-level manpower can lead to excessive response.

The federal government entered a new educational realm in 1965 with the passage of the Elementary and Secondary Education Act which, for the first time, made federal funds available for the support of general education below the college level, with special emphasis on strengthening schools in low-income areas. On the surface, this type of support has no direct impact on manpower, except for the employment of additional teaching staff. However, federal governmental financing occurred in large measure because of the growing recognition that many adults were experiencing difficulties in the labor market as a result of serious deficiencies in their early schooling. It was hoped that massive injections of money ($2 billion in fiscal 1972) into school systems with substantial numbers of pupils from deprived backgrounds would provide a stronger foundation for later skill acquisition, and thereby help to upgrade the caliber of future workers.

Immigration. The curtailment of immigration to the United States placed restrictions not only on the size of the manpower inflow from abroad, but also on its source and character. Quotas based upon national origin were imposed as early as the 1920s, limiting immigration largely to Europeans and North and South Americans; no more than 100 Asians per year were admitted to the United States.

While the formula was adjusted in subsequent decades, the first major revision did not occur until 1965, when quotas based on occupational skill were substituted for those based on national origin. This resulted in the admission of thousands of foreign professionals who helped to meet an expanding demand for scientists, engineers, physicians, and nurses. As a partial consequence, the annual addition of immigrants to the domestic physician supply is approximately equivalent to the yearly total of graduates from American medical schools. Although the decline in demand for professional workers after 1969 resulted in a drastic curtailment of labor certification for aliens, physicians and four other types of health workers still receive automatic certification.

At the lower end of the occupational scale, recent immigration policies have operated to control the agricultural labor force. Legislation that had authorized the admission of Mexican farm workers expired at the end of 1964. Instead of the 300,000 seasonal farm laborers who had been admitted annually since 1960, their numbers dropped precipitously and since 1968 none have been legally admitted. Nevertheless, illegal immigrants, primarily from Mexico and other Latin American countries, continue to enter the United States; a substantial number find a temporary or quasi-permanent place in the labor force. Although about 420,000 illegal aliens were apprehended in 1971 alone, millions of others remain undetected.

Social Security.   Laws and regulations governing the conditions under which workers are entitled to retirement benefits have important manpower consequences. The availability of such benefits has acted to decrease the labor force participation of persons over 65, and amendments permitting earlier retirement with lower benefits have resulted in a significant drop in the proportion of workers between 62 and 65.

On the other hand, periodic increases in the ceiling on earnings after retirement without loss of benefits (presently $2,400 a year) have added somewhat to the numbers of older workers, although by no means sufficiently to offset the effect of early retirement.

Policies Affecting Manpower Demand

One of the principal ways in which the federal government influences the demand for manpower is through appropriations for the purchase of goods and services. The government may be the primary or sole supplier of funds or a major purchaser; in either case its expenditures are bound to have significant sequellae in terms of the manpower requirements of different employers, industries, occupations, and regions.

Defense.   The rapid expansion of defense spending after 1964 had important manpower consequences. Defense spending increased from $51 billion to $78 billion between 1964 and 1968. As a result, almost two million more jobs were created in defense or defense-related industries. This was relatively high-paid work, which frequently required considerable overtime at premium pay. In addition, the rising demand for workers in these industries provided blacks and other minorities with new employment opportunities.

The rapid decline in defense spending after 1968 resulted in a decrease of about two million jobs, corresponding to the earlier increase. Clearly, the defense budget has a major impact on manpower demand.

Space.   The experience in the defense arena is paralleled by the history of the space program. Total expenditures for space grew from about three-quarters of a billion dollars in 1961 to $6 billion in 1966. Accompanying this rise was an increase in employment, primarily among NASA contractors, from 47,000 to 410,000.

Subsequently, the space budget was cut drastically and, as a consequence, NASA-supported employment in 1971 dropped to 144,000. Scientists and engineers were severely affected; half as many were employed in 1971 as in 1966. The unemployment rate for displaced engineers rose to over 6 percent, more than twice the rate for the entire profession. In recognition of the federal responsibility for the curtailment of engineering jobs, a number of special programs were established to provide assistance in reemployment, relocation, and retraining.

Research and development.   The demand for highly trained technical personnel was also expanded in the wake of increased federal expenditures for research and development (R&D). Federal appropriations for R&D increased at an annual average rate of 16 percent in the 1950s and 8 percent between 1961 and 1967. Over the next four years, the growth rate dropped to one-half of one percent in current dollars which, when corrected for inflation, actually meant a yearly decline of about 4 percent. Such an expenditure curve cannot fail to have the most serious repercussions on employment of specialists, especially in an area in which the federal government has accounted for the bulk of the total national expenditure (almost two-thirds at the peak in 1964).

It is clear that shifts in major federal programs can lead directly to the employment or unemployment of large numbers of workers. Moreover, since government contractors and subcontractors frequently are concentrated in a limited number of locations, shifts in the level and direction of federal expenditures can have severe repercussions on local and regional economies.

Health.   The expanded role of the federal government in health programming has had a profound effect upon the demand for manpower. By 1970, five years after the introduction of Medicare and Medicaid, personal expenditures for health care in current dollars had risen from $35 billion to $62 billion; 40 percent of the increase reflected expanded federal outlays. The infusion of so much additional money partially reflected a greater need for employees in all health occupations, particularly for hospital support personnel, because of higher demand for services by the aged and the low-income beneficiaries of these programs.

Policies Affecting Manpower Utilization

In addition to programs that directly influence the supply of or the requirements for various types of manpower, a number of federal policies also affect the utilization of manpower. Three illustrations relate to farming, residents of suburbs and inner cities, and special groups such as youth and women.

Agricultural supports.   At no stage in this country's long-term efforts to raise farm incomes through the use of commodity price supports and incentives for crop limitation has there been a systematic assessment of the manpower implications of these support policies. Yet they have had a pronounced impact upon the farm labor force.

Agricultural workers in 1930 represented 20 percent of the total civilian work force; by 1950, their proportion was 12 percent; and by 1970, the figure had dropped to 4.5 percent. Although rapid advances in agricultural technology stimulated by government-financed research, changes in marketing arrangements, and the expansion of nonfarm employment contributed to this decline, many experts are convinced that by reducing the cost of capital relative to labor, the government's subsidization policies sped the decline in farm labor.

The large-scale and more affluent farmers received the bulk of the cash benefits; as they made greater investments in fixed capital, they sought well-trained managers, supervisors, and equipment operators. Many farm owners and laborers were unable to compete with graduates of specialized agricultural courses. Hence this form of federal subsidy not only reduced the number of those directly employed in agriculture, it accelerated the migration of rural workers to the cities.

Housing and transportation.   Residential housing loans underwritten by the Federal Housing Administration increased from under $1 billion in 1940 to more than $13 billion in 1971. An additional $4 billion in mortgage loans was provided by the Veterans Administration. The availability of liberal federal loans to home purchasers and substantial tax benefits to homeowners facilitated the flight of middle-income whites to the suburbs. Left behind in the central cities are minorities and the poor.

Federal aid to state and local governments for the expansion and improvement of highways also contributed to the suburbanization of the middle class by facilitating their commuting to work. Annual federal assistance for highway construction rose from half a billion dollars in the early 1950s to a level of about $4 billion a year.

Although differences among metropolitan areas prevent generalizations about the employment implications of suburbanization, certain tendencies can be identified. Minority and low-income groups have largely been excluded from access to the burgeoning manufacturing and service jobs in the suburbs, among other reasons because of the scarcity of public transportation and the high cost of suburban housing. Thus new suburban employment opportunities are available mainly to middle-class workers living in adjacent communities. Simultaneously the highway network assures suburbanites of access to desirable jobs in the central city where they constitute a preferred labor supply.

Wage policies.   Periodic increases in the minimum wage under the Fair Labor Standards Act have had important effects upon manpower. With rises in the minimum, some marginal jobs may be eliminated and employers will seek more productive workers for their lowest-paid jobs. As a consequence, although many marginal workers may gain from an increase in the statutory minimum, others may encounter added difficulties in finding jobs. This is especially true in a loose labor market—and most often with respect to new entrants into the labor force, particularly those from minority groups.

Tax policies.   Major changes in tax legislation can have significant manpower implications. Changes in tax rates, joint filing, and business deductions are likely to have some influence on the number of employed workers, as well as upon hours of work. Tax credits to stimulate new investment or to encourage the employment of certain kinds of workers, such as welfare recipients, can have a direct impact upon utilization. Moreover, recent action to increase deductions for child care should serve to raise the labor force participation of younger women, as well as to assist those in the labor force who desire to continue working.

Conclusions

This review of selected federal policies is designed to demonstrate some of the ways in which diverse governmental actions affect the nation's manpower resources. A myriad of other policies could be cited, since every decision of the federal government is likely to have some manpower implications.

Although there is little question that a wide variety of federal policies affect manpower, there has been no systematic assessment of these consequences. There are several ways in which this might be accomplished.

Each major federal agency should be required to establish a manpower analysis unit charged with assessing the manpower implications of significant changes in its prospective expenditure pattern. In addition, a government-wide mechanism should be established, preferably in the Office of Management and Budget, to examine the analyses of the individual agencies and to explore the range of compensatory actions that might be taken to avoid negative consequences on particular industries, occupations, and communities.

Through a broadening of its own staff and closer liaison with the Department of Labor, the Council of Economic Advisers should give greater consideration to the employment effects of alternative economic policies. The days are over when a preoccupation with fiscal, monetary, and budgetary policies was sufficient to assure a noninflationary high-employment economy.

The report of the Commission on Population Growth and the American Future has drawn attention to the urgent necessity for a national policy combining considerations of population growth, economic development, and manpower decisions. The fact that we are very far from producing an adequate theory, much less an adequate policy, for regional development underscores the need for additional effort in these directions.

Finally, leadership is required to explore how the federal budget can be translated into manpower terms. Such an attempt holds promise of a substantial gain in public understanding and the national welfare. President Nixon in 1972 directed the Secretary of Labor to determine how such a translation might be accelerated. *The Manpower Report of the President, 1975* contains an interim report on the progress to date. Those in high policy positions must recognize the close linkages between this translation effort and the maintenance of a high-employment economy, and make more resources available to develop an appropriate methodology. Otherwise progress is likely to be slow, for the difficulties are substantial.

20

Urban Manpower: A Research Strategy

The views of the public and of specialists about the manpower problems of large cities are dominated by the following assumptions:

——There is an insufficiency of jobs in the cities for all who are able and willing to work.

——A large number of jobs pay so poorly that they do not enable the incumbents to support their families.

——Many families live under dysfunctional conditions that diminish their lives and prevent the development of their children's potential.

—— Serious inequities among different groups tend to persist despite society's commitment to equality of opportunity.

——Even with the passage of time, those trapped in the city's slums will not be able to extricate themselves.

Such gloomy diagnoses can lead to passivity and inaction, thereby becoming self-fulfilling prophecies. Since no city can look to time alone to cure its ills, it must organize to make sounder decisions today so that a better future will emerge. Admittedly, cities are part of a larger economy and society and as such are exposed to many forces over which they have little or no direct control—forces emanating from state capitals, from Washington, from myriads of corporations, even from the domains of King Faisal and the Shah of Iran.

Even if a city is unable to set its own course and pursue it without reference to these powerful forces, it constantly has opportunities to respond to what is happening on both the inside and outside, and the nature of its response is not preordained. The greater the degree to which a municipal leadership is able to articulate plans for the future, secure a broad consensus in support of its goals, and achieve an effective decision-making apparatus, the more influence a city will be able to exert over its own destiny. These basics are the preconditions for a manpower research strategy; unless they exist, there is little prospect that any research strategy will be successful.

Framework for a Strategy

There are diverse approaches to the study of critical urban manpower issues that must be included within a research framework. One element must be methodology, to determine the extent to which studies of the metropolis are constrained by existing data and to explore the potential for strengthening the data base. Next, historical studies of individual cities and comparative analyses of different cities can provide new and deeper insights. Examinations of employer behavior should be within the framework, because decisions made by the private sector can influence the future of the metropolitan area for good or for ill. In addition, studies of public programming are necessary, because the shape of every city's future in a pluralistic economy and society will be materially affected by the quality of decisions at each level of government.

Research in relation to policy also must be undertaken in order to consider the current and potential impact of new knowledge on decision-making in the entire range of policy arenas—private, nonprofit, and governmental. Finally, an effort must be made to explore the role of planning by distinguishing the decisions that can best be left to the individual and to the nuclear family from those that require communal and governmental intervention if the city is to progress.

Methodological Considerations

The way in which the census bureau collects and publishes data concerning (*a*) central cities and their suburban rings, (*b*) place of residence in relation to employment, and (*c*) employees' journey to their work has determined the analysis of interactions between manpower resources and metropolitan economies. The present statistical reporting must be broadened and refined in order to improve our exploration of the complex changes occurring with respect to these critical urban issues. One of the most serious shortcomings of the present data is that the geographic criteria used to distinguish the central city from neighboring counties do not permit sharp distinctions about the intensity of economic activity in different areas, or about the flows of people, jobs, and income among these areas.

Problems also exist in probing the residential, employment, and income characteristics of the inner city, especially in the cases of the largest metropolitan centers where, instead of a single labor market, there are a number of loosely interdependent labor markets that correlate with patterns of industrial concentration, housing, and availability of transportation.

When we consider the predominant role that the metropolitan economy has come to play in the United States, a twofold requirement emerges. The census bureau should explore how it can reform its data collection so that the resulting information can better illuminate changes in the dynamics of metropolitan economies; at the same time, the research community must address itself to studying the several labor markets within the central city and its suburban rings and their interactions. With a few notable exceptions, this arena of research remains terra incognita.

Both private and public decision-makers need better guidance concerning the future directions of manpower supply and demand within the metropolitan area. Admittedly, there are inherent difficulties in the use of any forecasting model, if only because of the openness of the city in terms of the number of people who are free to move in and out. Still, such movements, especially in the near and intermediate term (five to seven years) are not likely to be so large as to vitiate projections that are restricted to directions and first-order magnitudes.

Among the approaches that warrant exploration are efforts focused on disaggregating a macromodel and, in the process, taking account of the most probable deviations in the metropolitan region. As long as the objectives of such an approach are geared to delineate broad directions and first-order magnitudes, the explorations may well be justified.

A related effort would be to construct a matrix of the most important metropolitan industry and occupational patterns on the assumption that these are likely to show considerable stability in the short and intermediate periods. Hence, if one could estimate the faster and slower growing (and declining) sectors of the metropolitan economy, it would be possible to get a first fix on both the types of manpower that might be in relatively short supply and the potential surpluses that are likely to occur. While such an approach, even if successful, could do little more than provide some general directions to policy-makers in the private and public sectors, such directions geared to near-term developments might prove quite useful.

In the face of the present paucity of metropolitan manpower data, it might be well for governmental and nongovernmental specialists to take another look at area-skill surveys to determine whether these might be improved to a point where they could help fill part of the void. The conventional approach of asking employers about their hiring intentions some months hence would have to be refined before the results could be useful. In the absence of clear-cut alternatives to assessing metropolitan manpower developments, however, it is questionable whether even this admittedly imperfect approach should be discarded before one more effort is made to improve it.

Still another possibility is to design a sample of key employers of varying sizes and occupational mixes and to monitor their employment changes with the aim of extrapolating from their experience to the larger community. Such a structured sample study might provide decision-makers with information about the broad directions of metropolitan manpower developments.

Although there is no basis for optimism that any of these approaches will yield significant new understanding of major metropolitan manpower developments, unless a serious research effort is made to explore how the existing lacunae about basic manpower facts and trends can be reduced, there is little prospect that our large cities will be able to improve the quality of their decisions.

More attention also should be focused on certain major demographic changes that have important implications for the future of our cities. To what extent can the nation's large cities look forward to a substantial reduction, even a potential drying up, of the streams of poor whites and blacks migrating from farm areas? Since the surplus population left on the farms has greatly diminished, consideration also must be given to whether the millions of underemployed and low-income earners now living in rural nonfarm localities will provide the principal source of future migrants to the city.

There is considerable evidence that a new pattern of internal migration has been created by people moving from one city to another. What are the magnitudes of these city-to-city movements; more particularly, what conditions accelerate or retard such movements; and what subgroups in the population are most likely to be involved? Conventional wisdom holds that many suburbanites return to the central city once their children are grown. Is this a fact, and are the numbers of sufficient magnitude to be an important factor in the future well-being of the central city?

What are the intermediate and long-term implications of a continuing and rapid decline in national and urban fertility? Do these population trends threaten the maintenance of the existing population base of many large cities? What does a slower-growing urban population imply for the reduction of some of the disabilities associated with urban density? Is there any likelihood that declines in both in-migration and fertility will result in a constriction of certain metropolitan labor markets so that it will be difficult for them to maintain their existing level of economic activity?

To what extent will those cities that serve as ports of entry—such as New York, Miami, San Antonio, New Orleans, Los Angeles, San Francisco—continue to attract large numbers of illegal immigrants who will find a place in the interstices of their labor markets?

The "urban problem" of the last two decades has been explained largely in terms of racial and ethnic difficulties growing out of an exchange of populations—middle-class whites moving to the suburbs and poorly educated and low-skilled minorities moving into the inner city. In the light of the fact that half of all blacks now reside outside of the South and they, like whites, are experiencing rapidly falling birth rates, are the exacerbated conflicts of the past two decades in northern and western cities likely to moderate as the result of demography alone?

Another line of inquiry that invites research concerns the extent to which economic events on the national and international scene will determine future levels of employment and income in large cities. Greater analytic efforts are required to delineate how different types of cities are able to influence the multitude of economic forces playing upon them from within and without. For example, with the economy of New York tied, (if only to a minor degree) to economic developments in Tokyo, Rio de Janeiro, and Johannesburg, those in decision-making positions must be aware of and responsive to such far-flung linkages.

The energy crisis points up the need for a better understanding of the ways in which jobs, transportation, and the labor force are interrelated. For instance, if schools are unable to operate five days a week because of a shortage of fuel, many mothers currently in the labor force may be forced to stay at home to look after their children.

Another methodological weakness that limits understanding, planning, and decision-making in large cities is the sparsity of longitudinal data. There is a widespread belief that cities are major transformers of manpower, taking in poorly educated and untrained people whose offspring, after one or two generations of improved schooling and employment, are enabled to move up the socioeconomic ladder. Most of the information available about the poor and near-poor, immigrants, and minority-group members is cross-sectional. Although we know a good deal about social pathology and human deprivation at one point in time, we need to know much more about what happens to families on an intergenerational basis. Such knowledge is not easy to garner, but it is not beyond the reach of modern research capabilities. It is also critical if the vast expenditures on health, education, welfare, and other social services are to be more effectively directed to the groups most in need of special assistance.

Another data problem arises from the limitations of the economist's approach to and assessment of the well-being of a metropolitan community. The economist looks at wages almost solely through the mechanism of the price system, where they serve as an allocative device. However, in evaluating urban development and well-being, wages must also be related to family structure and need. A job at the minimum wage may be a satisfactory opening position for a 17-year-old high school dropout living at home; it is unsatisfactory for a head-of-household with three dependents. In short, social scientists must learn to regroup the data about the city and its people in many different ways in order to assess their many different meanings. To return to the example of wages: while wages provide a key measure of labor costs, they also must be assessed from such vantages as the local cost of living, the manner in which they attract or discourage various groups of potential workers (such as youth and married women), the role they play in race relations, and the way in which they are related to welfare standards.

One more methodological issue reflects the fact that cities have been and will certainly continue to be major arenas of social experimentation involving efforts to improve education, health, welfare, social security, race relations, and other critical aspects of contemporary life. There is a crying need for researchers to become engaged to a much greater degree in the design and evaluation of such experiments; for unless they do, taxpayers will remain in the dark about the outcomes. The research community faces the even broader challenge of helping to design outcome measures so that the routine expenditures of local governments can be more effectively assessed. With local governments responsible for spending ever-larger sums—in New York, for example, local government accounts for about one-quarter of the income of the population—the establishment and use of outcome measures for public services is urgently needed if elected and appointed officials are not to continue to make decisions solely in response to political pressure.

These are some of the more important areas in which new and improved data and studies are required if the quality of metropolitan decision-making is to be enhanced. The remedies will not be easy or cheap, since our strongest data base is national rather than metropolitan and since social scientists are conditioned to study macroissues and are relatively unsophisticated in approaching problems on a metropolitan level. Yet a major shift is urgently required, for to a large extent the future well-being of our cities depends upon strengthening their informational mechanisms.

Historical and Comparative Studies

A second important avenue for progress in metropolitan studies is through historical and comparative research. There is no single prototype of a large city. The largest urban agglomerations are characterized by a high degree of diversity, reinforced by the size and diversity of the country of which they are a part. With the single exception of Russia, the United States is the only industrialized nation in the world of continental scale. This suggests the need for caution in drawing comparisons among American cities and such principal European cities as London, Paris, Rome, Amsterdam, Brussels, or Stockholm, each of which is the national capital of a relatively small country with a much more homogeneous population. One need only name some of our largest cities—New York, Chicago, Los Angeles, Houston, Detroit—to appreciate the need to study them in sufficient depth to capture their uniqueness, which at a minimum encompasses marked differences in ethnic and racial distributions, industrial structure, political leadership, and cultural ambience.

Much the same point about diversity and uniqueness can be made about our suburban areas, that is, the perimeters of our large metropolitan centers. There is a need for developing a typology to group these areas according to whether they are growing or have leveled off; whether they are centers of manufacturing or primarily bedroom communities; whether they are well on the way to becoming satellite cities or whether they are, at the opposite extreme, highly restricted residential areas for the upper-middle class and the wealthy. This does not mean that aggregative analysis is undesirable, but the disaggregation must be a first step. Unless researchers proceed in this fashion, they run the risk of dealing with such heterogeneous aggregations that they will unwittingly wash out most of the details that contain within themselves the power to account for metropolitan changes.

In addition to putative gains from well-structured comparative analyses, there is need for more historical studies. Despite the contemporary bias in favor of econometric analyses, historical investigations can make a useful contribution to the understanding of urban dynamics by highlighting some of the mechanisms that earlier helped to transform the urban economy and population. It is still moot whether the urban poor today face comparable or different conditions from the urban poor of the middle and late nineteenth century. Clearly the labor markets have changed, but so has access to preparatory institutions. Earlier, the poor were immigrants from western, central, or southern Europe; now they are likely to be black or Latin American. How much importance should be ascribed to this difference? And what about the increased opportunities for today's urban women to work outside of the home? Does this imply that families are able to escape from poverty sooner?

While one should not look to history to answer the more complex issues of contemporary metropolitan life, a deeper comprehension of the evolution of our older cities cannot fail to illuminate their present condition and to offer some clues to the directions in which they are headed.

Employer Behavior

The next rubric under which research should be conducted relates to the behavior of private employers. Academicians have been slow to explore and exploit this arena for research purposes, in part because of a generic distrust of what goes on in the profit-seeking sector, but equally important, because those who have sought to use corporate data have encountered serious and often impassable obstacles in gaining access to records or in receiving permission to publish their findings.

However, past difficulties do not justify future neglect. Corporate behavior provides a major clue to the understanding of urban dynamics. One specific advantage of looking at the forces that impinge on the employer and how he deals with them is that it provides a sharpened focus on the decision-making process, albeit at a micro level. But many micros may provide a first clue to the macro. We know that more and more central city employers, particularly banks, department stores, utilities, hotels, restaurants, and hospitals have been forced to adapt their manpower and personnel policies and practices to the new urban labor force. Hence a study of their adaptations would provide a critical view of manpower and the metropolis. The research challenge is twofold: first, to develop some case studies in depth of those adaptations whereby employers have sought to deal more effectively with their new labor sources; second, to look for significant generalizations underlying their experience.

Another aspect of employer behavior that invites study relates to the matrix of forces that plays upon the decision to remain in the city or to move out—more particularly, the extent to which manpower resources influence the outcome. Many stories make the rounds about firms that have moved from a central business district over the last few years because they were unable to get the trained personnel they needed. A variant thereof stresses the pressures upon firms by their own staffs who dislike their urban location. Occasionally, the stories also refer to adverse labor costs in the form of high wage structures; more generally, the emphasis is on low productivity and trade union constraints. For the most part, however, complaints center on the difficulties of attracting and retaining an adequate supply of competent people.

It may well be that difficulties anchored in the manpower arena explain the flight of many large and small entrepreneurs from city centers; however, in the absence of carefully executed investigations, to accept this conclusion is an act of faith.

The suspicion that there is more to the story is reinforced by two newspaper accounts on the same day, in late 1973: Cities Service was reported to be leaving New York to consolidate its headquarters in Tulsa, while Delta Airlines was relocating a large number of its executives to New York so that they could be closer to where the action is. Economists have no difficulty in recognizing that two large companies, one an integrated oil firm, the other a large airline, may reach diametrically opposite conclusions about the advantages of a particular metropolitan location. But if our understanding of urban dynamics is to be deepened, we need studies in depth so that the role of the interacting variables can be correctly assessed.

Since some large companies unquestionably will continue to leave the central business district to relocate in the suburban ring or in smaller cities, the principles that guide their relocation should be a matter of both academic and public concern. If a large national corporation accepts, without protest, the practices prevailing in the community where it considers relocating, it may reinforce discriminatory patterns in employment and housing. On the other hand, if it is determined to use its bargaining strength to the full, it can lean against discriminatory patterns by making their abolition a precondition for relocation. The fact that minority groups have taken several large corporations to court to stop their flight from the racially mixed central city to outlying white enclaves adds relevance to these considerations. If the courts should decide that company relocation jeopardizes the constitutional rights of those presently on the payroll, the trade-offs between staying and leaving the city may change radically. In any case, here is yet another unexplored aspect of the interfacing of manpower and the metropolis.

There are two further facets of employer behavior that warrant attention. For the last decade the federal government has been expanding its funding for manpower training and related services in order to assist the hard-to-employ to link more effectively into the labor market. In the last few years the U. S. Department of Labor has been moving in the direction of decentralizing responsibility for planning and implementation of these programs to states and localities, a move that was accelerated by the passage of new comprehensive manpower legislation in 1973.

There is a great deal that employers may be able to do cooperatively via consortia and other devices to put training monies to more effective use to help the poorly educated inner-city labor force prepare for current job openings. A careful search will reveal several such cooperative experiments. These should be assessed and lessons extracted so that future plans may be strengthened. In our largest metropolitan communities more attention should be focused on the potential of employers in the same or adjacent neighborhoods—including those in the not-for-profit sector—to engage in cooperative training, placement, and upgrading efforts (for instance, among institutions comprising an educational park or a medical center).

The multiple interdependencies within the large city point to yet another arena where employer behavior may offer opportunities for constructive study and action. To illustrate: the ability of employers to attract workers, particularly in off-hours, may depend on heightened security, improved transportation, and the availability of local services such as eating places. It may not be feasible for any one employer, even a large one, to create the conditions that would assure him of the amenities he needs; yet cooperative action among a group of employers in the same area may prove successful. The potential for cooperative efforts of this nature should be reviewed and assessed. Moreover, analysis should be directed to the possible impact of a radical change in conventional working practices, such as a reduction to the four-day week. Clearly, there are a great many different fronts on which urban employers interact with the metropolis, and there is a great deal we still need to learn about this relationship.

Public Programming

The arena of public programming is critical in shaping the future of our major metropolitan communities. To begin with, one must note that municipal governments are spending large sums on human betterment and that in a political democracy such spending inevitably reflects the distribution of political power. Yet the researcher has a contribution to make by helping to sharpen the goals of such undertakings, by delineating the preferred methods of pursuing them, and by critically assessing the results.

Major efforts have been under way to evaluate the impact of income supplementation on incentives to work. These demonstrations have been carefully planned, and great care taken in selecting participants and controls. The ultimate findings may provide the American people with the type of guidance they so badly need when it comes to assessing the costs and benefits of social intervention.

The size of the country and the diversity of its people and problems speak to the desirability, in fact the necessity, of experimenting carefully before entering upon large new programs of social intervention. The only possible way for legislators and the public to secure the necessary guidance and feedback is through trial efforts under a diversity of circumstances accompanied by management data systems to summarize and evaluate outcomes. The shortcomings of the Great Society programs we shall discuss in our final chapter were less a matter of lack of accomplishment than failure to learn what worked, what did not work, and why.

The problems of the city are compounded because of the high degree of interdependency that exists among such major subsystems as employment, housing, and transportation—to isolate but three. While there may be good reasons why a government should hesitate to subsidize intra- or interurban transportation, no arguments from economics alone can settle the issue of subsidization a priori until one takes into account the employment and income-earning opportunities that might be jeopardized if the transportation network of a large metropolitan area were permitted to fall apart. It requires analysis and judgment for a balanced assessment of the short- and long-term consequences of such subsidization.

A related area concerns the policy to be pursued with respect to abandoned or about-to-be-abandoned land. Since land is the basic limiting resource of all cities, how it is handled will have a major impact on the future of the metropolis. Inevitably, there will be difficult trade-offs between social benefits and social costs. Real estate interests keep looking to government for actions that will facilitate their making windfall profits, but if the city fails to put together parcels of abandoned land and if it fails to offer various inducements to bring such land back into productive use, it may erode its economic and employment base. Helping real estate promoters is not necessarily faulty public policy.

Large cities are not only large employers themselves, accounting for about 15 percent of all urban jobs, they are also dispensers of transfer payments which provide essential income to large numbers of people who are not working but who, under supportive arrangements, might be able to work. One of the challenges cities face is to explore how some of the transfer income under their control might be used to encourage potential employables who are on welfare to enter productive work, even if the municipal authorities must initially establish both the job opportunities and ancillary support. There is nothing easy about going down this road, but there is also nothing easy about the city's continuing to support potentially employable adults in idleness. Since most municipalities have a great amount of public work that needs doing, the conversion of persons on welfare into productive workers commends itself, surely on an experimental basis.

There is widespread belief that the large city is an inhospitable environment for manufacturing, especially in an era of heightened concern about pollution and other environmental dangers. Nevertheless, those directly concerned with the economic welfare of the city worry every time a manufacturing unit closes down its operations. The right kinds of manufacturing can provide good jobs and clean jobs, which can be absorbed safely within the city's borders. We simply have not studied adequately the types of manufacturing employment that have moved out of our large metropolitan centers together with the considerable flow of new, if different, manufacturing jobs that have moved in. Once again, gross categories hide more than they reveal.

Since so many of our large cities' problems are directly or indirectly related to racial and ethnic discrimination, more attention should be aimed at identifying the high costs in terms of losses of efficiency and equity that derive from the persistence of discrimination, and at analyzing how certain accelerated programs can lower the barriers that hobble the progress of individuals and the community.

The city's future also will be affected by developments beyond its borders. The position of the suburbs has an important influence upon the urban condition. More must be learned about protection of the suburban turf. If the suburbs continue to be controlled by the affluent, who place a high price upon the environment in which they live, the use of land for industrial and commercial purposes will be restricted and the erection of housing for low-income groups will be discouraged. To the extent that this occurs, the expansion of the suburbs will be seriously constrained, thereby contributing indirectly to assuring the future vitality of the city. We need to know much more about the relative strength of the various interest groups which, by determining what happens in the suburbs, will have great influence upon the economic future of the cities.

Another external parameter is the strength and direction of national economic policy. No city can solve its manpower and economic problems and assure its future unless the federal government pursues policies that are both supportive of economic growth and nondiscriminatory against the nation's largest cities. More analysis is required of the interplay between federal policies and metropolitan well-being. The mayors of our largest cities are convinced that the federal government has not dealt fairly with their constituencies. Their argument has less to do with abstract justice and more with the belief that the principal problems our large cities face cannot be solved without substantial federal assistance. Clearly, when our national unemployment rate exceeds 6—not to mention 8—percent, there is little any large city can do by itself to assure employment opportunities for all of its residents. It must depend heavily upon the federal government.

The probable emergence of a much-improved fiscal position in many states resulting from revenue sharing and declining rates of population growth calls attention to a third externality that will affect the future of our large cities. The largest cities must develop alliances with other urban communities in their state and with their neighboring suburbs, many of which are also seeking an increased share of state aid. While such coalition-building is primarily the task of the politician, the analyst can help by exploring the extent to which the difficult problems encountered first by the large city are emerging increasingly in smaller cities and in many of the larger suburbs. It is probably not true that the problems of the large city are unique; they only appear to be for reasons of timing and scale.

The thrust of these comments has been to highlight many dimensions of public programming, and to point out how a stronger data base, better analysis, and carefully controlled experiments can contribute to better decision-making. Admittedly, decisions are currently being made, and must continue to be made, in the absence of adequate information and knowledge, but that should only encourage the researcher to increase his contribution.

Research in Relation to Policy

Although considerations of the relation between research and policy have been touched upon in all the preceding sections, we shall now focus directly upon this area of concern.

The first point is that all metropolitan studies must make room for the individual, as a source of information and as the recipient of feedback from completed research. The simple fact is that no study can have a positive effect on outcomes unless the findings are understood and accepted by those who must eventually act on them.

To clarify this point: if most of the people living in a neighborhood are firmly opposed to moving away and are organized to back up their determination, there is little purpose in a study of alternative land use that hinges on their relocation.

A closely related reason for making the individual a principal center of any research effort is that many residents of large metropolitan centers do not necessarily share the dominant value system. Accordingly, studies predicated on rationalistic economic theorizing are likely to lead to erroneous results if they fail to consider the cultural values that determine the behavior of specific groups. A finding that young black girls can earn good wages as domestics is irrelevant because they will not accept employment as maids no matter what the wage analysis shows. They have not waited three hundred fifty years for a long-delayed revolution only to accept what they view as degrading work.

Another shortcoming of much policy research is that investigators often do not anticipate the policy implications of their inquiries. To make matters worse, many investigators fail to consider whether their research is designed to deal with a problem of real importance. Clearly, if they slip at these initial points, there can be no recovery down the road; good answers and good liaison with policy-makers will not suffice to enhance trivia.

The politics of the metropolis is never static, and the recent reshuffling of population makes it more dynamic than ever. The new in-migrants and their children are making strenuous efforts to organize themselves in order to exert more leverage on their own lives and to expand their opportunities. They may not always succeed in advancing their own interests, but they are determined to keep trying; and no studies of the metropolitan environment should fail to take their strivings into account.

All urban research is seriously handicapped by the fact that social scientists have never developed sophisticated techniques for extracting information from people, and it is even more handicapped with respect to extracting information from people who have a cautious if not hostile stance toward the larger society. The 1970 census was unable to derive an accurate count of population in large metropolitan centers; the undercount, especially among certain minority groups, reached a distressingly high percentage. Not only are we unable to count the urban population accurately, we are even farther behind when it comes to understanding the values of many residents, the ties that bind them to relatives and neighbors, and their plans and goals. Here is a major drawback to an understanding of the metropolis and to the shaping of policies to improve its functioning. The day-to-day lives of many of its inhabitants are shrouded from view—and in the place of knowledge the leadership operates upon assumptions that are almost certain to be faulty, since they grow out of a different social experience.

Urban research is hobbled not only by unfamiliarity with cultural diversity and alienation, but also by a lack of attention to the ramifications flowing from the city's considerable reliance upon state and federal actions. Many of the difficulties cities experience result from insufficient articulation among the three levels of government. For instance, although the state is the agency that is ultimately responsible for the development of educational opportunities, it is the rare state that has used its constitutional authority to exert leverage on those of its cities that demonstrate serious educational shortcomings. The subject of intergovernmental relations and its import for an improved urban environment is a largely unexplored domain that warrants systematic analysis and evaluation.

Potentialities and Limitations of Planning

No city can survive, much less prosper, without planning. A great many decisions made today will have long-term consequences. The real challenge to urbanologists is to identify which issues fall within the realm of planning and to indicate the locus of decision-making. The individual and his family will continue to be relied upon to make critical decisions about education, training, and employment. In the area of land use and transportation, municipal government clearly must be the final arbiter. Other decisions fall within the domain of intermediary institutions, such as employers, trade unions, and voluntary agencies. Research can help to distinguish the roles of the different actors, and to show how improved communication among them can make planning more effective.

Despite the large, some might even say horrendous, problems our big cities face, it is important to recall that most people who live and work in the metropolitan area are able to take care of themselves, plan their own lives, and realize many of their goals. Yet if this sanguine assessment holds for the majority, there is a considerable minority that is not so well situated; that lacks the capacity or the resources to plan for the future; and that requires help. One of the principal challenges large cities face is to design programs of social intervention that are truly responsive to the needs of those who require help, so that they can be assisted to become independent. The success of such programs should be measured by the numbers who are enabled to care for themselves and the speed with which they do so.

To increase the ability of the urban population to earn its livelihood, reliance can be placed on market mechanisms so long as the leadership recognizes that the existing market structures are imperfect and that they fail, sometimes abysmally, to meet the minimum needs of some of the population. In short, while a city has every reason to rely on tested institutions, it must not ignore the challenge to build new structures more responsive to unmet needs, and to improve linkages among all institutions, both old and new. Here too the student of urban affairs has a major task. He must help identify the institutions that need to be modified and recommend the new ones that should be established if the full potentialities of the city's human resources are to be developed and deployed.

The critical characteristic of the modern metropolis is the variability of its institutions and its inhabitants. At no point can one rely on gross diagnosis and traditional therapies. The stress on research should not imply an exaggerated respect for the potentialities of social science, but rather an appreciation of present shortcomings in the information base and analytic structures which handicap the search for solutions to urban problems. Clearly, no one group can find the answers by itself, for the future of every large city depends on continuing accommodations among many different groups—accommodations that are rooted in political power, economic advantage, and cultural hegemony. In this complex environment, there is a place for the social investigator who can help to narrow differences by substituting knowledge for opinion, reality for fantasy, the realizable from the ideal.

21

Government: The Fourth Factor

I owe the title of this chapter to a Nigerian student who was in the audience when I lectured at the University of South Carolina in the early 1960s. In light of his knowledge about his own country, where government dominates the raising and allocation of capital, the exploitation of natural resources, the control of foreign trade, and the level and distribution of services directed to improving human resources, he wondered how economists in the Western world could ignore the dominant role of government in economic development. He had heard me say that, according to my calculations and those of my colleagues, the not-for-profit sector (government and nonprofit institutions) in the United States accounted for between one-third and two-fifths of all employment, and between one-fourth and one-third of the GNP. Why then, he asked, did economists—particularly those reared in the Anglo-Saxon tradition—ignore the fact that government was a factor of production? Was it, he continued, because of their political bias? Were they unable to acknowledge the potency of government in economic development because this would place them on the same side as Marxists, who look to government as the primary instrument for reforming and improving the operations of the economy?

The student's questions intrigued me at the time and they have intrigued me since. In a more complete answer than I was able to give him at that time, I shall treat the following facets of the problem: the forces that led the classical economists to ignore or minimize the role of government; the failure of Keynesian macroeconomists to understand the structural changes in the post-World War II American economy; and the need for a dynamic model of societal behavior if the relations between government and economic development are to be seen with clarity. This chapter, then, seeks to describe how economists went far astray in appraising the role of government; why most American economists have continued to rely on the earlier model of competitive markets; and the new framework that must be constructed if the interactions between government and the economy are to be understood.

The Neglect of Government in Traditional Economic Thought

The fact that the discipline of economics was developed as a counterpoint to mercantilism, which emphasized centralization, bureaucracy, and regulation, helps to explain why Adam Smith's successors tended to slight the role of government in their analyses. The author of *The Wealth of Nations* demonstrated to his own satisfaction, and that of his enthusiastic disciples, that governments had the unique capacity to waste scarce resources and to distort the goals of national economic policy. While Smith and his followers, from Ricardo to Pigou, acknowledged that on occasion governments should intervene in the allocation and distribution of resources on grounds of efficiency or equity, most economists believed that a strict limit should be set on such interventions.

Smith saw a role for government in defense, navigation, the development of human resources (education), and the establishment and maintenance of domestic security and tranquility, all of which are essential preconditions for economic development. His successors, concerned with analyzing the ways in which the competitive market calls forth scarce resources, prices them, and allocates them, directed their major energies to perfecting the competitive model.

The economists who dissented, from the early Christian Socialists through Marx to Veblen (purists may prefer to call them political scientists, historians, or sociologists), conceived of government as the key institution affecting the ownership of property and the distribution of profits. But, as Veblen demonstrated in his devastating attack on the major tradition, the classical and neoclassical economists refused to consider how government, with the aid of law, police power, and value reinforcement, helps to determine the structure of production and the distribution of rewards. By eliminating government from their analytic schema, the main-line economists were able to elaborate and refine their analyses of the laws of production while, at the same time, neglecting distribution.

A second reason why the economists gave government short shrift is that their models ignored all significant change; yet government is the instrument through which nations modify their institutions to cope with change. Economists deliberately omitted consideration of the impact of changes in population, technology, and tastes upon the structure and functioning of the economy. They recognized (as evidenced by Ricardo's revision of his chapter on machinery and Marshall's treatment of the Malthusian laws of population) that changes in these parameters could have important consequences for both production and distribution; still, they disregarded these forces in order to achieve determinate results.

Economists' concern with analyzing conditions of equilibrium, departures from equilibrium, and returns to equilibrium, within a substantially stable system, led them to place government beyond their purview. An exploration of the effect of changes in the governmental structure upon production and distribution would have required a historical, developmental, institutional, or—as Veblen phrased it—an evolutionary bias.

Beyond the authority of the founders of the discipline and the limitations of their own methodology, there were additional influences that deterred economists from considering the role of government in economic development. One such influence was their philosophical-psychological orientation. They saw society as a free association of independent human beings, operating under the dictates of rationality, and fixated on the accumulation of wealth. In exploring the dynamics of specialization, the economists used as their prototype, not the caste system of India, but a Robinson Crusoe setting. They were the direct descendants of the Romantic revolutionaries of the eighteenth century who saw society in terms of a social compact or contract. In their view, the economy was propelled by self-reliant individuals who freely entered into contracts to their mutual advantage. They considered the outcomes of competition as natural, inevitable, and desirable, and regarded Marx and his ilk as deluded in viewing workers as industrial slaves exploited by capitalists.

Since their concepts envisaged the individual as the prime mover in society, social organizations as contractual arrangements among individuals, maximizing of wealth as the primary goal of life, and man as a rational being, their decision to exclude government from their system was reinforced. There was no need, in their view, to analyze the political arena characterized by conflicting groups that pursue such nebulous ends as power and prestige, and a leadership that engages in questionable activities to obtain and maintain its position. To include government in their model would have sounded the death knell to the economists' efforts to build a new science.

Scholars have always disagreed about the design and improvement of the models with which they work. But there is consensus that the investigator's intent is less relevant than the ability of his model to illuminate reality. For this reason British economists were smug and secure: it was clear to them, at least up to World War I, that competition was the mainspring of their economy, and it was competition that they had been able to study in depth. When some continental followers of Karl Marx began to explore the linkages between foreign trade and domestic prosperity in advanced competitive economies, and pointed to the marriage of convenience between business and the Foreign Office in determining British policy in India, Southwest Asia, the Middle East, South Africa, and Latin America, most economists paid no attention. They did not want to complicate their increasingly tidy model of competitive markets with the dirty dynamics of imperialism.

The American experience was more equivocal. Most American economists were willing to follow in the footsteps of their British cousins, although a minority recognized early that the economic development of the United States was affected substantially by governmental decisions involving land distribution, protective tariffs, internal improvements, slavery, free immigration, the financing of higher education, agricultural extension services, and much more.

Recognition of these important arenas of governmental action was not sufficient, however, to wean the majority of American economists away from their preoccupation with the neoclassical model of the competitive market. They remained impressed with the wide disinclination of government to interfere with the operation of the marketplace, at least with the hiring of workers and with the output of goods. Resources continued to flow to where the opportunities for profits were greatest. The country grew; individuals prospered. The successful performance of the competitive economy gave economics its internal security and its external strength. No one, not even Karl Marx, had developed a model with greater explicatory power. In the competitive world of scholars, the best model, however flawed, remains ensconced as long as no one conceives of the need for or succeeds in producing a better one, and the entrenched American model had no place for government.

The Changing American Economy

A serious assessment of the relevance and utility of the Marshallian system for the analysis of British and American capitalism up to World War I, or shortly beyond, has yet to be made. Suffice it to say that by the late 1930s, as the New Deal sought to rebuild an American economy that had all but collapsed from several years of cumulative shrinkage of output, prices, and employment, there was a crying need for a new model. This

Keynes provided. Within a few years of publication of the *General Theory,* the Keynesian revolution was victorious. Except for a small minority who were too old or too cranky to go along, the economics profession accepted the new system, which gave the government a dominant role in assuring an adequate level of investment to keep the economy at full employment. Two decades of chronic underemployment in Great Britain, and a decade in which unemployment in the United States never fell below a rate of 10 percent, convinced economists that the free market alone was no longer capable of performing the critical function of utilizing all available resources effectively.

With the passage of the Employment Act in 1946, Keynesian macroeconomics became institutionalized in the United States. At the same time, American economists continued to make use of the competitive model, increasingly utilizing the modern and sophisticated econometric version. However, the structure of the American economy was being transformed in response to new opportunities on the domestic scene and to threats presented by international events.

The old theory, the new theory, and the new reality have lived cheek by jowl during the last three decades, and politicians and professors pick and choose among the disparate elements in seeking understanding and guidance. For instance, J. M. Clark found it necessary to write an explanatory note to the United Nations Report on Full Employment in the early 1950s, in which he warned his enthusiastic Keynesian colleagues not to expect too much from government spending. He insisted that, unless cost and price mechanisms continue to perform effectively, no economy would be able to operate continuously at or close to full employment. Clark's reservations were politely noted but disregarded.

The Eisenhower years revealed structural faults in the economy. The President, by instinct and background, was attuned to the McKinley economics of his Secretary of the Treasury, George M. Humphrey. His pragmatic chairman of the Council of Economic Advisers was Arthur F. Burns who, while criticizing Keynes in scholarly journals, borrowed liberally from him in fashioning his policy recommendations—which Eisenhower followed.

The Kennedy-Johnson decade revealed a similar dissonance. In an address at Yale, President John Kennedy insisted that management of the American economy is not a proper subject for political debate, but a matter that should be left to the economists, who know how to use fiscal and monetary policy to establish and maintain the economy at a high level.

At about the same time James Tobin, a member of Kennedy's Council of Economic Advisers whose roots were in Yale, sought to allay the fears of American businessmen about the expansion of the federal government into their domain by presenting data that pointed to a *decline* in the role of government in the generation of GNP. He argued that, although the federal government was seeking to deploy the instruments of fiscal-monetary policy more effectively, this effort was not, and should not be considered, a threat to the decision-making powers of businessmen.

During the next administration, while his economists sought to fine-tune the economy, President Johnson continued to talk of the strengths of our free-enterprise system in terms not greatly different from those of his immediate predecessors, Kennedy and Eisenhower, or from those of his successor, Richard Nixon.

Only small differences separate the approach of the Kennedy-Johnson economists, who looked to fiscal-monetary policies to relieve the country of excessive unemployment, and the early game plan of the Nixon administration, which sought to bring mounting inflation under control by resorting to the classic remedies of tight money, reduced governmental expenditures, and higher unemployment. A wide spectrum of academic economists looked to a combination of fiscal-monetary policy and the free market to keep the economy moving onward and upward.

In the 1960s a few dissenters questioned whether this combination would in fact be powerful enough to overcome structural impedimenta that appeared to lie beneath the excessively high unemployment rates of the disadvantaged. John K. Galbraith, impressed with the growth of private power centers in corporations and trade unions, ridiculed those who continued to look to market mechanisms for salubrious effects. And it was Arthur F. Burns, the consulting architect of the Nixon anti-inflation strategy, who realized early in 1970 that policy was out of phase with reality; in the face of high and rising unemployment, prices were moving upward, imports were increasing, and improved liquidity was failing to stimulate investment. By 1971 he put the matter simply: the economy was not responding as anticipated; new institutions and mechanisms were required.

For three decades major changes had been taking place in the structure and functioning of the American economy, primarily the steadily expanding role of government, a role which successive Presidents understandably sought to minimize in their concern about public and business confidence, and which most economists ignored in their infatuation with Keynesian macroeconomics and their investment in Marshallian microeconomics.

The steady expansion of the role of government during these decades can be read in the following summary record: direct employment by government and government's contribution to GNP increased several-fold; government set the pace for technological innovation via defense and space expenditures (air transportation, electronics, computers); it aided major industries that had fallen on hard times, such as agriculture and shipping; its expenditures for highways and subsidies for construction altered the location of people and industries; its foreign aid programs— insurance against expropriation, import controls on petroleum, stock-piling of strategic materials, and limitations on foreign investments by domestic corporations—increasingly changed the structure of foreign trade. Moreover, several government regulatory commissions exercise leverage over such critically important institutions as capital markets, stock exchanges, trade unions, communications and other utilities, and influence the speed with which new opportunities are opened to minority groups. Furthermore, government has been continuously involved in new arenas, from satellite communications to ecology.

When the Penn Central Railroad collapsed in the late spring of 1970, the Federal Reserve Board acted to prevent a financial panic, and when Lockheed was threatened with bankruptcy in the summer of 1971, Congress helped to bail it out. A spokesman for the banking syndicate, testifying on behalf of federal aid to Lockheed, stated that since the government is in every nook and cranny of the economy, there is good reason for it to save a major company whose collapse would have disastrous repercussions. That spokesman was a senior officer of the nation's second largest bank!

In August 1971 President Nixon announced his new economic program—a price-wage freeze, a special import levy of 10 percent, cutting the dollar loose from gold, new tax concessions for business and the consumer—and stated that these proposals represented the most significant departure in national economic policy in forty years. Regardless of the outcome, there is little reason to argue with Nixon's declaration that the introduction of wage, price, and dividend controls in a peacetime economy represents a major break with tradition. An interesting question, however, is why only a few economists understood that cumulative structural transformations would force the President to adopt such a policy, even a President who believed firmly in a free-enterprise economy.

The principal explanation of the economists' failure to foresee this change in policy lies in their continued allegiance to an outmoded methodology based on faulty assumptions spiced with a conservative-optimistic tilt. Competitive price theory, in its simple or sophisticated version, was the professional economist's major inheritance. This is what he had learned and what he knew how to use. Since an operational theory of oligopoly had not been adumbrated, economists made do with what they had, occasionally warning their students to take note of the gap between the assumptions of the theory and the realities of the moneymaking world. This gap was accentuated by their devotion to mathematical model-building and econometrics. Sophisticated theoreticians devote their energies to designing complex models; they pay little attention to the quantity and quality of the data that determine the relevance of their results.

Economists continued to postulate that individualism, voluntarism, and rationality provide a working model of man and society, although the overwhelming weight of scholarship has denied each in turn. However, these traditional assumptions made it easier to deprecate the growing role of government in charting the direction of an economy which the economists saw as responding primarily to entrepreneurial profit maximization and consumer utility maximization.

The post-World War II American economic fraternity had felt comfortable with the main thrust of economic and social policy, with its reformist orientation and avoidance of radical reforms. To them, the grafting of Keynes's model to the free market was preferable to experimentation with major institutional changes involving private property, corporate control, and income redistribution.

Prior to his retirement from Columbia University, Arthur Burns called attention to a paradox. In an era when economics in the real world has become political economy, in the halls of academe it was transforming itself into an increasingly esoteric discipline. This would be difficult to understand were it not for the fact that once before, in the formative years of Ricardian economics, when England was being buffeted by war, inflation, enclosure, blockade, industrialization, urbanization, and other major socioeconomic changes, the classical economists had developed a model that omitted these realities. By ignoring such structural changes, they were able to build a discipline with increasing powers of analysis at the price of a growing distortion of reality. The continued neglect of government as a critical decision-making center by contemporary American economists has resulted in the entrenchment of outmoded theory and the establishment of defective policies. Although improved theory does not guarantee sound policy, without a perspective that includes the ever-increasing role of government in shaping the goals and influencing the operations of the contemporary economy, policy is bound to go astray.

The Functions of the Governmental System

The following discussion summarizes the principal ways in which the governmental system interacts with the economy. Its purpose is to demonstrate that these interactions are critical to the understanding and formulation of policy.

In both autocratic and democratic regimes, those in power want to maintain public support. Politicians do not press for economic policies that are likely to lead to widespread discontent, which may take the form of industrial sabotage or noncooperation or lead to defeat at the polls. In a democracy, elections are the principal instrument for arriving at consensus about the intermediate and long-run goals that the society seeks to achieve and about the preferred ways to accomplish them. When those in power lose the support of the public, the consensus essential to economic growth and development is lacking; the result is confusion and uncertainty among decision-makers in both government and the economy. Since so much economic activity is geared to the future, a loss of confidence means that consumers and investors are likely to sit and wait and watch, with the result that the economy loses momentum.

Nor is the centrality of government much different in controlled societies. When the leadership is under pressure, riven by conflict, or uncertain about its next move, the cues that bureaucrats depend upon to guide them on the economic front, ranging from investments to price adjustments, will be equivocal and result in slippage, slowdowns, bottlenecks.

The maintenance of public support and confidence is the first and overriding task of government in nurturing a successful economy. In the absence of competent government whose authority is respected even if its leaders are not loved, no economy can long prosper.

Among the criteria that a government must meet to pass the test of competence is its ability to raise the substantial sums required to develop the infrastructure for sustained economic development. Private savings have a role to play in the process of growth, but unless government and large intermediate bodies (corporations) are able to deflect a substantial proportion of current output from consumption to investment, the economy will drag. The principle of complementarity in public and private investment has not received its due. A single illustration: the dynamism of the automobile industry is predicated upon a continuing high level of public investment in highway construction.

A parallel challenge can be subsumed under the term "equity." All governments represent a balancing of conflicting interest groups. Some groups are always in a better position than others to benefit from state action. In a democracy where those in opposition to government are able to voice their views and organize to replace those in power, elected officials must always be alert to adjust to the changing views of the public. Although alterations in the societal value structure are made slowly, there are stages in the development of nations that are associated with new value orientations. While it is true that momentum builds up only over a period of time, such circumstances as a severe depression, racial conflict, or the aftermath of a war often act as precipitants. A major test of political competence is the ability of the leadership to recognize turning points and adjust to them. Accommodation to new conditions can shorten the period of acute conflict and can mitigate political exacerbation. If the government is successful in this task, the economy will suffer less disturbance.

Another arena where government action can facilitate or retard economic development pertains to its policy regarding the development of human resources. The acquisition of skill depends, among other factors, upon access to education and training facilities. Unless these facilities are provided by government, they will not be broadly available. If the population can rely only on the family and on job mobility to develop its skills, its level of competence will be raised quite slowly. Consequently, the ability of government to expand and improve training institutions so that they will be available to a steadily increasing proportion of the population can affect the rate at which the economy grows.

In these several ways—facilitating consensus, building infrastructure, responding to demands for equity, providing opportunities for skill acquisition—governments engage in functions that are critical to the performance of the economy. The effectiveness with which they operate in these several realms will significantly influence performance of the economic system.

Government as a Factor of Production

Alfred Marshall was not satisfied with the old trilogy of land, labor, and capital as the factors of production: he added management. Joseph Schumpeter moved in the opposite direction: he reduced the trilogy to two, arguing that land is a form of capital. Karl Marx had earlier focused on one factor: he postulated that all surplus value stems only from labor.

There is no a priori method whereby the number of factors of production can be determined. It depends on the model employed by the economist. We have seen that the major tradition did not consider government specifically as a factor of production. In our view, that was an error. That error is compounded today when, at least in the United States, government has the following roles:

——It is the nation's largest employer. Together federal, state, and local governments employ more than 13.5 million persons, or nearly one of every six employed persons. This is more than *ten* times the number of workers in America's largest private firm, the American Telephone and Telegraph Company.

——It is the nation's largest investor. The Office of Management and Budget estimates that the federal government alone will have nearly $70 billion in investment outlays during fiscal 1974. This far exceeds the annual investment of any single private enterprise.

——It is the nation's largest consumer. Government purchases of goods and services in 1973 totaled over $277 billion, or more than one-fifth the total Gross National Product.

——It is the nation's largest supporter of science and technology. The federal government alone accounts for more than half of the $30 billion spent on basic and applied research in the United States during 1973.

——It provides transfer income to a large part of the population. With the Social Security system providing cash to over 28 million beneficiaries and state public assistance programs benefiting another 11 million, government directly supplements the income of roughly 15 percent of the population.

——It determines in large measure the level at which the economy operates. Total government expenditures including both transfer payments and purchases of goods and services are the equivalent of more than 30 percent of the GNP. With control over this large a share of the total economy, government is a major determinant of the level of demand and of employment.

——It sets the limits within which businessmen cooperate and compete. Through enforcement of antitrust, minimum wage, occupational safety, and consumer protection legislation, the government sets various standards for private market behavior.

——It controls the profitability of many large industries. Not only does government control the rates of return for various public utilities, through cost-plus contracts for defense purchases, cost reimbursement including fixed rates of return for hospital and nursing home services, subsidy of numerous agricultural commodities, and price regulation for various forms of transportation, it directly affects the profit rate of important sectors of the economy.

——It can expand opportunities for the disadvantaged. With public schools enrolling roughly 90 percent of the nation's elementary and secondary students and public funds accounting for more than 45 percent of all expenditures for higher education, government influences these critical developmental opportunities. Moreover, through the provision of nearly one million work and training program enrollment openings, the federal government provides additional opportunities to many disadvantaged youths and adults. Finally, through enforcement efforts under the Civil Rights Act of 1964 the government helps assure that job opportunities for minorities will be available in the private sector.

—— It exercises a dominant influence on the changing patterns of consumption. Through a combination of direct, guaranteed, and insured loans, the federal government advanced over $26 billion in credit to the public in 1973. Much of this credit was supplied to support consumer demand for housing and higher education. With its support for highway construction, government has significantly encouraged the purchase of private automobiles over other modes of transportation.

Since government does all of these things and many more, we must agree with the Nigerian student who saw government as a fourth factor of production. When economists recognize this fact, they will be able to develop a more realistic model that will facilitate more effective policy.

22

Some Lessons of the Great Society

Two lessons can be extracted from President Lyndon Johnson's broad program of social reforms, which he termed
the "Great Society." One lesson has to do with the general
process of social reform in a middle-class democracy, or at
least in this middle-class democracy. The second concerns
the specific legislative programs that made up the Great
Society. We shall concentrate our attention on the more
general implications for social intervention and social reform that can be derived from this recent experience.

No one who reads the evidence can seriously subscribe to
either of the extreme, simple, fashionable dogmas: that
social legislation is merely a sham, aimed at camouflaging,
not solving, problems; or that all major political intervention in social problems is a mistake, bound to fail, and is
better left to local government, private charity, or the free
market. Contrary to these dogmas, the evidence seems to
show that the problems are real, that political pressure to
do something about them is often irresistable, and that
many partial but genuine successes have been achieved.

Often, though not always, the intended beneficiaries of
social legislation do benefit. There are sometimes unin-
tended and unwanted side effects; and some public programs simply do not work or prove too costly. But there is
nothing in the history of the 1960s to suggest that it is a law
of nature that social legislation cannot deal effectively with
social problems, or that state and local governments or
private enterprise will always do better than the "feds."

There is no obvious support for such sweeping generalizations. Case-by-case judgment seems far more appropriate.

Goals

A first lesson is that the public will accept large-scale programs of social intervention only at long intervals. One measure of time is the generation that elapsed between the New Freedom of Woodrow Wilson and the New Deal of Franklin Roosevelt, and again between the New Deal and the Great Society. There is nothing inherently cyclic about such a pattern; only special circumstances—like the breakdown of the economy in the Great Depression, or the rise of the civil rights movement and the political awakening of the black population—with an assist from strong leadership can set the stage for major social reform. At other times, a piecemeal approach is the only kind possible.

Indeed, social progress in a democracy depends on its ability to recognize and respond to challenges that require governmental intervention in the interests of economic performance and social justice. If the government avoids piecemeal remedial action when and where the facts warrant, it is likely to be forced later on to mount more ambitious programs of social intervention when the constraints of time, resources, and tolerance will be more painfully binding. Prolonged neglect is costly. Most social problems do not fade away; they become more acute when neglected.

Piecemeal reform is not easy. The public has limited tolerance for reform at any time. More often than not, it is the quiet life that appeals to the Congress and to the voters. In a democracy whose political and economic systems are functioning reasonably well, the disadvantaged (those who can expect to gain directly from political or economic or social reform) will usually be a minority, and generally a weak or powerless minority. Social legislation needs a constituency broader than its direct beneficiaries. A larger public must share the goals of social intervention before political reform becomes possible. In the American system of government the President therefore becomes a key figure. No one else is likely to be able to fashion the required public consensus on goals and to get and maintain the required congressional support—especially on those occasions when the situation calls for major reforms on several fronts.

Even a President who can successfully use all his arts of persuasion and all his instruments of power to induce his countrymen to change their values, attitudes, and behavior toward the disadvantaged must reckon with intrinsic limitations. Even a President who begins with a smashing electoral victory—as Lyndon Johnson did—will find that he has only a finite stock of political capital to spend and, as he runs into opposition, he depletes it. A President who takes the lead in a broad program of social reform must anticipate mounting opposition from groups who balk at paying the price for progress, especially the progress of others. He must also reckon with increasing frustration among the potential beneficiaries, whose expectations are likely to outpace the improvements in their circumstances.

In the case of Johnson and his Great Society there was another factor. More than anything else, the Vietnam War was the enemy of the Great Society. We shall see later that the war stole resources that might otherwise have gone to finance social programs on a scale sufficient to show results. For now, let us recognize that the bitterness, hostility, and disillusionment generated by Johnson's prosecution and escalation of an unpopular war destroyed the consensus on social goals that he had earlier managed to create. And the problem was compounded by the fact that the natural antiwar constituency was also the natural constituency for social and economic reform.

Promises

It is hard enough for a reformist government to set realistic goals. It is almost impossible for it to limit itself to realistic promises. Here the social engineers of the 1960s clearly failed. The administration's spokesmen promised to undertake and win the war on poverty; to assure every American family an adequate home; to relieve old and poor people of the financial burdens of illness; to widen the educational opportunities of poor children; to speed the integration of the black community into the mainstream of American life; and to provide skill training so that those on the periphery of the economy could get better jobs. A democracy with a two-party tradition is inured to exaggerated promises and claims, especially in an election year. But the mid-1960s saw the President, his advisers, and the congressional leadership wantonly blur the distinction between campaign promises and legislative commitments. From one point of view, the Great Society programs were doomed from the moment of their enactment: there was no prospect that any government could deliver on such ambitious promises, certainly not within the time limits that an impatient public would allow.

It is easy to see how damaging this kind of puffery can be to the good name of sensible social policy. It will not be easy to kick the habit. One has the impression that nothing less than a Crisis can any longer attract political attention. The Urban Crisis, the Environmental Crisis, the Energy Crisis are only the latest in a long line. If verbal overkill were merely a device to attract attention, that would perhaps not be so bad. The distortion goes deeper. One can hardly respond to a Crisis with small-scale experimental programs to test out the nature of the problem and accumulate knowledge that can ultimately lead to the design of better policy. A Crisis has to be met on a grand scale. Of course, before one Crisis has been resolved the next Crisis is on the scene, and each is blown up so as to demand all available attention and resources. This sort of atmosphere is hardly conducive to the rational allocation of public funds and administrative capacity.

We can conclude, then, that especially if the issues are complex and if they have been ignored or minimized earlier, it is important that the leadership's promises of results be realistic rather than extreme. A public that has been encouraged to expect great things will become impatient, critical, and alienated if the progress that is achieved falls far short of the rosy promises. A wise leadership is careful to pledge no more than it feels moderately sure it can deliver within a reasonable time.

Knowledge

The social problems requiring remedial action by government are usually complicated. Their causes are not understood in their entirety, and the proposed cures are of uncertain efficacy. There is likely to be no firm body of knowledge and experience that explains how to shape manpower programs, carry out a war on poverty, or ensure that children in the ghetto will learn to read—certainly not at the moment when the problems gain visibility and attention and the demand for action becomes irresistible.

A selective review of the Great Society's social interventions exhibits a wide range in the quality of the intellectual base on which programs were erected. The Social Security Administration provided what turned out to be realistic estimates of the increased utilization of hospitals resulting from Medicare. The same experts were far off the mark when it came to estimating unit costs. As a result, Congress and the public had the unpleasant experience later of having to cover the much-enlarged costs of the program through higher payroll taxes and larger copayments. Since Medicaid legislation was enacted with even less study and discussion, it is not surprising that its open-ended commitment of federal funds for health care for the poor did not survive for more than two years before Congress was forced to limit eligibility.

Not only the design, but also the operation and administration, of public programs require a base of knowledge and experience that may well be lacking at the start. It took several years, for instance, for the U.S. Office of Education to recognize that much of the money it was allocating to states and localities for compensatory education was not being spent on the targeted population. It took even longer for the educational authorities to learn to distinguish between attractively packaged programs that would later prove ineffective, and less exciting but more productive approaches to improving the learning skills of poor children.

Let us take one last but very important example. The course of welfare reform would have been much smoother had expert knowledge been able to foretell the massive welfare drift of the 1960s. As things turned out, the modest reforms of 1962 and 1967 were simply obliterated by the rise in the welfare rolls. This unexpected result certainly contributed to the inability of a more substantial reform program to capture the support of a majority of legislators.

Almost by definition, a new social program is likely to be hobbled at first by the lack of knowledge and experience of those charged with its design and operation. A sensible public and its legislative representatives will allow time and resources for the knowledge and experience to be accumulated. But if the new programs do not command sufficient support, or if the initial enthusiasm that led to their enactment is dissipated, the minimum stability and learning time that is essential may not be available. As a consequence, the President, those charged with administering the program, and the legislators who control its finances will be caught up in a public relations charade in which the rules of the game are continually changed so that it is impossible to keep score. In the manpower arena, the White House has sought each year to launch "exciting new" programs by repackaging funds appropriated a year earlier. This is no way to run a railroad, much less a manpower program.

The conclusion to be drawn is not that our government should delay action in critical areas until it has all the knowledge and techniques to fashion a successful solution. In the first place, the required knowledge can be generated only by action, at least on an experimental scale. Moreover, a democracy really has no option but to act while it learns. It must run risks to meet the needs and desires of its citizens as best it can. The most one can say is that a responsible leadership will proceed with caution in areas where it lacks adequate knowledge and experience, in the expectation that second efforts at social intervention will be improved by what is learned from the initial trials. Perhaps the idea of the frankly experimental public program can be made politically viable. It is worth a try. There is an important corollary, however: social problems must be tackled early. After a time even a poorly functioning system acquires constituencies, at which point the pressure for a remedy cannot be put off by talk of experimentation and learning. The base of knowledge must be compiled beforehand. There is correspondingly less reason, even for conservatives, to oppose experimental programs of social intervention, except perhaps on the overriding principle that nothing new should ever be tried.

Resources

In judging the record of the 1960s, it is useful to keep in mind that a social program is usually better defined by its budget than by the language
of the enabling legislation. Certain programs in the fields of health, education, and manpower never command resources commensurate with
their expressed goals. When this occurs, it is not necessarily an accident
or a miscalculation. When Congress feels pressure to do something about
which it is skeptical, or in which it is uninterested, or toward which it is
ideologically hostile, one tactic it often adopts is to pass a bill containing
high-sounding language, establish an agency, and starve it for funds.
Thus one can say about many a program of the Great Society what G. B.
Shaw said about Christianity: it has not failed; it has never been tried.

In some cases underfunding is a concomitant of overpromising. When
a program has been puffed up beyond reason as the cure for everything,
its appropriation is bound to be too small. Here the habit of Crisis-mon-
gering is an important part of the difficulty. When every problem is
blown into a Crisis, the government must promise to do everything in
order to be permitted to do anything. And the budget can never be sufficient for doing everything.

The dangerous habit of underfunding has longer-run consequences.
New programs can be started modestly, but it is dangerous and often
fatal to hide from the legislature and the public the scale of resources that
will be required if significant progress is to be achieved. Unless the necessary resources are stated realistically, a multiplicity of programs may be
encouraged; and if, as is likely, each of them is undernourished, the
eventual failure of all of them is assured.

In the case of the Great Society, the Vietnam War was an independent
cause of underfunding for social programs. The increase in military
spending was large in comparison with the amount of resources allocated
to new social programs. President Johnson apparently refused to ask
Congress for a tax increase to finance the war for fear his request would
erode support for an already unpopular conflict. In the end the adventure
was financed by inflation. So convoluted did this commingling of politics
and economics become that when a large group of academic economists
tried to drum up support for an anti-inflationary tax increase, they were
opposed by others who did not disagree with their analysis, but who argued that a tax increase would only make it easier for the administration
to continue the war. And in turn, this argument was rebutted by the contention that failure to increase taxes would only lead to the sacrifice of
more of the budget for social programs, in favor of military funding.

One of the by-products of a policy of tackling emergent social problems early, with frankly experimental programs, is that it yields better

information about the cost side of a benefit-cost analysis. There can still be errors in extrapolating the costs of small-scale pilot programs to full-scale social intervention. But we would certainly be on firmer ground.

Administration

Among the scarce resources necessary to the success of any complicated enterprise, private or public, are organizational and administrative talent and will. In a federal system of government like ours, much of what happens in the public domain requires the cooperation of state and local governments. Even where the federal government is the initiator and funder, day-to-day planning and operations will often be in other hands. In area after area, in such diverse fields as education, manpower, welfare, and housing, there is relatively little that the federal government can do on its own. It is not able to deliver services to large numbers of citizens in their home communities. It can mail checks to beneficiaries of the Social Security program, or to the recipients of one or another type of educational grant or loan; but when it comes to organizing a Head Start program or to establishing and operating a skill-training center to assist employable people on the welfare rolls to move into productive employment, the federal government must work through state and local agencies and, to a lesser extent, through contractors in the private or nonprofit sectors of the economy.

The last decade has demonstrated that the strengths and weaknesses of the intermediaries through which the federal government must operate determine in considerable measure the success of its program efforts. It is clear that the best-conceived federal program will falter or fail if the agencies charged with implementing it lack initiative or competence. And the sorry fact is that most state and local governments—with some notable exceptions—are poorly structured and poorly staffed to carry out new and innovative tasks. They have a hard time meeting even their routine commitments.

In all fairness, the record of performance of government's contractors in the private and nonprofit sectors also leaves much room for improvement. The runaway inflation in medical care costs after the passage of Medicare-Medicaid does not reflect much credit on either the voluntary hospitals or on the health professionals, though it must be said that the legislation helped to provide perverse financial incentives to patients and suppliers. The best that can be said for the manpower programs that engaged private employers is that the performance record is mediocre. The firms that accepted performance contracts to teach the hard-to-teach have folded their tents and slipped away. There are many reports of sharp practices, shoddy workmanship, and outright fraud involving real estate brokers and builders working with federal funds to provide housing for poor families.

·The Nixon administration, committed to the doctrine that anything is better than the interference of a too-large federal government in the affairs of the individual citizen, opted in favor of general and special revenue sharing. The stated objective was to encourage state and local governments to play a larger role in determining program priorities and in operating those found worthy of funding.

Decategorization and decentralization of federal programs in education, manpower, health, urban development, and other areas are attractive goals once one recognizes the inherent incapacity of the federal government to be directly involved in the delivery of services to millions of beneficiaries. If the transfer of responsibility is a matter of political convenience and ideological rectitude, however, the weight of recent evidence should not be ignored. Most state and local governments must be substantially strengthened if they are to discharge their expanded functions effectively. In the meanwhile, and perhaps in perpetuity, the federal government must continue to insist on certain priorities, exercise surveillance over the execution of programs, and maintain financial control. It is the height of political naiveté or cynicism to assume that those who effectively control state and local governments will look out solicitously for the interests of the designated beneficiaries of federally financed programs in the absence of a check by the federal government. It would be an even bigger mistake to take it for granted that state and local governments will care as much for the redistributional design of social programs as the federal providers of the funds would wish.

The Record

As we review the record of the 1960s, we cannot fault President Kennedy's efforts to embody advances in economic knowledge in policies designed to speed the country's growth and reduce its excess unemployment. One could hardly argue that his modest initiatives in the areas of manpower training, welfare, reform, or civil rights were focused on issues better left alone, or that the remedies he sought were extreme. It was generally felt at the time, and has since been amply confirmed by historians, that the first Kennedy administration, whatever its other strengths and weaknesses, was characterized on the domestic front by caution and restraint. The enthusiasts promised much broader action for the second Kennedy administration.

While several of the Great Society programs had their roots in staff studies initiated during the Kennedy years, it was President Johnson's leadership that turned these modest beginnings into legislative realities, primarily in 1964 and 1965. It is difficult to argue that Johnson's decisions were unreasonable either, with respect to the problems he singled out or the legislative reforms he recommended.

As for Medicare, we need only recall the sudden and dramatic shift by House Ways and Means Chairman Wilbur Mills and by the American Medical Association from their long-time opposition, to appreciate the strength of the accumulated forces demanding remedial action. Congress had to act. If an error was made, it was not in passing Medicare, but in adding Medicaid as an afterthought.

Nor do we disagree with the executive and legislative decision to put special funds into elementary and secondary schools to provide compensatory education for the hard-to-instruct. Over the years, the federal government had made funds available to accomplish high-priority national educational objectives. It was a logical next step for it to help raise the educational achievement of children from low-income families. It is true that this effort was both administratively and substantively inadequate. Time and experience have seen many weaknesses removed, although no educational system has yet designed an effective remedial program. It is a fair guess that in the absence of a federal initiative we would be much farther from a solution today. This is clearly a case in which it is better to have tried and failed (and learned something) than never to have tried at all.

Of all the Great Society programs, the war on poverty is most open to criticism. The promises were extreme; the specific remedial actions were untried and untested; the funds were grossly inadequate; the political structuring was so vulnerable that it had to be radically reformed within a few years after the program was launched. Despite these weaknesses, we cannot argue that poverty is not a subject worthy of national concern and federal intervention; that many components of the specific Office of Economic Opportunity legislation, from the Job Corps to Operation Mainstream, were not sensible first efforts; that without presidential leadership and congressional support for social intervention the nation would be better off today. The prolonged economic prosperity of the 1960s helped to lift many families out of poverty, but this longest boom in the nation's history also proved that economic growth is not the answer to the problems of all who lack an adequate income.

With respect to federal efforts in housing and urban development, the record is mixed. Much that was attempted succeeded, such as facilitating home ownership among the middle class. On the other hand, suitable housing for low-income families remains a serious challenge. Even more difficult has been neighborhood preservation in urban centers, since large numbers of minority-group members must have access to housing that formerly was not available to them. The specialists agree that the federal government has an important role to play in housing and urban development. They differ only about the approaches the government should follow. As is frequently the case in complex arenas of societal change, there are no right or wrong answers; there are only cautious or radical experiments, the outcomes of which must be assessed before the next round of plans and policies is implemented.

We come to the last of the major interventions, which was directed toward improving the position of the black minority. While the Kennedy administration made a few moves on this front, it was Johnson's leadership that brought about major improvements in race relations. Today, a decade after the effort was mounted, there is no agreement about what he ventured and what he accomplished. A few facts are incontrovertible: the black population has made striking gains in occupational status and in income, in political participation and as office holders, in residential options and in treatment by law enforcement authorities and the courts. Blacks remain a disadvantaged minority suffering from the cumulative effects of more than three and one-half centuries of racism, segregation, and exploitation. But the gains over the last decade have been large and give promise of being sustained. Here in particular, presidential leadership played a critical and constructive role, even though some believe that President Johnson did not go far enough and others are convinced that he lost his followers because he moved too rapidly.

The record of the Great Society is one of successes and failures, of experiments that proved themselves at least partly successful and experiments whose returns do not appear to have justified the effort. In other words, it turned out much as any sensible person should have expected.

Acknowledgments and Sources

Index

Acknowledgments and Sources

Many of the chapters in this book have been substantially altered since their prior publication in various books and periodicals. Permission to publish in revised form has been graciously granted by the following: Academic Press, Free Press, Johns Hopkins Press, McGraw-Hill, Olympus Press, Prentice-Hall, *Challenge, The Columbia Forum, Humanitas, Industrial Relations, Phi Delta Kappan, The Public Interest, Saturday Review-World, Teachers College Record, Thrust,* and *Vocational Guidance Quarterly.*

Detailed sources of earlier publication are indicated below by chapter.

Chapter 1: Distinguished Lecture Series No. 1 (Columbus, Ohio: Center for Vocational and Technical Education, Ohio State University, 1972-73). Reprinted in *Teachers College Record* 76 (September 1974).

Chapter 2: Based on "Challenge to Education," *Thrust* 1:6-8 (April 1972); and Letter 32, *Manpower Advice to Government,* U. S. Department of Labor, Manpower Administration (Washington, D. C., 1972), pp. 139-143.

Chapter 3: *Phi Delta Kappan* 52:176-179 (November 1970).

Chapter 4: *Teachers College Record* 72:373-382 (February 1971). Reprinted in *Educational Vouchers: Concepts and Controversies,* ed. George La Noue (New York: Teachers College Press, 1971), pp. 98-108.

Chapter 5: *Vocational Guidance Quarterly* 20:169-176 (March 1972). Reprinted in *Counseling for Careers: Selected Readings,* ed. Stephen Weinrach (New York: MSS Information Corporation, 1973), pp. 39-66. See also *Counseling and Guidance in the Twentieth Century: Reflections and Reformulations,* ed. William Van Hoose and John Pietrofesa (Boston: Houghton Mifflin, 1970), pp. 58-67.

Chapter 6: *Manpower* 4:3-6 (February 1972). Reprinted in Weinrach, *Counseling for Careers,* pp. 166-174. See also "Is Career Guidance Worth Saving?" *Impact* 1:4-15 (fall 1971); and "The Interface Between Education and Guidance," *Phi Delta Kappan* 54:381-384 (February 1973).

Chapter 7: *Humanitas* 7:227-242 (fall 1971).

Chapter 8: *The Worker and the Job: Coping with Change,* ed. Jerome M. Rosow (Englewood Cliffs, N. J.: Prentice-Hall, 1974), pp. 49-71.

Chapter 9: *Quality of Working Life: Problems, Prospects, and State of the Art,* ed. Louis Davis (New York: Free Press, forthcoming), vol. 1.

Chapter 10: *World* 1:22-26 (September 26, 1972). Reprinted in *Humanizing Organization Behavior,* ed. H. Meltzer and F. Wickert (Springfield, Ill.: Charles C Thomas, in press).

Chapter 11: Based on *The Public Interest* 26:100-111 (winter 1972). Reprinted in *Engineering Management Group Newsletter* 80:1-4 (May/June 1972), and *The Columbia Forum* 13:12-16 (fall 1970).

Chapter 12: See *Perspectives in Defense Management* (spring 1972), pp. 15-24; and *Manpower Research and Management in Large Organizations,* Report of the Task Force on Manpower Research (Washington, D. C.: Defense Science Board, Office of the Director of Defense Research and Engineering, June 1971).

Chapter 13: A much-reduced version of *Blue Collar Workers: A Symposium on Middle America,* ed. Sar Levitan (New York: McGraw-Hill, 1971), pp. 20-46.

Chapter 14: *Industrial Relations* 7:193-203 (May 1968). Reprinted in *Contemporary Personnel Management,* ed. M. Matteson, R. Blakeney, and D. Domm (San Francisco: Canfield Press, 1972), pp. 265-274. See also "Public Policies and Womanpower," *Public and Private Manpower Policies,* ed. Weber, Cassell, and Ginsburg (Madison, Wis.: Industrial Relations Research Assn., 1969), pp. 165-190.

Chapter 15: *Corporate Lib: Women's Challenge to Management,* ed. Eli Ginzberg and Alice Yohalem (Baltimore: Johns Hopkins Press, 1973), pp. 140-152. See also "Women Managers: From Expectations to Reality," presentation at the Symposium on the Advancement of Women in Industry, sponsored by the Advisory Committee on the Economic Role of Women to the Council of Economic Advisers, September 1972, offset.

Chapter 16: *Challenge* 16:52-56 (September/October 1973). See also *Federal Manpower Policy in Transition* (Washington, D. C.: U. S. Department of Labor, Manpower Administration, 1974), pp. 67-77.

Chapter 17: *Federal Manpower Policy in Transition,* pp. 51-61.

Chapter 18: With James W. Kuhn and Beatrice G. Reubens. Prepared for the National Commission on Productivity (Washington, D. C.: U. S. Government Printing Office, 1972).

Chapter 19: Based on *Manpower Report of the President, 1972* (Washington, D. C.: U. S. Government Printing Office, 1972), pp. 7-24 (substantially edited version of original draft prepared by Eli Ginzberg), and *Manpower Policy Perspectives and Prospects,* ed. Seymour Wolfbein (Philadelphia: Temple University School of Business Administration, 1973), pp. 209-217.

Chapter 20: *The Future of the Metropolis,* ed. Eli Ginzberg (Salt Lake City: Olympus Press, 1974), pp. 145-163. See also Eli Ginzberg et al., *New York Is Very Much Alive* (New York: McGraw-Hill, 1973).

Chapter 21: *Nations and Households in Economic Growth—Essays in Honor of Moses Abramovitz,* ed. Paul David and Melvin Reder (New York: Academic Press, 1974), pp. 279-289.

Chapter 22: With Robert M. Solow. *The Public Interest* 34:211-220 (winter 1974). Reprinted in *The Great Society—Lessons for the Future,* ed. Eli Ginzberg and Robert Solow (New York: Basic Books, 1974).

Index